CHRISTIAN HERITAGE COLLEGE
2100 Greenfield Dr.
El Cajon, CA   92021

THE END
OF NEUTRALITY

THE END
OF NEUTRALITY

✿

The United States, Britain, and Maritime Rights

1899-1915

✿

JOHN W. COOGAN

Cornell University Press

ITHACA AND LONDON

CORNELL UNIVERSITY PRESS GRATEFULLY ACKNOWLEDGES
A GRANT FROM THE ANDREW W. MELLON FOUNDATION THAT
AIDED IN BRINGING THIS BOOK TO PUBLICATION.

For information address
Cornell University Press, 124 Roberts Place, Ithaca, New York 14850.
First published 1981 by Cornell University Press.
Published in the United Kingdom by Cornell University Press Ltd.,
Ely House, 37 Dover Street, London W1X 4HQ

International Standard Book Number 0-8014-1407-5
Library of Congress Catalog Card Number 81-66645
Printed in the United States of America
Librarians: Library of Congress cataloging information
appears on the last page of the book.

Contents

5

Acknowledgments

A personal expression of gratitude to everyone who aided in the research, writing, and publication of this book would require a second volume. Special thanks are due, however, to Michael Hunt and Calvin Davis, to Judith Johnson and to Mary Anna Bird, to Frances and Peter Coogan, and to Bernhard Kendler and the rest of the staff at Cornell University Press. Without their assistance and encouragement, this work could not have been completed.

For assistance in examining or for permission to quote from essential materials I thank Her Gracious Majesty Queen Elizabeth II, the Controller of Her Majesty's Stationery Office, the Duke of Hamilton, Lord Esher, Lord Fisher of Kilverstone, Lord Haig, Lord Lansdowne, the late Lord Mountbatten, Lord Salisbury, Lord Selborne, Lord Simon, Mark Bonham Carter, Michael Brock, Somerset de Chair, Alistair Elliot, Milton Gendel, Martin Gilbert, A. R. B. Haldane, L. P. Scott, E. J. Vernon, and Major Cyril Wilson, and the staffs of the Beaverbrook Library, the Birmingham University Library, the Bodleian Library, the British Museum, the Cambridge University Library, the Christ Church Library, the Churchill College Library, the Georgetown University Library, the Houghton Library of Harvard University, the Imperial War Museum, the India Office Library, the Labour Party, the Library of Congress, the National Archives, the National Library of Scotland, the National Maritime Museum, the National Register of Archives, the Naval Historical Library of the Ministry of Defence, the United States Naval War College, the

United States Navy's Operational Archives Branch, the New College Library, the Newcastle-upon-Tyne University Library, the Nuffield College Library, the Public Record Office, the St. Andrews University Library, and the Yale University Libraries. I also wish to beg the indulgence of those copyright owners whom I was unable to trace or to contact despite the most strenuous efforts.

JOHN W. COOGAN

Durham, North Carolina

Abbreviations

Adm	Admiralty (Great Britain)
AM	British Museum, Additional Manuscripts
BEF	British Expeditionary Force
British Documents	Gooch and Temperley, eds., *British Documents on the Origin of the War, 1898–1914*
CAB	Cabinet (GB)
Cape	Cape of Good Hope Station, Royal Navy
CB	Sir Henry Campbell-Bannerman
CIC	Commander in Chief
CID	Committee of Imperial Defence (GB)
CO	Colonial Office (GB)
CRES	Committee on Restriction of Enemy Supplies (GB)
Debates	*Debates in the British Parliament, 1911–1912, on the Declaration of London and the Naval Prize Bill*
DMO	Director of Military Operations, War Office (GB)
DNI	Director of Naval Intelligence, Admiralty (GB)
Eur MSS	India Office Library, European Manuscripts
FO	Foreign Office (GB)
FRUS	United States, Department of State, *Papers Relating to the Foreign Relations of the United States*
LO	Law Officers (GB)
(M)	Microfilm
MS	National Library of Scotland Manuscript
ND	Navy Department (United States)
NF	Numerical file

PRO	Public Record Office (GB)
Proceedings	Scott, ed., *The Proceedings of the Hague Peace Conferences*
RG	Record group
Savage	Savage, ed., *Policy of the United States toward Maritime Commerce in War*
SD	State Department (US)
tel	telegram
TR Letters	Morison et al., eds., *The Letters of Theodore Roosevelt*
WO	War Office (GB)

THE END
OF NEUTRALITY

Introduction

Historians traditionally have seen the period 1914–1920 as a turning point in the development of American foreign policy. Although some recent scholars have emphasized economic continuities in American diplomacy before and after 1914,[1] the consensus remains that Woodrow Wilson's plunge into making war and peace on a global scale did constitute, as the title of the best survey of the period asserts, "the great departure" in American relations with the rest of the world.[2] During Wilson's presidency, the United States abandoned the path of political isolation from Europe which it had followed since the days of George Washington to set out on a new path of global involvement.

This concept of historical periodization has been a primary factor in the way historians have sought to explain American intervention in World War I. Today's standard accounts—Ernest May's *The World War and American Isolation, 1914–1917,* Arthur Link's *Wilson,* Daniel Smith's *Robert Lansing and American Neutrality, 1914–1917,* Ross Gregory's *The Origins of American Intervention in the First World War*—begin with the outbreak of war in Europe in August 1914. Their common underlying assumption is that, although prewar attitudes and relationships played some role in shaping the nature of American neutrality and the final decision for war, the primary determinants, and therefore the proper

1. E.g., William Appleman Williams, *The Tragedy of American Diplomacy,* rev. ed. (New York: Dell, 1962), esp. pp. 86–92.
2. Daniel Smith, *The Great Departure* (New York: Wiley, 1965).

focus for historical study, were the events from August 1914 to April 1917. The emphasis has been on how and why American foreign policy shifted toward intervention in a European war, not on the ways in which prewar events and perceptions shaped wartime neutrality policies.[3]

This concentration on events after the outbreak of war in Europe has obvious intellectual and organizational advantages. It has, however, resulted in a substantially distorted view of American neutrality. This distortion is particularly evident in questions involving neutrality and international law. Although maritime rights had often been a vital issue in American diplomacy before 1914, even the most highly regarded accounts of American neutrality during World War I are characterized by misunderstanding and error in regard to basic matters of international law. Link has written of the "existing statutes" of a law which, by its very nature, is conventional and customary rather than statutory.[4] Other scholars err or unintentionally mislead when discussing the Declaration of London, a document vital in the evolution of American neutrality policies.[5] In general, modern historians have considered the international maritime law existing in 1914 "ambiguous," "obsolete," and a "quaking surface" offering no firm

3. The most widely accepted studies of American neutrality and intervention are Daniel Smith, *Great Departure* and *Robert Lansing and American Neutrality, 1914–1917* (Berkeley and Los Angeles: University of California Press, 1958); Ernest R. May, *The World War and American Isolation, 1914–1917* (Cambridge: Harvard University Press, 1959); Arthur S. Link, *Wilson*, 5 vols. (Princeton: Princeton University Press, 1947–1965); Ross Gregory, *The Origins of American Intervention in the First World War* (New York: Norton, 1971); and Patrick Devlin, *Too Proud to Fight* (New York: Oxford University Press, 1975).

4. Link, *Wilson*, III, 107. A "statute" requires an authority possessing sovereignty, whereas international law, which regulates relations between states possessing sovereignty and admitting no higher authority, consists of customs and conventions.

5. E.g., John Milton Cooper, *Walter Hines Page* (Chapel Hill: University of North Carolina Press, 1977), p. 290, which mistakenly asserts that the declaration was drafted by "an international conference dominated by trading nations likely to be neutral"; Samuel F. Wells, Jr., in Wells et al., *The Ordeal of World Power* (Boston: Little, Brown, 1975), p. 81, which confuses the Declaration of London with the 1856 Declaration of Paris; May, *World War*, p. 43, which gives a misleading impression of the British government's justification for the declaration; Barbara Tuchman, *The Guns of August* (New York: Macmillan, 1962), p. 333, which incorrectly places food on the free list and contains several inaccuracies concerning the doctrine of blockade; Peter Rowland, *The Last Liberal Governments*, 2 vols.

foundation for policy makers.[6] Few have given the legal issues in debate between the British and American governments more than passing attention, and none has attempted to reconstruct maritime law as perceived by those governments.

This lack of attention would have surprised most of the men who shaped British and American foreign policy during the first eight months of World War I. Sir Edward Grey, the British foreign secretary, and Robert Lansing, the counselor and often acting secretary at the United States State Department, devoted enormous amounts of time to questions of contraband, visit and search, and continuous voyage. The number of man-hours their staffs spent on such questions, reflected in the volume of papers in the Foreign Office and State Department archives, is staggering. Prime Minister Herbert Henry Asquith and President Woodrow Wilson, though less continually involved, also were forced by the importance of the disputes to give considerable attention to the issues of belligerent and neutral rights. The statesmen of 1914 might try to evade established doctrines of maritime law or argue as to the precise definition of those doctrines, but unlike the modern historian they could not simply dismiss the law as "obsolete" or "ambiguous."

To understand American neutrality during World War I and the reasons for its breakdown, it is necessary first to understand the legal as well as the strategic and political contexts in which British statesmen evolved the blockade of Germany and American leaders responded to the consequent curtailment of trade. The historian may agree with George Kennan that "looking backward today on these endless disputes between our government and the belligerents over neutral rights, it seems hard to understand how we could have attached so much importance to them,"[7] but he must recognize that the Anglo-American leaders

---

(London: Barrie & Rockliff, 1968 and 1971), II, 40, which inaccurately states that the declaration forbade seizure of absolute contraband under the doctrine of continuous voyage; and Samuel R. Williamson, Jr., *The Politics of Grand Strategy* (Cambridge: Harvard University Press, 1969), p. 241, which confuses the separate legal doctrines of contraband and blockade.

6. Quotations from Link, *Wilson*, III, 105; George F. Kennan, *American Diplomacy, 1900–1950* (Chicago: University of Chicago Press, 1951), p. 64; and Devlin, *Too Proud*, p. 167.

7. Kennan, *American Diplomacy*, p. 64.

of 1914 did regard those issues as vitally important and must attempt to view events and motives from their perspective rather than his own. The maritime issues in dispute between Britain and the United States, and later between Germany and the United States, were not new. The doctrines of continuous voyage, visit and search, retaliation, contraband, and blockade had been a source of international controversy before the American Revolution. Washington and London had bickered and even fought over them for more than a century before 1914. Two wars and three international conferences in the fifteen years prior to Sarajevo had emphasized the importance of maritime rights and shaped both the law and the perceptions of statesmen.

The present book is an effort to place the origins of the British blockade and of American neutrality policy back within this historical context. Its conclusion, briefly stated, is that a viable system of international law did exist in 1914. This system offered the United States a realistic opportunity to maintain effective neutrality, to mitigate the horrors of war for other neutrals and for belligerent civilians, and perhaps to create a favorable position for mediation. But this legal order crumbled, and the opportunities were missed, because Woodrow Wilson ultimately placed preservation of Anglo-American friendship above preservation of American neutrality under the rules of international law. By April 1915, the United States was no longer entitled to the legal status of "neutral."

CHAPTER ONE

✿

Maritime Law to 1899

The first principle of international maritime law was that the seas were free to the ships of all nations. This rule had been established during the sixteenth century by the English and Dutch seamen whose cannon shattered Spain's claim to oceanic sovereignty, and it remained the basis of all maritime law in 1914. Nations possessed sovereignty over their territorial waters and their ships on the high seas, but all nations possessed an equal right to sail the seas in peace.[1]

Over the centuries, however, this principle had been limited to some degree by the doctrine of belligerent rights. Warring nations had fought each other at sea as well as on land and had seized each other's merchant ships as freely as they seized each other's territories. Although some nations, including the United States, had advocated abolition of the right to capture the private property of enemy citizens at sea,[2] none had argued that the right did not exist.

Had belligerents been content to seize each other's merchant

1. There is no reliable modern account of the evolution of international maritime law, but see Max Savelle, *The Origins of American Diplomacy* (New York: Macmillan, 1967), pp. 215-224 and passim; also Philip C. Jessup, ed., *Neutrality*, 4 vols. (New York: Columbia University Press, 1935-1936).

2. Carlton Savage, *Policy of the United States toward Maritime Commerce in War*, 2 vols. (Washington: U.S. Government Printing Office, 1934, 1936) [Savage], I, 119-121 and passim; cf. Great Britain, FO, "Selected Papers and Correspondence respecting the Capture of Private Property at Sea in Time of War, 1854-1906," printed March 1906, CAB, 17/85.

ships, the doctrine of belligerent rights would have remained a matter between enemies rather than a question of international law. But belligerents insisted that they also possessed the right to seize a neutral ship which aided their enemy. Such seizures not only challenged the neutral's understandable desire to continue to trade without interference from a war in which he was not a participant, but struck at the principle of freedom of the seas and the sovereignty of the neutral flag. Not a few belligerents, including Britain in 1812, had found their interference with neutral commerce bringing new enemies into the field against them. This basic contradiction between the belligerent's desire to cut off outside assistance to his enemy and the neutral's desire to continue trading while maintaining neutrality never was to be completely resolved.

Nevertheless, trial and error over centuries had established certain guidelines on the respective rights of neutral traders and belligerent navies. The essence of these guidelines was stated by the dean of American international law scholars, John Bassett Moore, in his 1907 *Digest:* "Neutrals have the right to continue during war to trade with the belligerents, subject to the law relating to contraband and blockade. The existence of this right is universally admitted, although on certain occasions it has been in practice denied."[3] This principle emerged by general consent, as belligerents balanced the value of overseas assistance to their enemies against the dangers of raising up new enemies and neutrals balanced their desire to continue trading against the prospect of going to war each time a merchant got caught running guns. The net result of this balancing was a series of compromise rules, which by treaty and custom defined the extent to which a belligerent could interfere with neutral shipping without giving the neutral government just cause for objection.

By the time George Washington became president of the United States, a general international consensus on these rules had evolved. Neutral merchant ships were liable to be stopped, visited, and searched by a belligerent warship in order to establish their identity, cargo, and destination. They were liable to capture

3. John Bassett Moore, *A Digest of International Law,* 8 vols. (Washington: U.S. Government Printing Office, 1906), VII, 382.

and confiscation if the belligerent could prove in prize court that they carried military dispatches or performed other unneutral service for his enemy, that they were running a legitimate blockade, or, under the doctrine of contraband, that they were carrying goods destined for the enemy armed forces. Britain claimed the right to seize enemy private property from neutral ships, a right France and the United States refused to recognize. France claimed the right to seize neutral property on enemy ships, a right Britain refused to recognize. Except for these belligerent rights, a neutral state's sovereignty over its ships on the high seas was absolute, and its government was legally justified in any action it took to assert and defend that basic neutral right.[4]

This system, comparatively simple in theory, had proved and would continue to prove complex and controversial in practice. Every nation recognized that a belligerent right of blockade existed; each nation, however, had its own definition of the rules under which such a stoppage of trade could legitimately be enforced. The same was true of contraband—little agreement existed as to what articles could be seized or the degree of proof necessary for condemnation. Thomas Jefferson might regard the American interpretation of maritime rights as "the law of nature upon the ocean,"[5] but he and other American presidents prior to 1815 had mixed success in persuading Britain or France to honor that natural law.

Despite difficulties, however, the basic balance underlying maritime law survived even at the height of the French Revolutionary and Napoleonic Wars. Britain and France extended the concept of belligerent rights enormously in their efforts to wage economic war against each other, but at each step they calculated potential military advantage against potential neutral resistance. The United States, on the other hand, employed every weapon in its arsenal to discourage inflated claims of belligerent rights and to resist enforcement of rules violating the American definition of

---

4. On visit and search, see Moore, *Digest*, VII, 473–487; on unneutral service, ibid., 410–415, 752–768; on blockade, ibid., 780–848; on contraband, ibid., 656–752; on the "free ship, free goods" vs. "enemy ship, enemy goods" dispute, ibid., 434–454. Cf. Savage, I.

5. Quoted in Lloyd C. Gardner et al., *Creation of the American Empire* (New York: Rand McNally, 1973), p. 64.

neutral rights. At various times between 1793 and 1812 the American government had used diplomatic protest, recall of consuls, breaking of diplomatic relations, economic sanctions up to and including general embargo, neutral convoy of merchant ships, armed neutrality, retaliatory capture of belligerent ships, and finally declaration of war to assert and defend American interpretations of neutral rights.[6] A modern British jurist and historian has commented that a belligerent's prize regulations constituted "a statement of the conditions under which it would permit neutrals to trade with its enemies,"[7] but it would be equally true to say that a neutral's position constituted a statement of the conditions under which it would permit belligerents to interfere with its right to use the high seas. If the world wars of 1793–1815 established one legal principle beyond challenge, it was that neither belligerents nor neutrals could dictate maritime law. Future law, like past law, would be shaped by belligerents and neutrals balancing contradictory interests on the seas against the political and strategic implications of possible policies.

Thus John Quincy Adams, one of the American negotiators, wrote of the "truce" rather than the peace of Ghent signed on Christmas Eve, 1814, ending the War of 1812.[8] Statesmen on both sides of the Atlantic shared this evaluation of a treaty that failed to resolve the disputes over maritime law which had driven the two nations to war. Britain continued to maintain that the dominant sea power possessed the right to close the seas to its enemy and that British doctrines of impressment, blockade, contraband, continuous voyage, and retaliation were justifiable corollaries of this basic right designed only to prevent neutrals from rendering unneutral assistance to the enemy. The United States responded

6. The best accounts of American efforts to maintain maritime neutrality during this period are Bradford Perkins, *The First Rapprochement* (Philadelphia: University of Pennsylvania Press, 1955), and *Prologue to War* (Berkeley: University of California Press, 1961); cf. Alexander DeConde, *Entangling Alliance* (Durham: Duke University Press, 1958), and *The Quasi-War* (New York: Charles Scribner's Sons, 1966).

7. Devlin, *Too Proud*, pp. 159–160.

8. Quoted on Kenneth Bourne, *Britain and the Balance of Power in North America, 1815–1908* (Berkeley and Los Angeles: University of California Press, 1967), p. 9.

that the seas were free to ships of all nations, subject only to closely defined belligerent rights, and that the British doctrines in question constituted an intolerable violation of the principle of freedom of the seas and of the sovereignty of the neutral flag. Twenty years of acrimonious debate, three years of war, and a year of peace negotiations had failed to resolve this dispute. Each nation believed its vital interests were at stake. Neither would compromise.[9]

Even as the ink dried on the Treaty of Ghent, its signers regarded another Anglo-American war over maritime rights as inevitable. Britain appeared determined to enforce belligerent rights in any future war, rights that the United States would not recognize. The American government strengthened its navy and refused to retreat on neutral rights. The precarious peace in Europe seemed likely to break down at any time, and both Americans and Englishmen believed that any British attempt to enforce belligerent rights against American commerce would mean war with the United States. Only the exact data of Britain's next involvement in a Continental war seemed in doubt.[10]

Yet the generally anticipated Anglo-American conflict to settle the disputed maritime rights issue never took place. The two nations found numerous other grounds for controversy after 1815, but none with the explosive potential of impressment or blockade. The assumption of inevitable conflict had been based on the expectation of continuing European wars in which Britain would seek to use the economic pressure of sea power against Continental enemies. This expectation proved false. Britain had no occasion to assert the controversial belligerent rights and the United States no occasion to resist them. The one war Britain did fight against a Continental enemy, the Crimean War of 1854–1856, actually produced a major step toward international agreement on maritime law. In the Declaration of Paris, part of the peace settlement of 1856, France abandoned its doctrine of "enemy ship, enemy goods" and Britain in return recognized the doctrine

9. For British and American views on maritime rights after 1815, see Bradford Perkins, *Castlereagh and Adams* (Berkeley: University of California Press, 1964), pp. 161–163, 168, 262; Savage, I, 39ff.
10. Bourne, *Britain and Balance of Power*, p. 7, n. 2, and passim.

of "free ship, free goods." Britain also accepted the principle that only "effective" blockades were legally binding.[11] All of these agreements were most satisfactory from the American viewpoint.

The United States did not formally accept the Declaration of Paris because of an article outlawing privateers.[12] Nevertheless, the increasing complexity of modern warships and the need for extensive training to manage their weapons and propulsion systems made the use of privateers, like the impressment of sailors from neutral merchant ships, increasingly unlikely. Technological advances during the mid-nineteenth century steadily reduced the apparent area of dispute between belligerent and neutral interpretations of maritime law. This shift was not always evident in theory, because no British statesmen could publicly admit that belligerent rights had been limited and no American Fourth of July oration was complete without a denunciation of continued British tyranny over the seas. Yet behind the theory and behind the rhetoric lay a steadily increasing agreement.

The degree of this de facto agreement emerged clearly during the American Civil War, when for the first time the United States found itself the dominant naval power in a major war. The Union immediately proclaimed a blockade of the Confederacy.[13] James Madison undoubtedly would have considered this blockade ineffective, and therefore illegal, because it did not bar access to each port, pier, and isolated stretch of beach along thousands of miles of coastline. But Abraham Lincoln took a more pragmatic view, arguing that a blockade did not have to be totally effective in practice to be legally "effective." The Supreme Court later confirmed this interpretation in formal prize rulings: effective blockade was a general concept, requiring a blockading force to present blockade runners with a significant danger—but not an absolute certainty—of capture.[14] By 1865 the United States, through its

11. For the text of the Declaration of Paris, see Moore, *Digest*, VII, 561–562.

12. President Franklin Pierce, Annual Message to Congress, 2 Dec 1856, ibid., 563–565; for subsequent negotiations see pp. 565–583.

13. President Abraham Lincoln, Proclamation, 27 Apr 1861, Savage, I, 420; Stuart Bernath, *Squall across the Atlantic* (Berkeley and Los Angeles: University of California Press, 1970), pp. 2–3.

14. Moore, *Digest*, VII, 708–715; Savage, I, 459–460, 465–466, 467–470; Bernath, *Squall*, pp. 11–14, 27–33, and passim.

Civil War precedents, and Britain, through the Declaration of Paris, were committed to essentially the same interpretation of the belligerent right of blockade.

The Lincoln administration also had found another British doctrine worthy of adoption. Before 1812 Americans had seen no justice in the principle of continuous voyage, under which the Royal Navy had seized American ships in transit between two neutral ports on the ground that they were in the process of a "continuous voyage" to a blockaded port.[15] The United States government took a different view, however, when Union warships intercepted British merchantmen carrying cavalry sabers stamped "CSA" from London to Nassau. The Supreme Court chose to accept the British rule that intent to break blockade or carry contraband was legally equivalent to commission of those offenses and exposed the neutral merchant to the same penalty of confiscation when captured at any point of a voyage. The American assertion of continuous voyage actually went beyond the precedents established in British prize courts, although Her Majesty's Government, aware of the potential value of the extended rule, made no complaint.[16]

By the fiftieth anniversary of the Treaty of Ghent, the progress toward Anglo-American agreement on maritime rights would have amazed John Quincy Adams or Lord Castlereagh. Technological change had made impressment and privateering obsolete, whatever the academic positions of the two nations. Britain had accepted the American doctrine that free ships made free goods, except for contraband and blockade runners. The British government had agreed that blockades must be "effective" to be binding on neutrals, while the United States had agreed that effectiveness was a general concept. Both the Lincoln administration and the Supreme Court had endorsed the doctrine of continuous voyage. British and American views on contraband also had moved closer to agreement. Although some differences be-

---

15. Moore, *Digest,* VII, 383–391, 697–744, 828–830.
16. Bernath, *Squall,* p. 12 and passim; James P. Baxter, III, "The British Government and Neutral Rights, 1861–1865," *American Historical Review,* 34 (1928):9–29; Baxter, "Some British Opinions as to Neutral Rights, 1861 to 1865," *American Journal of International Law,* 23 (1929):517–537.

tween British and American prize law remained, the yawning gaps that had seemed so wide in 1815 had largely disappeared by 1865.

Perhaps the most remarkable aspect of this shift was the way it had taken place. The general assumption that Anglo-American differences could be settled only with the cannon had proved false. The United States had offered little objection to Britain's limited enforcement of belligerent rights during the Crimean War; Britain had made little protest against the Union blockade during the Civil War. The Lincoln administration correctly concluded that Britain, the only neutral with a significant interest in trade with the Confederacy, would not object to enforcement of traditional British rules of blockade. The British foreign secretary who assented to the "free ship, free goods" principle in 1856, on the other hand, did so because he believed that Britain must abandon its traditional practice of seizing enemy property from neutral ships or have "all mankind against us" in future wars.[17] In each case the belligerent balanced its interest in halting neutral trade with its enemy against its interest in avoiding provocation of powerful neutrals.

This continuing process of balance and realistic compromise between contradictory interests was the essence of international maritime law. A belligerent could disregard this law if he were willing to pay the price in neutral opposition, just as a neutral could disregard it if he were willing to take whatever steps might be necessary to defend his merchant shipping against enforcement of belligerent rights. But for the vast majority of belligerents, who wanted to defeat one enemy rather than raise up others, and for the vast majority of neutrals, who sought only to continue their legitimate trade without involvement in other nations' conflicts, maritime law seemed to offer a system that balanced the vital interests of both combatants and noncombatants and produced a compromise generally acceptable to both.

Ironically, however, this progress toward agreement on the

17. Lord Clarendon to Lord Palmerston (prime minister), 6 Apr 1856, G. P. Gooch and Harold Temperley, eds., *British Documents on the Origins of the War, 1898–1914* [*British Documents*], 11 vols. (London: His Majesty's Stationery Office, 1927–1938), VIII, 204.

principles of maritime law took place at a time when the entire question seemed to be growing less important in international relations. The United States made little effort to rebuild its merchant marine or maintain its navy after 1865. Instead it withdrew behind the Monroe Doctrine into what amounted to unilaterally disarmed isolation. After Lord Palmerston's Danish fiasco of 1864, Britain moved away from participation in the European balance of power and redefined its national interests in maritime and imperial terms. The new policies precluded large-scale Continental intervention, which often in the past had led Britain to broad assertions of belligerent rights. Technological improvements in land transportation seemed to make the European Great Powers less dependent on sea transport vulnerable to enemy interception. The Austro-Prussian War of 1866 and the Franco-Prussian War of 1870–1871 appeared to establish a new pattern for Great Power wars: sharp but short conflicts settled by a few decisive battles soon after the mass national armies had completed mobilization. As the nineteenth century drew to a close, the possibility of a war in which sea power would generate decisive economic pressure against a Great Power appeared increasingly remote. Controversies over blockade and contraband seemed well on their way to the obsolescence that had already claimed privateering and impressment.

This perception was reinforced by the Spanish-American War of 1898. The United States and Spain could strike at each other only through sea power. Both presumably had an incentive to make a broad assertion of belligerent rights. Yet the American government authorized its naval forces to exercise extreme care in dealing with merchant vessels and allowed capture only of Spanish ships, of blockade runners, or of ships carrying contraband directly to the enemy. Although the United States had asserted the doctrine of continuous voyage during the Civil War, it disclaimed that right in 1898. The only belligerent rights enforced were those so well established in international law that no honest neutral could have grounds for objecting.[18] American

18. Secretary of the navy, "Instructions to Blockading Vessels and Cruisers," 20 Jun 98, Savage, I, 489.

warships seized ten British merchantmen during the conflict, but their condemnation or release with compensation aroused no excitement from the people or the government of either nation.[19]

President William McKinley decided to take advantage of this apparent trend toward greater freedom for wartime commerce by seeking to realize the old American dream of immunity for private property at sea. In his Annual Message to Congress in December 1898, McKinley proposed an international agreement that would make all property owned by individuals, whether neutral or belligerent in citizenship, free from belligerent capture.[20] American statesmen had offered this proposal in varying forms since the days of Benjamin Franklin, with a notable lack of success. In 1898 William McKinley, a most cautious man, believed that the goal was within reach at last.

This confidence was not entirely misplaced. Immunity found an unexpected and powerful champion when McKinley's proposal reached London. Arthur James Balfour, leader of the House of Commons and heir apparent to his uncle's premiership, argued that adoption of immunity would improve Britain's relative strategic position.

> In my judgment the question of capture of private property at sea, and certain allied problems, deserve and require immediate consideration. I am inclined to think that our national interests would gain by the change; they would almost certainly gain if the change was limited to the relief of commerce *not attempting to run effective blockade.* . . .
> We have recently had some debates in Parliament on the subject of national food supply, Government insurance of merchant-ships in time of war, &c. These debates, from my point of view, have been unsatisfactory, as I have been obliged to expound the policy of a Government which had none.

Whereas McKinley's message had justified immunity as a humanitarian reform, Balfour's sole consideration was British na-

---

19. R. G. Neale, *Great Britain and United States Expansion, 1898–1900* (East Lansing: Michigan State University Press, 1966), pp. 93–94, n. 12; H. C. Allen, *Great Britain and the United States* (New York: St. Martin's Press, 1955), pp. 576–577.

20. McKinley, Annual Message to Congress, 5 Dec 98, Savage, I, 490–491; for background see Boston Chamber of Commerce to McKinley, 2 Jan 99, and New York Chamber of Commerce to McKinley, n.d., United States, SD, (M), M-179/1023.

tional interest. Britain, with the world's strongest navy, presumably would be able to blockade its enemy and thus seize both enemy and neutral merchantmen for blockade running. Immunity would safeguard the immense British merchant marine, however, because no enemy could blockade Britain effectively. Balfour concluded that immunity would protect British commerce while not hindering British sea power and should therefore be supported by the British government.[21]

Had the author of this paper become prime minister in 1899 rather than three years later, a revolutionary change in maritime law might have ensued. But "Dear Uncle Robert" was not yet ready for either retirement or immunity. Lord Salisbury did not disagree with his protégé's arguments. He did note, however, that in his career as premier and foreign secretary he had seen a good many solemn and sensible paper agreements torn up. Could immunity, even if embodied in an international convention, survive the test of war?

> Like all stipulations which are supposed to hold good when the parties making them are at war with each other, I do not see how the exemption is to be enforced. Contraband of war and ships trying to run a blockade will still be liable to seizure. It will be easy for a captain to shelter himself under one of these exceptions in most cases. And to whom is the captured vessel to appeal?
> Prize Courts in France would be a poor reliance.[22]

Salisbury had pointed out an important distinction between neutral rights per se, which the neutral could enforce by threatening sanctions against the offending belligerent, and immunity for enemy private property, which could have no force but neutral disapproval of the offending belligerent's bad faith and the offended belligerent's ability to retaliate.

The prime minister's opposition seems to have ended discussion of the American immunity proposal on the cabinet level. But the idea that Britain might gain from immunity, or from some limitation on belligerent rights, lived on. Commercial interests lobbied for stronger safeguards to protect British shipping, and

21. Balfour, 24 Dec 98, minute on Sir J. Pauncefote (British ambassador, Washington) to Lord Salisbury (prime minister and foreign secretary), 8 Dec 98, FO, "Selected Papers," CAB 17/85.
22. Salisbury, n.d., minute, ibid.

though these efforts provoked salty language at the Admiralty, they forced many people to think about the issues involved.[23] Within a few years other influential Englishmen had joined Balfour in wondering if it were not time for a reexamination or even reversal of Britain's traditional maritime rights policies.

Rebuffed in this informal approach, McKinley now sought a means to bring the American proposal on immunity formally before the Great Powers. An international peace conference initiated by the Czar, which was to meet at The Hague during the summer of 1899, seemed to offer the perfect opportunity. Secretary of State John Hay instructed the American delegation, which was headed by Andrew Dickson White and included the famous naval strategist and historian Alfred Thayer Mahan, to commend to the conference "the principle of extending to strictly private property at sea, the immunity from destruction or capture by belligerent Powers which such property already enjoys on land as being worthy of being incorporated in the permanent law of civilized nations."[24]

White learned soon after he reached The Hague, however, that neither immunity for private property nor any other proposal for reform of maritime law evoked enthusiasm from the other delegations. There was even opposition within the American delegation, with Mahan, who favored broader rather than more restricted belligerent rights, working to defeat his own nation's resolution.[25] The chief Austro-Hungarian delegate assured his American counterpart that his nation certainly would support President McKinley's noble humanitarian proposal. He then predicted, correctly, that Britain and Russia would not allow an im-

23. E.g., Liverpool Chamber of Commerce to FO, 23 Mar 99, with minutes by first sea lord, 30 Apr 99, and director of naval intelligence, 22 Apr 99, on FO to Adm, 19 Apr 99, Adm 1/7422B; Balfour to Captain Alfred T. Mahan (American naval historian and strategist), 20 Dec 99, Balfour Papers, AM 49792; Balfour to G. Goschen (first lord of the Admiralty), 14, 15 Dec 99, and Goschen to Balfour, 16 Dec 99, ibid., AM 49706.

24. Hay, "Instructions to the American Delegates to the First Hague Peace Conference," 18 Apr 99, Savage, I, 491; Calvin D. Davis, *The United States and the First Hague Peace Conference* (Ithaca: Cornell University Press, 1962), pp. 76–80.

25. White, diary entries, 19 Jun 99 and passim, Andrew Dickson White, *The Autobiography of Andrew Dickson White*, II (New York: Century, 1905), 316–317 and passim.

munity resolution to reach the floor.[26] After considerable effort, White secured passage of a recommendation that a future Hague conference consider the American proposal. McKinley and Hay reluctantly admitted defeat.[27]

Significantly, immunity had not been defeated on its merits. It had been tabled for future consideration. Most nations at The Hague in 1899 seemed to recognize that some aspects of international maritime law did remain vaguely defined and that some reform was necessary. But at a time when the Ottoman and Chinese empires seemed on the verge of disintegration, the Great Powers had more urgent concerns than abstract questions of law. The pattern of short wars without significant controversy over maritime rights, confirmed only the year before by the Spanish-American War, seemed to prove that the necessary reforms could be postponed safely until another Hague conference an indeterminate number of years in the future. The events of the next fifteen years were to demonstrate how badly this confidence was misplaced.

26. White, diary entry, 22 May 99, ibid., p. 317.
27. "Proceedings of the International Peace Conference," 5 Jul 99, SD/RG 43/E2; Davis, *First Hague*, pp. 134-135.

CHAPTER TWO

✿

Maritime Rights and the Test of War, 1899–1904

Even as the Hague Conference tabled immunity for private property at sea, events in South Africa had begun to demonstrate that the delegates had seriously underestimated the continuing potential for international controversy in disputes between belligerents and neutrals over maritime rights. Within months the Boer War would bring a dangerous confrontation between British sea power and the determination of the United States and Germany to protect neutral trade. Five years later Britain and the United States would come to the very brink of war against Russia in defense of their neutral rights. In both crises more serious consequences were avoided only by the belligerent's decision to abandon "rights" that neutrals refused to recognize. When the Second Hague Conference met in 1907, the experience of these two wars would assure maritime law a place among the most urgent items on the agenda.

The Anglo-Boer War, which began in October 1899, initially seemed likely to confirm rather than discredit the view that maritime rights was an obsolete issue. The Boers had no navy to attack British shipping, no merchant ships to capture, and no coast to blockade. Article II of the Declaration of Paris protected their few exports, which were shipped under neutral flags from the neutral port of Lourenço Marques in Portuguese Mozambique. Britain could claim a right to seize enemy imports of a contraband nature, but only by applying the controversial doctrine of continuous voyage to goods destined to Lourenço

Marques for transshipment overland. After considering the difficulties of enforcing belligerent rights under such circumstances and the assurances of the British War Office that the Boers did not require imported arms,[1] Lord Salisbury decided that the best action was no action. The Admiralty instructed its commander in South African waters, Admiral Sir Robert Harris, that "no vessel of a foreign state should be searched."[2] Britain had decided not to enforce its belligerent rights.

Had this decision remained in effect, there would have been no dispute over maritime rights, and the belief that the entire question was obsolete would have been confirmed. But bureaucratic blundering and exaggerated estimates of enemy vulnerability to economic warfare led almost immediately to a reversal of policy. Over the next three months a confused and divided British government drifted into an international crisis that would have enormous impact on the nation's maritime rights positions over the next fifteen years.

Salisbury's order not to interfere with neutral shipping was telegraphed to Capetown on October 11. Before it arrived, however, Admiral Harris had wired London to ask whether "warlike stores" destined for the enemy were contraband.[3] The prime minister explained to the Admiralty that receipt of the earlier order should answer Harris's query. "Warlike stores" destined for Lourenço Marques might well be contraband in law, but "Her Majesty's Government . . . propose for the present to interfere as little as possible with neutral vessels."[4] Unfortunately, a literal-minded Admiralty clerk transmitted only one of Salisbury's three paragraphs to South Africa. The telegram informed Harris that he possessed a legal right to seize contraband, but failed to tell him that the government had decided not to exercise that right.[5]

The dangers of this confusion quickly became evident. Sir

---

1. Great Britain, WO, Intelligence Division, "Military Notes on the Dutch Republics of South Africa," revised Jun 1899, General Sir John Ardagh Papers, PRO 30/40/16; J. A. S. Grenville, *Lord Salisbury and Foreign Policy* (London: Athlone, 1964), pp. 260–261.

2. Adm to CIC, Cape, tel, 11 Oct 99, Adm 116/107/1; Sir Francis Bertie (FO official) to Salisbury, 11 Oct 99, FO 2/267.

3. CIC, Cape, to Adm, tel, 11 Oct 99, Adm 116/111.

4. FO to Adm, 13 Oct 99, ibid.

5. Adm to CIC, Cape, tel, 14 Oct 99, Adm 116/107/1.

Alfred Milner, British high commissioner in South Africa, had been convinced for months that only a flood of men and supplies from overseas encouraged the Boers to resist British pressure.[6] Irritated by the initial decision not to halt this supposed flow by enforcing belligerent rights but pleased by the apparent reversal, Milner wired Colonial Secretary Joseph Chamberlain on October 19 that a Dutch ship was approaching Lourenço Marques with a cargo of food. Because Harris had been authorized to seize contraband, and the Cape attorney general had declared food to be contraband, instructions had been given to seize the ship.[7]

Chamberlain received Milner's telegram the same day the Crown's Law Officers submitted a formal opinion on the status of food shipments under the doctrine of contraband. The attorney general and solicitor general warned that "provisions can only be stopped if there is reasonable ground for believing that they are directly destined for the supply of the enemy's forces."[8] By this standard, capture of a neutral ship under the circumstances Milner had outlined would be a flagrant violation of international law. The high commissioner had cited as authority an order to Harris of which the colonial secretary knew only that it contradicted the Government's official policy. After sorting out the confusion, Chamberlain ordered Milner to take no action without specific instructions from London.[9] He then suggested that the separate government departments leave all questions involving maritime law "for Lord Salisbury's decision."[10]

This delegation of authority reached a prime minister already experiencing doubts about his decision not to enforce belligerent rights. The war was going badly, with Boer commandos striking deep into British territory.[11] Milner's pessimism had proved a more realistic evaluation of enemy capabilities than Colonial Of-

6. E.g., Milner to Lord Selborne (CO parliamentary undersecretary), 18 Oct 99, Selborne Papers, 11; Milner to Chamberlain, 23 Aug 99, CO 417/265.

7. Milner to Chamberlain, tel, 19 Oct 99, FO 834/19.

8. LO, Report, 20 Oct 99, ibid.

9. Chamberlain to Milner, tel, 21 Oct 99, CO 879/60/605; cf. Adm to CIC, Cape, tel, 22 Oct 99, Adm 116/111.

10. CO to FO (copies to WO and Adm), 21 Oct 99, CO 879/60/605.

11. On the unfavorable British military situation in October 1899, see Rayne Kruger, *Good-bye Dolly Gray* (London: Cassell, 1959), pp. 65–97, and Byron Farwell, *The Great Anglo-Boer War* (New York: Harper & Row, 1976), pp. 39–84.

fice optimism.[12] Although still anxious to avoid friction with neutrals, Salisbury had to give more weight to warnings that importation of men, munitions, and food would enable the enemy to prolong resistance indefinitely. On October 21 the prime minister proposed a limited assertion of belligerent rights. The new policy would authorize Harris to search neutral ships destined for South African ports and detain for the prize court any that carried contraband if "reasonable ground" existed for suspecting enemy destination. The list of contraband would include not only arms and munitions, but "food suitable for feeding troops."[13]

Salisbury did not intend to implement this policy without extensive consultation among the departments concerned. He was especially anxious that the proposed regulations should be reviewed by the Law Officers before any attempt was made to enforce them.[14] But events outstripped deliberation. On October 23 Harris wired that "a large amount of munitions of war and foodstuffs" was nearing Lourenço Marques. The prime minister on his own authority ordered the draft instructions enforced on a "provisional" basis. British warships were to examine all neutral ships in South African waters and to seize any that carried contraband suspected of enemy destination.[15]

Harris had been ordered not to search on October 11, to search on October 14, not to search on October 22, and to search on October 23. Nor was the confusion at an end. Chamberlain had declared himself "ready to carry out at once any decision arrived at by Lord Salisbury,"[16] but the Law Officers and the first lord of the Admiralty took quite another view. The decision to enforce belligerent rights, even on a provisional basis, provoked an internal dispute that quickly reached the cabinet.

In a formal report dated October 26, the Law Officers deli-

12. E.g., Milner to Selborne, 11 Oct 99, Selborne Papers, 11; cf. Chamberlain to Selborne, 5 Oct 99, ibid., 9, and Chamberlain to Lord Lansdowne (secretary of state for war), 7 Oct 99, J. Chamberlain Papers, 5/51/88.

13. Salisbury to Bertie, 21 Oct 99, FO 2/268.

14. Ibid.; Bertie to LO, 23 Oct 99, FO 834/19.

15. Bertie to LO, 23 Oct 99, FO 834/19; Adm to CIC, Cape, tel, 23 Oct 99, Adm 116/111.

16. Chamberlain, 21 Oct 99, minute on Bertie to Chamberlain, 21 Oct 99, FO 2/268.

cately explained that the maritime rights policy currently in effect was in their view both illegal and inexpedient. The order authorized capture of food if "reasonable ground" existed to suspect an enemy military destination; international law required absolute proof. The order made a sweeping assertion of the doctrine of continuous voyage which British prize courts were likely to repudiate. Other aspects of the current policy, though legal, could not be enforced effectively. The Law Officers' overall opinion was that Salisbury's instructions were not in the national interest and should be withdrawn immediately.[17]

This conclusion was echoed by the first lord of the Admiralty. George Goschen complained that the prime minister should not have taken upon himself the decision to enforce questionable belligerent rights. For a nation that must import food to live, any decision affecting the legal status of food on the high seas was the proper responsibility of the cabinet, not of its chief alone. The present policy risked confrontation with neutrals and created unfortunate precedents, but gained only a negligible military advantage. "Is it worthwhile to run the risk of friction with neutrals if it can be avoided? Is it really worthwhile? Would French or German shipowners, & their Governments, not loudly protest? . . . Whatever we do, let us avoid friction with the Powers except for the strongest reasons." Goschen closed ominously: "There are some of the Cabinet who hold the same view as I do."[18]

Salisbury tried to justify his action, but would not withdraw the provisional orders to Harris. Goschen responded with an appeal to the full cabinet.[19] The first lord had not exaggerated the degree of support for his position. Salisbury was able to avoid complete reversal of the provisional orders pending a review of the Law Officers' report by the lord chancellor, but his colleagues demanded immediate withdrawal of the section making food contraband.[20] As Chamberlain explained to a disappointed Milner, seizure of food "might form a dangerous precedent and the game

17. LO, Report, 26 Oct 99, FO 834/19.
18. Goschen to Salisbury, 26 Oct 99, Salisbury Papers, Hatfield House MSS, 3M/E/Goschen.
19. Goschen to Salisbury, 28 Oct 99, ibid.
20. Adm to CIC, Cape, tel, 1 Nov 99, Adm 116/111.

is not worth the candle, as we intend not to starve the Boers but to beat them."[21]

For the next six weeks the British government allowed maritime rights policy to drift. The cabinet majority apparently continued to accept War Office assurances that the enemy did not require imported supplies. It certainly respected the Law Officers' opinion and desired to avoid friction with neutrals.[22] But this attitude could not survive the series of mid-December military disasters known as "Black Week."[23] During the next week the speed of the retreating British armies in South Africa would be matched only by the speed with which officials in London scrambled to avoid responsibility for the debacle. The prime minister complained on December 15 that the navy had let the army down by allowing contraband to slip through its patrols.[24] Goschen protested that the fleet had acted as rigorously as the cabinet permitted and argued that incompetent British generals were to blame for the defeats. To avoid any appearance of naval culpability, however, he had sent private instructions to Harris to supplement the official orders: "You may read between the lines that the Govt. will not complain if importations into Delagoa Bay are materially hampered by the uncertainty of the new definition applied to contraband in foodstuffs." The first lord also had assured Harris that "officers will not be censured for over-zeal, nor if the prize courts give judgments against them."[25] The British public would demand a scapegoat for defeat, and Goschen was determined that it not be the Admiralty or its first lord.

These private instructions had an obvious potential for provoking friction with neutrals. But in the aftermath of Black Week, few in the British government were concerned. When a Colonial

21. Chamberlain to Milner, tel, 2 Nov 99, CO 879/60/605.
22. Sanderson, memo of conference, 2 Dec 99, FO 2/274.
23. On "Black Week" and its psychological impact in London, see Farwell, *Anglo-Boer War*, pp. 127–147; Kruger, *Good-bye Dolly Gray*, pp. 122–159; and John Wilson, *CB: A Life of Sir Henry Campbell-Bannerman* (New York: St. Martin's Press, 1973), pp. 320–322.
24. Salisbury, 15 Dec 99, minute on draft memo to General Sir Redvers Buller (British military commander in South Africa), *British Documents*, I, 243.
25. Goschen to Salisbury, 15 Dec 99, Salisbury Papers, E/Goschen. Lourenço Marques was the major port on Delagoa Bay.

Office clerk warned that diplomatic difficulties were likely, a colleague remarked that prize court appeals would require "several months, by which time the war ought to be over."[26] Salisbury circulated a warning from the Belgian foreign minister that "the only danger which England runs of the war being transferred to Europe would arise from incautious handling of the question of Delagoa Bay,"[27] but saw no contradiction between it and Goschen's tough orders to Harris. Although the British government still had no evidence that the enemy was importing contraband through Lourenço Marques, there seemed to be unanimous agreement that only the unfair advantage of possessing an unblockadable port could explain Boer victories. Doubts as to how the supposed flood of contraband could evade Harris's search at sea, a Portuguese embargo on munitions shipments, and the host of British agents in Lourenço Marques were swept away in the haste to use sea power to dam the flood.[28] The result was a potentially explosive dispute with the United States and a crisis with Germany.

On December 5 a British warship had seized the British merchantman *Mashona* on a voyage from New York to Lourenço Marques. Although most of the cargo was owned by Americans and the ship was sailing from one neutral port to another, both ship and cargo were placed in the prize court for violation of British laws against trading with the enemy.[29] American exporters who failed to understand how their goods could be captured on the high seas for violation of British municipal law protested to the State Department.[30] Hay instructed his ambassador in London, Joseph Choate, "to inquire as to the circumstances and le-

26. H. Lambert and H. Just, 20 Dec 99, minutes on FO to CO, 19 Dec 99, CO417/274.

27. Quoted in Salisbury, "Occupation of Delagoa Bay," cabinet memo, 27 Dec 99, CAB 37/51/102.

28. E.g., Milner to Chamberlain, 27 Dec 99, J. Chamberlain Papers, 10/9/76; Ardagh, memo, 23 Dec 99, WO 108/81; Casement (British agent, Lourenço Marques) to Foley (FO official), 25 Dec 99, Salisbury Papers, A/98/95.

29. Stowe (American consul-general, Capetown) to Crindler (assistant secretary of state), 6 Dec 99, United States, Department of State, *Papers Relating to the Foreign Relations of the United States* (Washington: Government Printing Office, 1861 *et seq.*), 1900, p. 529 [hereafter *FRUS*, year].

30. E.g., Hopkins & Hopkins to Hay, 12 Dec 99, ibid., 529–530.

gality of the seizure. If it was illegal, you will request prompt action and restitution."[31]

News of the capture appeared in the American press and stirred a strong public reaction. John Hay, who had written privately three months earlier that "as long as I stay here no action shall be taken contrary to my conviction that the one indispensable feature of our foreign policy should be a friendly understanding with England,"[32] had led the McKinley administration into a position of benevolent neutrality toward Britain.[33] But Hay knew that nothing could wreck his prized rapprochement faster than an old-fashioned confrontation over freedom of the seas. He instructed Choate to warn Salisbury that British actions had provoked "considerable public feeling" in the United States and that the matter would require delicate handling by both governments.[34]

A measure of British confusion in December 1899 is that Goschen had ordered Harris to search vigorously for contraband before the government had agreed on rules to govern such searches. The Admiralty maintained that the size of modern merchant ships made search at sea impossible and that the right of search must therefore be enforced in British ports.[35] The solicitor general maintained that the right of search existed only within the system of international law, which allowed diversion of a neutral ship into a belligerent port "only for the purpose of Prize Court proceedings." There could be no legal justification for speculative capture of neutral ships in the hope that a thorough search in port would reveal evidence to justify prize court charges.[36] Before the government could resolve this dispute, however, events once again outpaced the bureaucratic process. On December 29 Harris informed London that one of his ships had seized the German merchantman *Bundesrath* and brought it into Durban for

31. Hay to Choate, 21 Dec 99, ibid., 534.

32. Hay to Henry White (American diplomat), 24 Sep 99, White Papers, 28.

33. Bradford Perkins, *The Great Rapprochement* (New York: Atheneum, 1968), pp. 94–97; John H. Ferguson, *American Diplomacy and the Boer War* (Philadelphia: University of Pennsylvania Press, 1939), pp. ix, 221, and passim.

34. Hay to Choate, tel, 29 Dec 99, SD(M)M-30/186.

35. Admiral Lord Walter Kerr (first sea lord), 29 Dec 99, minute on FO to Adm, 27 Dec 99, Adm 1/7425.

36. Sir Robert Finlay to Bertie, 28 Dec 99, FO 2/279.

search.[37] As Goschen wryly told Salisbury, "the fun (?) has begun."[38]

Among those who saw nothing funny in the situation was Kaiser Wilhelm II. Germany had built up its shipping routes in South African waters at great expense. The shippers assured the Foreign Ministry that the *Bundesrath*'s cargo was entirely innocent.[39] On the morning of December 31 Count Hatzfeldt, the German ambassador in London, appeared at the Foreign Office to make a polite request for the ship's release. Sir Thomas Sanderson, the permanent undersecretary, assured him that the British government had no desire to interfere with legitimate German trade and that the *Bundesrath* would be released at once if the search revealed no contraband.[40]

Despite Sanderson's promise, and despite the solicitor general's opinion that seizure of neutral ships for search in port was a violation of international law, the prize authorities in South Africa went about their business without haste. The *Bundesrath* sat in Durban for a week while the court enjoyed a leisurely New Year's holiday. The search did not begin until January 6.[41] Long before it was complete, German patience was exhausted.

American patience was growing thin as well. Choate warned Salisbury on January 3 that the United States could not accept the detention of American property from the *Mashona* "under any belligerent right of capture." When the prime minister argued that the prize court was the proper authority to determine if the detention was legal, Choate disagreed. Britain had no right, he stated, to extend its own municipal law to justify capture of neutral property on the high seas. That aspect of international law was so clear that the American government saw no justification for judicial review. Unstated, but unmistakable after earlier warnings, was the threat that the American people might become so outraged by the British violations of neutral rights that the adminis-

37. CIC, Cape, to Adm, tel, 29 Dec 99, Adm 116/108.
38. Goschen to Salisbury, 30 Dec 99, Salisbury Papers, E/Goschen.
39. Sir Frank Lascelles (British ambassador, Berlin) to Salisbury, tel, 30 Dec 99, FO 2/434.
40. Hatzfeldt to Sanderson, 31 Dec 99, ibid.; Sanderson, memo of conversation, 31 Dec 99, ibid.
41. Hely-Hutchinson (governor, Natal) to Chamberlain, 13 Jan 00, CO 879/60/605.

tration would be forced to abandon the benevolence in its neutrality.[42]

Although Choate's January 3 statement was the most forceful from the United States to Britain since the Venezuelan boundary crisis of 1895, it paled before the note presented by Hatzfeldt the next day. The German ambassador simply announced that his government considered the *Bundesrath* innocent and its detention illegal. Germany would recognize no prize court proceedings, but instead would hold the British government directly responsible. If the Foreign Office wished to know the law relevant to the *Bundesrath* case it should consult the Royal Navy's own official prize manual: "The destination of the vessel is conclusive as to the destination of the goods on board." Germany would recognize no attempt by Britain to rewrite international law to the detriment of neutral rights in the middle of a war. The message closed by repeating the demand for the *Bundesrath*'s immediate release.[43]

Salisbury, although furious at the Admiralty for giving official sanction to a prize manual that did not recognize the doctrine of continuous voyage, refused to acknowledge that neutral protests were sincere: "The Kaiser's object of course is to pass his naval estimates."[44] The situation deteriorated still further. Capture of another German ship, the *General*, brought Hatzfeldt back to the Foreign Office on January 5 to present a note which Sanderson characterized as "of a nature not usual except in cases of Admirals addressing South American Republics."[45] The ambassador demanded immediate release of the *General*. He then formally requested the British government to "cause explicit instructions to be sent to the Commanders of British ships in African waters to respect the rules of international law."[46]

Salisbury must have recognized at this point that his position was becoming untenable. Hatzfeldt's "curt and peremptory tone" had wounded the prime minister's pride, however, and he refused to release the ships until a thorough search had established

---

42. Quotation from Hay to Choate, tel, 3 Jan 00, SD(M)M-30/186; see also Choate to Hay, tel, 4 Jan 00, ibid.; Choate to Hay, 6 Jan 00, Hay papers, (M)7.
43. Hatzfeldt to Salisbury, 4 Jan 00, FO 2/434.
44. Salisbury, n.d., minute on Bertie to Salisbury, 5 Jan 00, FO 2/434.
45. Sanderson to Lascelles, 6 Jan 00, FO 800/9.
46. Hatzfeldt to Salisbury, 5 Jan 00, FO 2/434.

their guilt or innocence. Grumbling that the German notes "do not deserve a civil reply," he gave them none.[47]

Release of the *General* after completion of a search on January 6 lessened Anglo-German tension,[48] but only for one day, until news of another capture brought the crisis to a head. The *Herzog* carried a Red Cross party personally sponsored by the Kaiserin. The German government had formally requested that the British government treat this party in the manner appropriate to its humanitarian mission and the rank of its sponsor. Yet the only special treatment the *Herzog* received was capture at sea and detention at Durban next to the *Bundesrath*.

The Kaiser was livid. Count von Bulow, the foreign minister, warned British Ambassador Sir Frank Lascelles that he had been able to persuade Wilhelm to appeal for arbitration rather than take unspecified direct action only with the greatest difficulty. Germany sought only friendship with Britain, but if such gratuitous insults continued public opinion would make good relations impossible. The German government would be forced to discuss British actions with other neutrals. Once such talks began, they might well extend to "other questions."[49] Bulow did not use the phrase "Continental coalition," but he scarcely had to in order to communicate his meaning.

Salisbury, however piqued, could not ignore the capture of the *Herzog*. The cabinet suddenly realized that its chief's stubbornness had plunged Britain into a crisis. Lord James of Hereford and other ministers who rarely showed interest in diplomacy complained that the prime minister had placed them "in a most untenable position."[50] Salisbury might ignore protests from Berlin and Washington, but when the chancellor of the Duchy of Lancas-

---

47. Salisbury to Lascelles, tel, 7 Jan 00, ibid.; Salisbury, n.d., minute on Barrington (FO private secretary) to Salisbury, 5 Jan 00, Salisbury Papers, A/96/101.

48. Lascelles to Sanderson, 6 Jan 00, FO 800/17.

49. Lascelles to Salisbury, tel, 7 Jan 00, FO 2/434.

50. Lord James to Lord Halsbury (lord chancellor), 7 Jan 00, Halsbury Papers, AM 56372; cf. Duke of Devonshire (lord president) as quoted in Eckardstein (first secretary, German Embassy, London) to Foreign Ministry, tel, 20 Jan 00, Johannes Lepsius et al., eds., *Die Grosse Politik der Europäischen Kabinette, 1871–1914*, XV (Berlin: Deutsche Verlagsgesellschaft für Politik und Geschichte, 1924), 481.

ter and the lord president of the council challenged his leadership
in foreign affairs he clearly had lost control of his cabinet. On
January 7 the Admiralty ordered "immediate release" of the *Herzog* whether searched or not.[51]

Only the *Bundesrath* now remained in British hands. Despite
Harris's promises, no evidence of contraband was forthcoming to
justify that capture.[52] By January 9, under heavy political as well
as diplomatic pressure, Salisbury was in full retreat. As a bid to
save face, he suggested that Britain might voluntarily refrain
from searching mail steamers.[53] Almost every ship that called at
Lourenço Marques carried mail, so the effect was to abandon the
effort to enforce belligerent rights. The British government continued to assert that it had the right to search neutral ships for
contraband and to enforce the doctrine of continuous voyage, but
while reserving the form it conceded the substance.

The same policy of retreat was evident when Salisbury met
Choate on January 10. The prime minister admitted that the
American goods seized on the *Mashona* could not be considered
contraband. The ship, he explained, had been seized for a violation of British municipal laws against trading with the enemy.
Unfortunately, the guilty ship could not be diverted without di-
verting the innocent cargo it carried. Charges had been dropped
against all American property, and it would be released to its
owners upon demand or purchased by the British government.
When Choate warned that the administration might present a
claim for damages, the prime minister's only comment was "very
likely."

Salisbury expressed particular approval of the American position that food for civilians could not be contraband. The panic of
Black Week was now a month past, and British statesmen were
returning to a more balanced view of national interests. The

51. Adm to CIC, Cape, tel, 7 Jan 00, Adm 116/108.
52. CIC, Cape, to Adm, tel, 8 Jan 00, ibid.; telegrams between Chamberlain
and Hely-Hutchinson, 9–28 Jan 00, CO 879/60/605; Chamberlain to Halsbury, 17
Jan 00, Halsbury Papers, AM 56372.
53. Salisbury to Lascelles, 9 Jan 00, FO 2/434; Bertie, "Memorandum as to
Belligerent Right of Search in case of Neutral Mail-Steamers," 10 Jan 00, with
minute by Salisbury, 12 Jan 00, ibid.; Adm to CIC, Cape, tel, 16 Jan 00, Adm
116/108; Salisbury to Lascelles, tel, 16 Jan 00, FO 2/434; Choate to Hay, 19 Jan 00,
Hay Papers, (M)7.

prime minister now upheld the doctrine that his Law Officers had advocated from the beginning of the war: "Foodstuffs with a hostile destination can be considered contraband of war only if they are supplies for the enemy's forces. It is not sufficient that they are capable of being so used. It must be shown that this was in fact their destination at the time of seizure."[54] The net result of the January 10 interview was British concession on every major point contested with the United States.

The decision to allow mail steamers to sail unmolested and the concessions to Choate produced an immediate easing of tension. Reports of vast arms shipments continued to reach London, but no longer were taken seriously.[55] The final indignity came when a secret service agent examined the books of the Boer commandant-general in March and reported that they contained no record "of any arms and ammunition having been received since the outbreak of war."[56] Chamberlain already had expressed the general feeling among his colleagues: "Personally I believe the seizure of foreign vessels has been a great mistake."[57]

This negative reaction is essential for understanding British maritime rights policy between January 1900 and August 1914. The generation that came to power in the aftermath of the Boer War, the generation of Balfour and Lord Lansdowne, of Herbert Henry Asquith and Sir Edward Grey, had only one experience with the exercising of belligerent rights. They had seen neutral ships detained without evidence and charged by incompetent prize authorities with "trading with the enemy,"[58] an impossible offense for any neutral by definition. They had seen a prime minister in humiliating retreat before angry neutrals and his own colleagues. They had seen all too clearly the difficulties of enforcing belligerent rights under modern conditions. These unpleasant memories were to have far-reaching consequences.

American leaders also learned from the Boer War experience.

54. Choate to Hay, tel, 10 Jan 00, enclosing Salisbury to Choate, 10 Jan 00, *FRUS*, 1900, pp. 549–550. The best historical account of the Boer War Anglo-American maritime rights dispute remains Ferguson, *American Diplomacy*, pp. 69–80.
55. E.g., CIC, Cape, to Adm, tel, 11 Mar 00, Adm 116/109/1.
56. Ross (British consul, Lourenço Marques) to Salisbury, tel, 13 Mar. 00, ibid.
57. Chamberlain to Halsbury, 17 Jan 00, Halsbury Papers, AM 56372.
58. CO to FO, 26 Feb 00, FO 2/435; Chamberlain to Hely-Hutchinson, tel, 15 Mar 00, ibid.

Before 1900 neither Britain nor the United States provided its naval officers with systematic training in maritime law, although the American Naval War College did offer an optional course. But in 1901 the Congress appropriated funds for a major effort to spread legal knowledge through the fleet. John Bassett Moore, the nation's most distinguished authority on international law, agreed to lecture at the War College. The next year Professor George Wilson of Brown University began offering an annual course structured especially for serving officers.[59] Graduates spread through the fleet, taking knowledge of maritime law with them, and the possibility that American naval officers would involve their country in a replay of Britain's fiasco was reduced correspondingly.

The Navy Department also ordered the president of the Naval War College to prepare a comprehensive code of maritime law as interpreted by the United States.[60] His draft was circulated to Mahan, to four eminent professors of international law, to the navy's General Board, and to the State Department for suggestions.[61] The president then declared the revised code in effect in June 1900.[62] The Boer War experience provided a strong impetus for these reforms.

The British government also sought to ensure that there would be no repetition of the maritime rights confusion so evident in 1899. Senior naval officers praised the American code,[63] and Professor Thomas Holland, author of the Admiralty prize manual, led a drive to reform British law along similar lines. Legislation was introduced in Parliament, but encountered insurmountable opposition.[64] The first lord of the Admiralty com-

59. House Resolution 13705, 11 Feb 01, with notes, Naval War College Archives, "International Law."

60. Secretary of the navy to Captain C. Stockton, 2 Nov 99, ND/RG45/VL.

61. Stockton to secretary of the navy, 19 May 00, Naval War College Archives, "Presidents: Stockton"; ND/RG45/VL.

62. United States, Naval War College, *International Law Topics and Discussions* (Washington: Government Printing Office, 1896 *et seq.*), 1903.

63. Clover (American naval attaché, London) to MacGregor (Admiralty Secretary), 2 May 03, Naval War College Archives, "Presidents: Stockton"; Chief, Office of Naval Intelligence, ND, to president, Naval War College, 19 May 03, ibid.; cf. U.S. naval attaché, Berlin, to Office of Naval Intelligence, ND, 8 Jun 03, ibid.

64. Naval Law Branch, Adm, "Short History of the Progress of the Naval Prize Bill," 15 Dec 03, with subsequent notes, Adm 116/1236.

plained that the Boer War experience was "sufficient to convince the most stupid Unionist member" of Parliament that "Naval Prize Law was not a subject on which the country can afford to trifle." He reluctantly admitted, however, that he could not pass the reform bill.[65] British statesmen had begun to reexamine traditional views on maritime rights, but the shock of another war would be necessary to crystallize these ruminations into action.

The Russo-Japanese War began on February 8, 1904, with a Japanese sneak attack prior to formal declaration of war. Despite this obvious breach of international law, no British or American statesman proclaimed that the date would live in infamy. On the contrary, President Theodore Roosevelt was "thoroughly well pleased" by the Japanese success.[66] The British Admiralty sneered at those "international purists" who were concerned at Japan's "technical violation of international law."[67] Anglo-American leaders regarded the war as a rematch of David and Goliath and believed that only Goliath himself, his fellow philistines, and a few unworldly "purists" could expect David to observe the international equivalent of the Marquess of Queensbury rules.

Russia quickly discovered, however, that these same Anglo-American leaders were less tolerant when Goliath committed the violations of international law. The Russian prize regulations announced on February 14 were extremely vague, but seemed to claim unprecedented belligerent rights. Russian officers were authorized to sink any ship, enemy or neutral, which they believed to carry contraband. The contraband list included food, fuels, and other items of general use, but made no clear distinction between absolute and conditional contraband. Prize courts were to be composed not of magistrates learned in the law of nations, but of Russian naval officers.[68] Japan had violated international law by attacking Russian warships, but Russia threatened

65. Selborne to J. Sandars (Balfour's political secretary), 22 Dec 04, Balfour Papers, AM 49708.
66. Roosevelt to T. Roosevelt, Jr., 10 Feb 04, Elting Morison et al., eds., *The Letters of Theodore Roosevelt [TR Letters]*, 8 vols. (Cambridge: Harvard University Press, 1951–1954), IV, 868.
67. Captain C. Ottley (director of naval intelligence), "Suddenness in Naval Operations," 1 Mar 05, Balfour Papers, AM 49710.
68. *FRUS,* 1904, pp. 727–729 (contraband list), and 736–754 (general prize regulations).

to attack neutral merchantmen. Britain and the United States were to resist with legal argument, diplomatic pressure, and finally the overt threat of force.

Lord Lansdowne, who had replaced Salisbury at the Foreign Office in 1900, considered the Russian prize rules so blatantly contrary to international law and detrimental to British interests that he determined to lodge an immediate protest. He instructed his ambassador in Washington, Sir Mortimer Durand, to sound out the American government on the possibility of joint representations. Secretary Hay declined this offer, stating that the United States would defend its rights against Russian actions but would not protest mere words in a proclamation.[69] The British government then acted alone. On June 8 Sir Charles Hardinge, the British ambassador in St. Petersburg, delivered a friendly but formal warning to Count Lamsdorff, the Russian foreign minister. International law drew a clear distinction between absolute and conditional contraband. Britain would hold Russia responsible for any violation of this principle.[70]

Ironically, Hardinge's warning was repeated in almost the same terms two days later in a circular from Hay to the American ambassadors in Europe. Although unwilling to give the appearance of collaboration with Britain, the secretary of state had been concerned by the Russian proclamation. By stating his objections in a circular rather than a bilateral note, he avoided a direct challenge to the Russian government and still made his point. The United States considered food, fuels, and cotton to be conditional contraband and would resist any attempt to treat such goods as absolute contraband.[71]

Russia had announced its prize regulations, and both the United States and Britain had placed themselves on record in opposition to certain aspects of those regulations. As long as the Russian navy refrained from any attempt to enforce the contested rules, the dispute remained academic. Fighting was limited to the

69. Hay, diary entries, 5, 10 Mar 04, Hay Papers, (M)1; Durand to Lansdowne, tel, 10 Mar 04, with minute by W. Davidson (FO Legal Adviser), 11 Mar 04, FO 418/18.

70. Hardinge to Lansdowne, 8 Jun 04, FO 46/625.

71. Hay to American ambassadors, circular dispatch, 10 Jun 04, *FRUS*, 1904, pp. 730–732; Hay, diary entry, 7 Jun 04, Hay Papers, (M)1.

Far East, where Japanese naval predominance left Russia little opportunity to enforce belligerent rights. A crisis flared in mid-July, when Russian ships that had passed the Turkish Straits as merchantmen began to intercept British shipping in the Red Sea, but the Czar agreed to end these operations voluntarily when Lansdowne warned they otherwise would be ended by the Royal Navy.[72] Because this dispute was more over the legal regime of the Turkish Straits than traditional maritime law, the controversial Russian prize regulations still had not been tested.

The test came with a vengeance on July 24, however, when a Russian squadron sank the British merchantman *Knight Commander*. London's initial reaction was disbelief. Young Lord Salisbury, who had inherited the title upon the former prime minister's death the year before and served as lord privy seal in his cousin's cabinet, exclaimed: "The idiots!! Let us hope that it is a lie."[73] It was not. A junior Russian naval officer had sunk a British ship, without trail in a prize court, because he had decided that it carried contraband. The attorney general advised that the British government would be legally justified in taking any action to protect neutral shipping.[74] Lansdowne expressed hope that the Russians would "climb down," but the Royal Navy remained on alert.[75]

The situation was complicated because, though the *Knight Commander* was British, most of its cargo had been owned by Americans. When Lansdowne told Choate that Britain would protest sinking of the ship in the strongest terms, the ambassador promised that the United States would be equally vigorous in regard to destruction of the cargo. When Hay sent his complaint to St. Petersburg on July 30, he authorized Choate to provide

72. John W. Coogan, "The End of Neutrality" (Ph.D. dissertation, Department of History, Yale University, 1976), pp. 50–52, 61–63; for further details see F. E. Smith and N. W. Sibley, *International Law as Interpreted during the Russo-Japanese War* (Boston: Boston Book Co., 1905), pp. 29–48.

73. Salisbury (4th Marquess) to Balfour, 25 Jul 04, Balfour Papers, AM 49757. On Russo-Japanese War maritime law, see C. J. B. Hurst and F. E. Bray, eds., *Russian and Japanese Prize Cases,* 2 vols. (London: His Majesty's Stationery Office, 1912).

74. CID, minutes, 27 Jul 04, CAB 2/1.

75. Lansdowne to Hardinge, 27 Jul 04, FO 800/140; Selborne to Kerr, "Decision of the Cabinet," 26 Jul 04, Selborne Papers, 154.

Lansdowne with a summary.[76] Russia thus produced what the best efforts of the British government had failed to produce: direct Anglo-American cooperation in defense of neutral rights. Hay remained wary of a public appearance of unity, and his chief subordinate gloated that "England is doing all the fighting and we shall reap our share of the benefits without making ourselves disagreeable."[77] But the Russian government could not ignore the obvious coordination of British and American responses.

The unwillingness of Hay and Roosevelt to appear too cozy with England in an election year did not prevent them from defending American rights. When Russia seized the *Arabia,* a German ship carrying American cargo, the State Department made no attempt to open polite negotiations. It stated bluntly that the cargo was not contraband and that the United States demanded its immediate release.[78] An aroused Theodore Roosevelt indicated to his secretary of state that he would go to any necessary length to safeguard American rights:

> I am not feeling any too kindly toward Russia, and I want you to think well what we shall do in case they [*sic*] seize any American ship. My own inclination is to notify them immediately that we will not stand it and to move our Asiatic Squadron northward. Of course I would put our statement in polite language, but very firmly, and I should do it with the intention of having our squadron bottle up the Vladivostok fleet, in case they attempted to cut up rough.[79]

This statement represented more than Rough Rider rhetoric; the president went on to instruct the Navy Department to prepare plans for a blockade of Vladivostok.[80] American cargoes seized under other neutral flags would be a subject of strenuous diplo-

76. Loomis (acting secretary of state) to Eddy (American chargé, St. Petersburg), tel, 30 Jul 04, *FRUS,* 1904, p. 734; Lansdowne to Durand, 27 Jul 04, FO 46/652.

77. Loomis to Hay, 28 Jul 04, Hay Papers (M) 20. Note the differences between the published version of McCormick (American ambassador, St. Petersburg) to Hay, 20 Aug 04, *FRUS,* 1904, p. 758, and the text in SD(M)M-35/61.

78. Adee (acting secretary of state) to Eddy, tel, 27 Jul 04, SD(M)M-77/93.

79. Roosevelt to Hay, 29 Jul 04, *TR Letters,* IV, 869.

80. Roosevelt to Captain J. Pillsbury (acting chief, Bureau of Navigation, ND), 29 Jul 04, ibid.

macy. Seizure or destruction of a vessel under the United States flag would be answered by the American navy.

The Russian government released the *Arabia* with a haste the jealous British considered indecent[81] and refrained from seizing any ships flying the American flag, so Roosevelt never had to implement his threat. The prize court condemned part of the American cargo on the *Arabia* as contraband, but Lamsdorff was careful to point out that the decision could be appealed.[82] Russia seemed so eager to placate the United States, in fact, that many in Britain suspected a deliberate plot to separate the Anglo-American powers by discriminatory treatment of British trade.[83] Austen Chamberlain, the young chancellor of the exchequer, urged a stronger effort to "flatter & engage American sympathies."[84] At the same time, pressure from the press, from commercial interests, and from Parliament pushed the Government toward a stronger stand with or without American cooperation.[85]

Early in August the cabinet decided that normal diplomacy had failed. The Foreign Office drafted a note reviewing previous attempts to reach a peaceful settlement, warning that Russia would owe British shippers compensation of "enormous dimensions," and threatening that the British government was no longer able "to rest content with the prospect of obtaining pecuniary compensation for the sufferers."[86] Prime Minister Balfour explained to King Edward why his Government had felt compelled to use such stiff language:

> The line taken is a strong one: but Mr. Balfour is of opinion that this is on the whole likely to conduce to peace rather than to war. The Russians are sometimes under the delusion that a *conciliatory* attitude is a *weak* attitude and that Great Britain is prepared to make any concession rather than defend her rights by force. So lamentable a misconstruction of the real feeling of this country is a

81. E.g., Lansdowne to Hardinge, draft dispatch, 6 Aug 04, CAB 37/72/114.
82. Lamsdorff to McCormick, 9 Aug 04, transmitted in McCormick to Hay, 10 Aug 04, *FRUS,* 1904, p. 756.
83. E.g., Liverpool Steam-Ship Owners' Association to FO, 19 Aug 04, printed in CID Paper 75B, 15 May 06, CAB 4/2; Hardinge to Lansdowne, 1 Sep 04, FO 800/140; Lansdowne to Balfour, 26 Aug 04, Balfour Papers, AM 49728.
84. Chamberlain, n.d., notes on Lansdowne to Hardinge, draft dispatch, n.d., A. Chamberlain Papers, 7/5B/10A.
85. See FO 46/618-656, esp. 625; Selborne Papers, 154.
86. FO, draft dispatch to Hardinge, n.d., FO 46/652.

serious menace to good international relations; and the sooner it is dissipated the better.[87]

Lansdowne meanwhile continued the effort to present at least the appearance of a common Anglo-American front to the Russian government. When Choate informed him of the American decision to protest condemnation of food on the *Arabia* on the ground that Russia had not proved destination to the Japanese armed forces,[88] the foreign secretary immediately demanded of his staff: "Is there not some British flour on board? Have we taken any steps?"[89] Informed that part of the condemned food had been consigned to a British firm, Lansdowne gleefully ordered Hardinge to submit a note "following as closely as possible terms of U. S. protest, which you can perhaps get from American colleague."[90]

These obviously concerted protests forced the Russian government to reconsider its policy. On March 7 Lamsdorff had assured the British ambassador that Russia considered food absolute contraband.[91] On August 16 Lamsdorff assured the British ambassador that Russia considered food conditional contraband. The foreign minister expressed regret that the prize court had so completely misinterpreted the meaning of the February 14 regulations in its recent decision. Hardinge predicted after this interview that Russia would soon accept the Anglo-American position, a change for which he credited "the firm and uncompromising attitude of the British and American Governments."[92]

Balfour assured the King upon receipt of this report that "there is some hope now that the most serious phase in our controversies with Russia as to her belligerent rights is at an end."[93] But before the American ambassador's equally optimistic report reached Washington, the patience of Hay and Roosevelt had been

87. Balfour to Edward VII, cabinet letter, 11 Aug 04, CAB 41/29/31.
88. Hay to Choate, tel, 11 Aug 04, SD(M)M-77/93.
89. Lansdowne, n.d., minute on Hardinge to Lansdowne, tel, 13 Aug 04, FO 46/628.
90. Lansdowne to Hardinge, tel, 13 Aug 04, ibid.
91. C. Scott to Lansdowne, tel, 7 Mar 04, Great Britain, Parliament, *Parliamentary Papers* (House of Commons and Command), 1905, vol. CIII, Cmnd. 2348, pp. 4–5.
92. Hardinge to Lansdowne, 16 Aug 04, FO 46/629.
93. Balfour to Edward VII, 21 Aug 04, Balfour Papers, AM 49684.

exhausted. The secretary of state recommended a protest so strong that Russia must respect it. The president replied: "I am delighted." The State Department solicitor drafted a note in "nearly as strong language as I could," and Roosevelt applauded his "admirable" refutation of Russia's "preposterous position."[94] Hay sent this dispatch to St. Petersburg the day before the report of Lamsdorff's conciliatory statements arrived. His message was nothing less than a lecture on civilized behavior:

> The established principle of discrimination between contraband and noncontraband goods admits of no relaxation or refinement. It must be either inflexibly adhered to or abandoned by all nations. There is and can be no middle ground. The criterion of warlike usefulness and destination has been adopted by the common consent of civilized nations....
>
> If the principle which appears to have been declared by the Vladivostok prize court ... is acquiesced in, it means ... the complete destruction of all neutral commerce with the noncombatant population of Japan; ... and is in effect a declaration of war against commerce of every description between the people of a neutral and those of a belligerent State.
>
> ... The Government of the United States regrets its complete inability to recognize the principle of that decision and still less to acquiesce in it as a policy.[95]

The new American note reinforced Lamsdorff's belief that Russia stood to lose far more by provoking Britain and the United States than it could possibly gain by seizing a few cargoes of food. On September 16 the foreign minister announced that new instructions had been issued to naval officers and prize authorities. The controversy apparently had been resolved to the satisfaction of the Anglo-Americans, although the new rules did seem to require that a neutral merchant prove his goods would not be used by the Japanese military. Lamsdorff explained that his government felt compelled to maintain its rule in principle, but he promised that "in the future there would be less ground for complaint" because Russia would not seek to enforce the disputed rule.[96]

94. Hay to Roosevelt, 25 Aug 04, Hay Papers, (M)4; W. Penfield to Hay, 29 Aug 04, ibid., (M)20; Roosevelt to Hay, 25, 29 Aug 04, T. Roosevelt Papers, (M)416.

95. Hay to McCormick, 30 Aug 04, *FRUS*, 1904, pp. 760–762.

96. Hardinge to Lansdowne, 15 Sep 04, FO 800/141; Hardinge to Lansdowne, tel, 16 Sep 04, FO 834/21; McCormick to Hay, 21 Sep 04, *FRUS*, 1904, pp. 767–768.

These concessions effectively ended the controversy between Russia and the United States. They also seemed to have resolved the difficulties over maritime rights between Russia and Britain, despite some continued difficulties concerning the status of Russia's Black Sea auxiliaries.[97] Differences in principle remained, but Russian promises not to enforce contested rules appeared to ensure that future controversies would be academic debates rather than diplomatic or military confrontations. On the night of October 21, however, a Russian fleet opened fire on British fishing boats in the North Sea.

Some points of maritime law were open to debate in 1904. The right of neutral fishermen to follow their perilous calling off their own coast without the added danger of slaughter by trigger-happy belligerents was not. Britain reacted to the Dogger Bank incident with a rage no Continental nation could understand. Arthur Balfour, who had a reputation for sang-froid even among his fellow British aristocrats, stormed that "my first thoughts are to stop the Russian Fleet at the first convenient place and exact explanations and reparation."[98] Lansdowne drafted an ultimatum. When one of his clerks tried to moderate the language, the foreign secretary insisted that the original text be restored. King Edward then inserted more threatening language. Hardinge read this note to Lamsdorff, then offered the personal observation that "the Russian fleet was behaving as though it were officered and manned by savages or lunatics."[99]

As the Russian fleet steamed down the Bay of Biscay, Gibraltar went under martial law. The British squadron stationed .there stood north into the Atlantic, ships darkened and live fuses on their shells. The commander's orders were to stop the Russians "by persuasion if possible but by force if necessary."[100] Before the two fleets met, however, the Czar backed down. The Russian ships had mistaken the fishing fleet for Japanese torpedo boats, and the Russian government would make full apologies and repa-

---

97. Coogan, "End of Neutrality," pp. 61–63.

98. Balfour to Selborne, tel, 24 Oct 04, Selborne Papers, 39.

99. Lansdowne to Hardinge, draft tel, 24 Oct 04, FO 65/1729; quotation from Eddy to Hay, 29 Oct 04, Hay Papers, (M)8.

100. Selborne to Admiral Lord Charles Beresford (CIC, Channel Fleet), tel, 27 Oct 04, Adm 116/969.

rations for the error. To the amazement of Theodore Roosevelt, the British accepted this settlement.[101] Whether because of Russian restraint or naval weakness, no further controversies developed over maritime rights.

Overall, the Russo-Japanese War confirmed the conclusions many British and American statesmen had drawn from the Boer War. Once again a belligerent had claimed broad rights, and once again neutral resistance had forced a retreat. For Americans, the two experiences seemed to support the traditional national position in favor of neutral rights. To Englishmen, the belligerent experience in 1899 and the neutral experience in 1904 seemed a strong argument for reexamining the old insistence on broad belligerent rights. In both countries the trend toward reform that began in 1899 gathered momentum.

The Boer and Russo-Japanese Wars also established legal precedents on several contested questions. In 1899 the British had claimed a right to capture neutral ships on the high seas and bring them into port for a thorough search. When Germany presented a bill for damages resulting from application of this rule to the *Bundesrath* and other ships, the Law Officers, who had regarded the practice as illegal all along, advised the Government to settle out of court.[102] No prize court decision explicitly repudiated this doctrine of speculative seizure, but the British government ordered Harris to refrain from attempting to enforce it and paid damages to Germany for prior cases of diversion for search.[103] These actions were in their own way as strong a repudiation as any formal statement or court ruling.

Both wars served to confirm the traditional distinction between absolute and conditional contraband, especially in regard to food shipments. Britain had asserted several rules of varying severity in 1899, but Salisbury's statement on January 10, 1900, swept all of these away. The cabinet had overruled the prime minister once and had been prepared to do so again to maintain

---

101. Lansdowne to Hardinge, 29 Oct 04, Hardinge Papers, Cambridge Collection, 7; Hay, diary entry, 25 Oct 04, Hay Papers, (M)1.

102. LO to FO, 1 Feb 00, CO 879/60/605.

103. Adm to CIC, Cape, tel, 16 Mar 00, Adm 116/108; Bertie to Salisbury, 1 Aug 00, FO 2/435; cf. damages paid to American shippers, Choate to Hay, 21 Nov 00, Hay Papers, (M)7.

the principle that food was conditional contraband and therefore could be seized only when the captor could prove destination to the enemy armed forces. Britain had joined the United States in defending this rule in 1904, and together they had forced Russia to accept their view in practice if not in theory. Not all nations would have accepted the rule stated by Hay, Salisbury, and Lansdowne, but by 1904 there could be no doubt in either British or American prize law that conditional contraband could be seized only when the captor could prove enemy military destination. Nor could there be any doubt that food constituted conditional, not absolute, contraband.

One point of law the Boer War did not resolve and the Russo-Japanese War did not test was the doctrine of continuous voyage. In 1900 Britain had refused to abandon its position that the doctrine was sound law and Germany had refused to recognize that continuous voyage had any legal existence.[104] McKinley had expressed regret that no agreement had been reached.[105] At the end of the Russo-Japanese War continuous voyage remained as it had been before the Boer War: a vaguely defined and controversial presence on the fringe of international law.

One principle not in doubt after 1904, however, was that the law of nations rather than the will of belligerents was the primary determinant of neutral rights on the high seas. As Salisbury and Lamsdorff could testify, maritime law was a vital reality which powerful neutrals would force belligerents to respect. There was a general international recognition of the need for a common code of law to define the precise limits of neutral and belligerent rights.[106] But after 1904 only a very brave or a very foolish statesman would have repeated Count Lamsdorff's assertion that a belligerent was free to establish whatever rules it wished for neutral commerce.[107]

Perhaps the most surprising aspect of the Boer and Russo-Japanese War experiences was the degree of accord and identity of interest they seemed to reveal between Britain and the United

---

104. E.g., Salisbury to Lascelles, 10 Jan 00, FO 2/434; Bertie, memo of conversation, 11 Jan 00, ibid.

105. McKinley, Annual Message to Congress, 3 Dec 00, *FRUS*, 1900, p. xxi.

106. E.g., Hay, circular dispatch, 21 Oct 04, ibid., 1904, pp. 10–13.

107. Reported in Hardinge to Lansdowne, 8 Jun 04, FO 46/625.

States on maritime rights. Two nations that traditionally had viewed their positions as poles apart found that they in fact had a remarkable degree of agreement. Britain had used American Civil War precedents to justify its position on continuous voyage in 1899, and Salisbury's statement on food might have served as the basis for the relevant section of the American Naval War Code announced that same year.[108] Roosevelt had been unwilling to sanction public cooperation with Britain against Russia in 1904 because of his fears of isolationist and Anglophobic reaction in an election year, but the two nations had coordinated their protests effectively in secret. They had taken essentially identical positions, particularly in regard to contraband and placing the burden of proof on the captor in prize court proceedings. An even greater degree of cooperation seemed likely in the future, as British statesmen continued to question past insistence on broad belligerent rights. Lansdowne privately assured Roosevelt in January 1905 that when the Second Hague Conference discussed the law of contraband, Britain would "be found on the side of neutral rather than belligerent interests."[109] An international code of maritime law along the lines traditionally favored by the United States had never seemed so close to realization.

108. United States Naval War Code of 1900, Article 34, Savage, I, 497.
109. Lansdowne to Balfour, 18 Jan 05, Balfour Papers, AM 49729.

✿

The United States and Maritime Rights, 1904–1907

The favorable international response to a call by John Hay in October 1904 assured the holding of a second peace conference at The Hague.[1] The disputes of the Boer and Russo-Japanese Wars ensured that maritime rights would have a high priority on the conference's agenda. Both Hay's dispatch and the course of American history seemed to indicate the position the United States would take. American delegates would propose, as they had in 1899, that all private property at sea except contraband or blockade runners be made immune from belligerent capture. If the other nations were so misguided as to reject this proposal, the American delegation would support a code of existing maritime law that provided strong safeguards for neutral commerce. The United States had advocated such a policy on maritime rights almost since its founding, and there was no apparent reason to expect a change as the twentieth century began.

The Naval War Code of 1900, as revised in 1903, provided a convenient summary of American interpretations of international law. Behind the code stood a century of prize court judgments and notes to other nations. The United States held that the sea was free to ships of all nations, except insofar as that freedom might be limited by certain belligerent rights sanctioned by law. These rights entitled a belligerent to seize ships of his enemy, to

1. Hay, circular dispatch, 21 Oct 04, *FRUS*, 1904, pp. 10–13; for background and international responses, see Calvin D. Davis, *The United States and the Second Hague Peace Conference* (Durham: Duke University Press, 1975), pp. 91–116.

seize neutral ships carrying contraband to his enemy, and to seize blockade runners. Belligerents possessed the right to stop neutral ships on the high seas and search them, but only when essential to enforce other belligerent rights. International law permitted no other interference with neutral commerce.[2] Should a belligerent exceed these established rights and refuse to make restitution for his violation, the offended neutral was justified in any action he chose to take in defense of his neutral rights.[3] American history had not been marked by a reluctance to take action under such circumstances.

The United States traditionally had favored even greater restriction of belligerent rights. American statesmen from Benjamin Franklin to William McKinley had advocated immunity for all private property at sea except contraband and blockade runners. Roosevelt had requested authority to negotiate an international agreement on immunity in 1903, and Congress had assented unanimously. Even the Supreme Court had expressed its approval.[4] As the United States began preparing for the Second Hague Conference in the wake of Hay's initiative, the Roosevelt administration was officially committed to advocate immunity.

At least one American was concerned that his nation might, in the international atmosphere following the Boer and Russo-Japanese Wars, prove too successful in limiting belligerent rights. Alfred Thayer Mahan, who had served as a delegate to the First Hague Peace Conference, warned his friend and fellow naval historian Theodore Roosevelt that adoption of immunity might prove a disaster rather than a boon for national security under modern conditions:

> The general situation of the United States in the world policy of today, appears to me to make most impolitic this change. Circumstances almost irresistible are forcing us and Great Britain, not into

2. Some highly technical doctrines not significant to this study, such as angary, are ignored in this generalization.

3. Naval War Code of 1900, Naval War College, *International Law Discussions,* 1903; Moore, *Digest,* VII, passim; Savage, I, passim.

4. Roosevelt, Annual Message to Congress, 7 Dec 03, Savage, I, 506–507; Senate and House, Joint Resolution, 24 Apr 04, ibid., 514; Justice Peckham for the Court, 11 Dec 99, ibid., 506. For the history of immunity before 1900, see Moore, *Digest,* VII, 461–473.

alliance, but into silent cooperation. . . . Our united naval strength can *probably* control the seas. . . . It may well be that under such conditions the power to control commerce,—the *lawful* right international precedent now hampers,—may be of immense, of decisive importance. . . .

The question is one of expediency, and what was expedient to our weakness of a century ago is not expedient to our strength today. Rather should we seek to withdraw from our position of the flag covering the goods. We need to fasten our grip on the sea.

Mahan's letter struck at the root of America's traditional support for restrictions on belligerent rights. Policy on maritime law, he warned, already was out of step with foreign policy and national interests. The belligerent rights the United States had sought to limit as a weak state trying to maintain isolation from Great Power conflicts were now essential for the security of a powerful state that no longer could maintain its isolation. Changing strategic conditions in the twentieth century demanded the sacrifice not only of youthful dreams such as immunity for private property, but of such basic American principles as "free ship, free goods." American policy at The Hague should reflect the necessity of belligerent rights rather than the hallowed but no longer appropriate tradition of neutral rights.[5]

Mahan's arguments convinced neither Roosevelt nor Hay. The secretary of state dismissed the letter as "the professional sailor's view" and concluded, "I do not think the considerations he brings to bear are weighty enough to cause us to reverse our traditional policy for the last century."[6] The president agreed. Immunity for private property and general limitation of belligerent rights remained official objectives.

Mahan did not regard this failure as final. He waited while the conference was delayed, then renewed his effort early in 1906. After drafting another letter to Roosevelt,[7] he decided to appeal instead to the new secretary of state, Elihu Root. This time he emphasized the importance of maritime rights to the United States and requested "a comprehensive examination" of the full

5. Mahan to Roosevelt, 27 Dec 04, Mahan Papers, 3.

6. Hay to Roosevelt, 31 Dec 04, Hay Papers, (M)4.

7. Mahan to Roosevelt, draft letter, n.d., Mahan Papers, 6; Robert Seager II, *Alfred Thayer Mahan* (Annapolis: Naval Institute Press, 1977), p. 509.

"civil, legal and military aspects" of American policy at the upcoming conference.[8]

Mahan's letter convinced the secretary of state that traditional maritime rights policy should be subjected to "the most careful re-examination" before he drafted the final instructions for the Hague delegation. Root's experience as secretary of war had forced him to recognize that even the oldest of policies could become obsolete.[9] He asked the navy's General Board for a systematic reassessment of immunity and its potential impact on national security under modern conditions.[10]

Mahan, a retired captain, could speak only for himself. The General Board, a committee of senior officers chaired by Admiral of the Navy George Dewey,[11] could speak for the navy. Its agreement with the main points of Mahan's argument thus was a potent blow against immunity. Dewey admitted that immunity would have been "advantageous to us from a military standpoint" during the years of American naval weakness, but insisted that "at the present time conditions are reversed." Rather than pursuing further limitation of belligerent rights, the United States should "advocate an increase in the list of contraband goods, thus limiting further the rights of neutrals, and . . . resist any attempt to further limit the rights of blockaders." The board did not endorse Mahan's recommendation for abandonment of the "free ship, free goods" rule, but it did conclude that "no considerations should be permitted to put the United States at a military disadvantage in any possible future war."[12]

Dewey cast his initial report in general terms and gave brief

8. Mahan to Root, 20 Apr 06, Admiral C. Sperry Papers, 9 (page 1) and 11 (remainder of letter and enclosures).

9. James E. Hewes, Jr., *From Root to McNamara* (Washington: U.S. Government Printing Office, 1975), pp. 6-13; Richard D. Challener, *Admirals, Generals, and American Foreign Policy, 1898-1914* (Princeton: Princeton University Press, 1973), pp. 23-25, 46-47; Philip L. Semsch, "Elihu Root and the General Staff," *Military Affairs*, 27 (Spring 1963):16-34.

10. Root to secretary of the navy, 21 May 06, Mahan Papers, 6.

11. J. A. S. Grenville and George Berkeley Young, *Politics, Strategy, and American Diplomacy* (New Haven: Yale University Press, 1966), pp. 299-300 and passim; Challener, *Admirals*, p. 47 and passim; Ronald Spector, *Admiral of the New Empire* (Baton Rouge: Louisiana State University Press, 1974), pp. 126-131 and passim.

12. General Board (signed by Dewey) to secretary of the navy, 20 Jun 06, Navy Department, Operational Archives Branch, General Board Letters, IV, 276-301.

consideration to possible wars with each of the leading maritime powers. In a supplemental memorandum submitted three months later, however, he justified the same conclusion in bluntly specific terms.

> The General Board is of the opinion that our interests are now so closely bound up with Great Briatin, that we should exert our diplomatic efforts to dissuade Great Britain from giving up the great advantage she now holds over Germany, due to her great Navy and her excellent strategical position in regard to Germany's commerce. This great advantage would be lost to Great Britain should she join with the United States in its previous mistaken policy of urging an international agreement to exempt private property from seizure in time of war. . . .
>
> Germany will fear our interference with her merchant marine to some extent in case of a war with the United States single handed, and of course if private property at sea is immune in time of war she need not fear it at all. But if the United States should secure Great Britain as an ally, Germany's shipping would be tied up no matter who Germany might secure as an ally. . . . Should private property at sea be immune in time of war this great advantage would be lost to Great Britain, as well as to the United States, and the immense assistance which we might expect to receive from Great Britain would be tremendously decreased. . . .
>
> The welfare of the United States and its immunity from entanglements with the other powers is greatly strengthened by strong ties of friendship and by unanimity of action with Great Britain. The two great English-speaking nations seem destined to exert a great influence on the conduct of war when war is inevitable. Nothing should be agreed to that will lessen that influence or, where our interests are in common, to take away so potent and influential a factor to prevent or shorten a war, as the liability to seizure of enemy's private property at sea in time of war.[13]

The General Board agreed with Mahan that a common Anglo-American interest in preserving the ability of sea power to strike at Germany required that the United States oppose immunity for private property or any other limitation of belligerent rights.

Root, obviously impressed by the navy's arguments, circulated them within his own department. They found an unexpected champion in the solicitor, James Brown Scott, a leading international lawyer, a pacifist, and a past supporter of immunity. He was

13. General Board to secretary of the navy, 28 Sep 06, ibid., 356–361.

careful now to avoid comment on the board's prediction of
Anglo-American conflict with Germany, such "policy" matters
being reserved "for the Secretary and the Assistant Secretaries."
Nevertheless, Scott admitted that Dewey's argument had convinced him that immunity was no longer in the national interest.[14]

When James Brown Scott agreed with George Dewey and
Alfred Thayer Mahan on a question of maritime law, Elihu Root
could not but be impressed. In October 1906 the secretary instructed his ambassador in London, Whitelaw Reid, to ask the
foreign secretary what position Britain intended to take on immunity. Root admitted that "I myself have grave doubts" about
the traditional American policy and referred specifically to the
danger that Germany might grow more aggressive should its vulnerability to sea power be reduced.[15] Two months later the
American military delegate-designate assured his naval counterpart that Root, along with Assistant Secretary Robert Bacon and
Hague delegate Horace Porter, was opposed to immunity.[16]
Mahan appeared to have won his fight.

When the Hague delegation met with Root in April 1907,
however, the secretary had changed his position if not his views.
He admitted that he was "not wholly clear" personally as to
whether immunity would be in the national interest. But as secretary of state he could not change such a traditional policy "at
this day." Admiral Charles Sperry, the naval delegate, protested
that if the United States did secure an international agreement on
immunity the major effect would be to jeopardize its own national
security. Choate, the former ambassador to London who was to
head the delegation, replied that America must press immunity at
The Hague because it had responsibilities to humanity and peace
as well as to security. The debate continued until Choate asked the
secretary whether further discussion was likely to change the outcome. An embarrassed Root then admitted that it was not. Despite
his own "great doubts on the question," he had no choice but to
instruct the delegates to support immunity.[17]

14. Scott to Adee, memo, 9 Oct 06, SD/RG59/NF 40/2½.
15. Root to Reid, 24 Oct 06, Reid Papers, (M)176.
16. General George Davis to Sperry, 12 Dec 06, Sperry Papers, 9.
17. Scott, minutes of meeting, 20 Apr 07, SD/RG59/NF40/210½. See also
Davis, *Second Hague*, pp. 170–173.

This revelation effectively ended the debate. Only Theodore Roosevelt could have overruled his secretary of state, and if the president had already rejected the arguments of Mahan, Dewey, and Root he was not likely to be swayed by the Hague delegates. The secretary of state issued his formal instructions on May 31. They directed full support for immunity, with the usual disclaimer as to contraband and blockade runners. The United States would favor defining contraband "as narrowly as possible." The Naval War Code of 1900 was commended as the model for the proposed international code. All in all, Root's instructions were in the American tradition of support for commercial at the expense of belligerent rights.[18]

Choate, delighted, assured the less-than-enthusiastic secretary of state that immunity was almost certain to win approval.[19] Others were less pleased with the instructions. Sperry approved of the narrow definition of contraband and was unconcerned about immunity because he was confident the British would veto it.[20] Mahan had planned a public campaign against immunity, but redirected his effort toward influencing the British government when he learned that Roosevelt had decided against his view.[21] The General Board, whose views had been disregarded on immunity, contraband, and most other matters, expressed no formal opinion.

The American decision to follow traditional policies on maritime rights in 1907 is most frustrating for the historian. Mahan had proposed a complete reversal of the national position, justified by an elaborate strategic analysis based on a revolutionary definition of national interests. The Navy and State departments and at least half of the Hague delegates accepted his conclusions. Only Hay and Choate had demurred, and neither made any systematic effort to refute Mahan's arguments. Nevertheless, Roosevelt rejected the overwhelming recommendation of his ad-

18. Root, Instructions, 31 May 07, Savage, I, 517–520; for earlier drafts see SD/RG59/NF40/unnumbered at end of file.
19. Choate to Root, 7 May 07, SD/RG59/NF40/230½.
20. Scott, minutes, 20 Apr 07, ibid. /210½.
21. Mahan to T. Roosevelt, draft letter, n.d., Mahan Papers, 6; Mahan to George Harvey (editor, *North American Review*), 17 Oct 06, Franklin D. Roosevelt Papers, RG7/"Mahan."

visers and directed that the established policy remain the American position at The Hague. He apparently left no record of his reasoning.

Mahan believed that Roosevelt privately agreed with the critics of immunity, but felt compelled to maintain the traditional policy because of Hay's 1904 circular and his own 1903 statement to Congress. The United States would make a show of supporting restriction of belligerent rights at The Hague, Mahan predicted, but "would not be greatly disappointed to meet an insuperable objection."[22] The leading historian of the American role at the Second Hague Conference supports this interpretation, suggesting that Roosevelt privately shared Mahan's view but was unwilling to reverse publicly the stance taken by the United States since Benjamin Franklin.[23] A gallant but foredoomed fight must have seemed far more attractive to the president than an attempt to explain to businessmen, peace groups, and an isolationist public that the United States must abandon its emphasis on commercial rights in order to strengthen the belligerent rights it would require in an Anglo-American war against Germany.

There is, however, another plausible explanation for Roosevelt's decision to continue supporting immunity. He may have rejected the advice of Mahan and Dewey because he did not consider it sound. The president had a high regard for professional opinion on strategic questions, but an even higher regard for his own opinion. Were Roosevelt convinced that broad commercial rights remained in the national interest, not even the most trusted subordinates could have moved him.

The essence of the Mahan-Dewey position was a series of assumptions about the course of international relations in the near future. An aggressive Germany, they argued, posed an inevitable threat to British and American interests in the Far East and in Latin America. This common threat would force the United States to abandon its historic isolation in favor of Anglo-American cooperation. Because neither the United States nor Britain pos-

---

22. Mahan to Leo Maxse (editor, *National Review*), 30 May 07, Mahan Papers, 4; cf. Mahan to Maxse, 30 Jul 07, in Robert Seager II and Doris D. Maguire, eds., *Letters and Papers of Alfred Thayer Mahan*, 3 vols. (Annapolis: Naval Institute Press, 1975), III, 221.

23. David, *Second Hague*, pp. 139, 171.

sessed a mass army, sea power was their only real weapon to deter or resist German aggression. Any weakening of the effectiveness of this weapon, such as restrictions on its ability to strike at an enemy's commerce, strengthened the relative strategic position of Germany and thus reduced correspondingly the security of Britain and the United States. Although the General Board had asserted that cooperation with Britain would strengthen American "immunity from entanglements with the other powers," the Mahan-Dewey analysis in fact advocated the most significant foreign entanglement for the United States since abrogation of the French Alliance.

Did Theodore Roosevelt accept the view that common interests would force Britain and the United States into a common front based on resistance to German aggression? His decision on maritime rights policy for the Second Hague Conference would seem to indicate that, at least in the spring of 1907, he did not. His personal view of American relations with Britain and Germany had oscillated wildly since he told a British friend in 1898 that prior to the Spanish-American War "the one desire of his life was to have a fight with the British."[24] Yet a year later he wrote that "the Navy is a unit in wanting to smash Germany" and left no doubt that he shared that desire.[25] British friendship and German hostility had "worked a complete revolution" in his feelings.[26]

Roosevelt brought this pro-British, anti-German attitude to the White House with him in 1901. Had Mahan and Dewey presented their analysis at that time, the president probably would have accepted it intellectually whether or not he was willing to pay the political price for implementing their conclusions. But the Venezuelan crisis of 1902–1903 had marked both the peak of Roosevelt's Germanophobia and the beginning of a better German-American relationship. He later described his actions and their result to a friendly English diplomat:

> When I first came into the Presidency I was inclined to think that the Germans had serious designs upon South America. But I think

24. Sir F. Villiers (FO official) n.d., minute to Arthur Lee (British military attaché with American forces in Cuba, 1898) to Villiers, 8 Dec 98, FO 800/23.
25. Roosevelt to Sir Cecil Spring Rice (British diplomat), 11 Aug 99, *TR Letters,* II, 1050.
26. Roosevelt to Lee, 25 Jul 00, ibid., p. 1362.

I succeeded in impressing on the Kaiser, quietly and unofficially, and with equal courtesy and emphasis, that the violation of the Monroe Doctrine by territorial aggrandizement on his part around the Caribbean meant war, not ultimately, but immediately, and without delay. He has always been as nice as possible to me since and has helped me in every way, and my relations with him and the relations of the two countries have been . . . growing more close and friendly.[27]

By November 1905, when Roosevelt wrote this letter, he had abandoned much of his simplistic antagonism and suspicion toward Germany. A senior British naval officer, Prince Louis of Battenberg, reported that same month that the president had spoken of "close friendship, and if necessary co-operation, between the three great Anglo-Saxon Powers—America, England and Germany—to whom the future belonged." Roosevelt "rejoiced" at the fall of Théophile Delcassé, the anti-German French foreign minister, and warned that Britain would have only itself to blame if it permitted the Anglo-French Entente of April 1904 to block rapprochement with Germany.[28] Although indignant when British friends suggested he was "under the influence of the Kaiser,"[29] Roosevelt's view of German policy did change after 1903. He did not become anti-British, as Lansdowne and others in the British government feared,[30] but unlike the General Board he

27. Roosevelt to Spring Rice, 1 Nov 05, ibid., V, 63.
28. Admiral Prince Louis of Battenberg to Edward VII, 5 Nov 05, extract FO 800/116.
29. Roosevelt to Spring Rice, 13 May 05, Roosevelt Papers, (M)416. On the overall evolution of Roosevelt's view of Germany, see Howard K. Beale, *Theodore Roosevelt and the Rise of America to World Power* (Baltimore: Johns Hopkins Press, 1956), pp. 390–447. Raymond A. Esthus, *Theodore Roosevelt and the International Rivalries* (Waltham, Mass.: Ginn-Blaisdell, 1970), pp. 23–24, 38–135, 149–150, is also useful, although the author errs in stating that "Roosevelt came to essentially the same conclusion as that reached by Eyre Crowe in his famous Foreign Office memorandum of January 1, 1907" (p. 135). Roosevelt agreed with Crowe that Britain should never allow the Royal Navy to fall behind the German navy, but his comments to Prince Louis on the fall of Delcassé prove that he did not share Crowe's conclusion that Wilhelmine Germany was driving for European hegemony in the footsteps of Philip II, Louis XIV, and Napoleon I, or that the proper policy for Britain was diplomatic and if necessary military intervention on the Continent to block this drive. Crowe's memo is printed in *British Documents,* III, 397–420.
30. E.g., Lansdowne to Balfour, 27 Apr 05, and minute, n.d., Balfour Papers, AM 49729.

did not believe that American friendship with England was incompatible with good German-American relations.

Certainly by the time Roosevelt made his decision to press immunity at The Hague he was no longer preoccupied with the supposed German threat to the Monroe Doctrine. Since the end of the Russo-Japanese War the focus of American defense planning had shifted steadily toward the Far East and Japan.[31] Dewey's brief and inconclusive analysis of the effects of immunity on a Japanese-American war[32] may well have seemed more relevant than his elaborate discussion of a German-American conflict. American relations with Germany in 1907 appeared friendlier than they had been at any time since 1898. Under these circumstances, there seems every reason to believe that the president rejected the Mahan-Dewey recommendation on maritime rights primarily because he did not accept the assumption of German-American hostility on which it was based.

Another factor, hard for the historian to evaluate but nonetheless real, may also have influenced Roosevelt's decision. The president had an exceptionally strong reverence for American history. The first words of *The Naval War of 1812,* which he had written a quarter of a century earlier, were: "Causes of the War of 1812—Conflicting views of America and Britain as regards neutral rights—Those of the former power right." He had depicted the Royal Navy as an arrogant bully taught respect for American rights in the only language he understood—the broadsides of American warships: "The principles for which the United States contended in 1812 are now universally accepted, and those so tenaciously maintained by Great Britain find no advocates in the civilized world. . . . Our sailors had gained too great a name for anyone to molest them with impunity again."[33] Although there is no evidence that these thoughts were in the president's conscious mind, Hay and Lamsdorff could testify that his emotional re-

31. Naval War College, strategic war games, 1906 and 1907, Naval War College Archives, General Correspondence, Boxes 46–47; Challener, *Admirals,* pp. 29–32 and 225–264; William R. Braisted, *The United States Navy in the Pacific, 1897–1909* (Austin: University of Texas Press, 1958), pp. 198ff.

32. General Board to secretary of the navy, 20 Jun 06, General Board Letters, IV, 298.

33. Theodore Roosevelt, *The Naval War of 1812* (New York: G. P. Putnam's Sons, 1882, reprinted 1910), p. 1.

sponse to maritime rights remained strong.[34] This same revulsion must have colored his reaction when Mahan and Dewey advocated that the United States abandon the rights it had fought to win a century before and join Britain in tyranny over the seas.

Was the General Board's recommendation on maritime rights sound professional advice unfortunately disregarded by a willful and uncomprehending civilian? Or was it, in Hay's words, simply "the professional sailor's view," too narrow to be of value to makers of foreign policy? Any historical evaluation of the decision to press for expanded commercial rights at The Hague requires answers to these questions. And such answers in turn depend on evaluation of the Mahan-Dewey analysis of changing national interests.

The critics of established American policy predicted that the United States would be drawn into war with Germany. Such a war would result either from a German attack on American imperial interests, most likely in Latin America, or from German aggression against British imperial interests shared by the United States. The essence of this analysis is best stated in the General Board's September 1906 memorandum:

> Germany is desirous of extending her colonial possessions. Especially, is it thought that she is desirous of obtaining a foothold in the Western Hemisphere, and many things indicate that she has her eyes on localities in the West Indies, on the shores of the Caribbean, and in parts of South America. It is believed in many quarters that she is planning to test the Monroe Doctrine by the annexation or by the establishment of a protectorate, over a portion of South America, even going to the extent of war with the United States when her fleet is ready.
>
> It is asserted on good authority that Great Britain does not wish to acquire any additional colonial possessions. At the same time Great Britain does not wish Germany to extend her colonial possessions.
>
> Should it be true that Germany wishes to extend her colonial possessions to the Western Hemisphere, our interests are here bound up with those of England and we can reasonably expect . . . assistance from Great Britain.[35]

34. E.g., Hay, diary entries, 17 Oct, 26 Dec 04, Hay Papers, (M)1.
35. General Board to secretary of the navy, 28 Sep 06, General Board Letters, IV, 356–361.

The General Board's prediction of Anglo-American cooperation in a war against Germany was to come true in 1917. Much of
the board's strategic analysis, however, seems wildly inaccurate.
Dewey had maintained that war would result from a German
assault on Latin America in violation of the Monroe Doctrine. No
evidence has appeared to demonstrate that the German government ever gave serious consideration to such an attack. Germans
did have extensive plans for commercial penetration of Latin
America, but not even Richard Olney's chauvinistic 1895 corollary
had suggested that the Monroe Doctrine precluded peaceful economic competition. The most reliable modern study of German
policy concludes that "German naval planners coveted a base
somewhere in the Western Hemisphere at *some* time and *some*
place." The Kaiser shared this desire and authorized his naval
staff to draw up detailed contingency plans for military operations in the Americas. But not even at the height of the Venezuelan crisis in 1903 did the German government discuss implementation of these plans. After 1905, Germany's deteriorating
position in Europe convinced "even the most militant and anti-
American officials of the Reich" that any challenge to the United
States in American waters was unthinkable.[36]

In another sense, however, Mahan and Dewey were correct.
They maintained that British and American interests were so in-
tertwined that enlightened self-interest would force either to aid
the other in a conflict with Germany. This view, held by Woodrow
Wilson and many of his subordinates, would prove the dominant
force in shaping American policy toward the belligerents during
World War I. The General Board had seen the United States and
Britain as sharing common interests because both were primarily
commercial and colonial powers, isolated from the "entanglement" of European alliances. The British government abandoned
its political isolation in August 1914, when it plunged into war for
causes—German invasion of Belgium and the Continental balance of power—that were entirely European. Nevertheless, the
Wilson administration bent and ultimately broke American neu-

36. Holger Herwig, *Politics of Frustration* (Boston: Little, Brown, 1976), pp.
13–92, quotations from pp. 67 and 91.

trality in favor of the Allies because it perceived the Anglo-American special relationship as absolutely vital. Ironically, the official American casus belli in 1917 would be an attempt by Germany to do precisely what Mahan and Dewey had advocated earlier: expand belligerent rights at neutral expense. The United States would be drawn into war with Germany not by Wilhelmine *Weltpolitik* in Latin America, but by the American policy of rapprochement with Britain.

Theodore Roosevelt certainly did not believe that his foreign policies were likely to involve the United States in a general European war, much less one begun by a political assassination in the Balkans. But his own intervention in the Algeciras Conference in 1906 proved a major step toward American involvement in such a war. Although nominally concerned with such issues as control of police in Moroccan ports, Algeciras was in fact a test of strength and will between Britain and France, on the one hand, and Germany on the other. The rising tide of Anglo-German hostility before 1906 had frightened Roosevelt, and he had done what he could to cool passions in both countries.[37] When Britain sided with France in the Moroccan crisis, however, the president forgot his doubts about the justice of the French case[38] and used his personal influence with the Kaiser to help secure a settlement favorable to France.[39] Roosevelt believed he could support Britain and France against Germany in a European quarrel without being caught in European entanglements. But as long as American leaders continued to regard the special relationship with Britain as the sine qua non of American foreign policy, the potential for entanglement existed.

The decision to support immunity for private property and

37. E.g., Durand to Lansdowne, tel, 26 Apr 05, FO 800/116; Roosevelt to Reid, 19 Sep 05, Reid Papers, (M)179; Roosevelt to Hay, 2 Apr 05, *TR Letters*, IV, 1157.

38. E.g., Roosevelt to Spring Rice, 1 Nov 05, *TR Letters*, V, 63.

39. On Roosevelt's role in the first Moroccan crisis and its settlement at Algeciras, see Esthus, *TR*, pp. 66-110, and "Isolation and World Power," *Diplomatic History*, 2 (Spring 1978):123-127. Other worthwhile accounts of this complex and controversial subject include Beale, *Roosevelt and the Rise to World Power*, pp. 354-389; Perkins, *Great Rapprochement*, pp. 259-265; George E. Mowry, *The Era of Theodore Roosevelt* (New York: Harper, 1958), pp. 192-196; and John M. Blum, *The Republican Roosevelt* (Cambridge: Harvard University Press, 1954), pp. 133-134.

general restriction of belligerent rights at sea at the Second Hague Conference was not Theodore Roosevelt's most important presidential decision, but it was one of his most revealing. The means by which the decision was made indicate the informal manner in which the United States government determined its strategic policies during the first decade of the twentieth century. A retired naval officer wrote a personal letter to the secretary of state, who referred it to the General Board of the Navy. The board recommended abandonment of the traditional policy on maritime rights and convinced the State Department that such a change was in the national interest. The president had followed the policy of de facto alliance with England advocated by the navy, but refused to accept the strategic corollary it drew on maritime rights. No record was made of his decision. The American delegation went to The Hague in 1907, as its predecessor had done in 1899, with a formal charge to secure approval for immunity and a naval delegate privately determined to defeat it.

The overwhelming impression is one of confusion. The foreign and military policies of the United States were in a state of transition in 1907 and so were the bureaucratic institutions charged with determining those policies. Traditional concepts such as political isolation from Europe, a coast defense and commerce raiding naval strategy, and immunity for private property at sea were being challenged by such new ideas as Anglo-American rapprochement and Mahan's sea command strategy. Yet American leaders failed to recognize the implications of the new ideas or the dangers of mixing them unsystematically with the old. There was no consensus definition of national interests to guide policy makers in 1907 and no government institution capable of formulating such a definition and imposing it on the bureaucracy. Understanding of American maritime rights policy during the period must begin with an appreciation of this haphazard style of policy making.[40]

40. Cf. Challener, *Admirals,* pp. 11, 45–80.

CHAPTER FOUR

✿

Great Britain and Maritime Rights, 1904–1907

Britain, like the United States, began reconsideration of maritime rights prior to the Second Hague Conference within the context of a traditional policy. The British Empire had been built on sea power, and the British position on maritime law reflected this heritage. Support for broad belligerent rights had been an article of faith for centuries of British statesmen. Doubts had begun to arise, however, regarding the value of those rights. Arthur Balfour had suggested in 1898 that Britain might benefit from immunity for private property at sea. Lord Lansdowne's January 1905 statement that his nation henceforth would favor limitations on the doctrine of contraband was positively heretical. Other leaders drew similar conclusions from their Boer and Russo-Japanese War experiences. By 1905 British maritime rights policy seemed more flexible than at any time during the previous century.

The primary force behind this shift was the belief that Britain was, in Balfour's words, "pre-eminently a great Naval, Indian and Colonial Power."[1] Although Balfour and Lansdowne had joined Joseph Chamberlain in leading the cabinet revolt against Salisbury's extreme interpretation of splendid isolation, all shared their mentor's basic view of Britain as an imperial rather than a European power. The Balfour Government's foreign policy rested

1. Quoted in Nicholas d'Ombrain, *War Machinery and High Policy* (London: Oxford University Press, 1973), p. 1.

on three assumptions: that Britain's vital interests lay outside Europe, that those interests could be defended by a small professional army and a predominant navy, and that Britain's only vital interest in Continental rivalries was to remain uninvolved in them. The importance of these assumptions cannot be overemphasized. Balfour and Lansdowne would make agreements and even alliances with other nations, but only as a way to strengthen Britain's colonial position. They would not make any agreement that committed them to military intervention in Europe.[2]

British defense strategy from 1902 to 1905 reflected this foreign policy. The Royal Navy guaranteed control of the seas and thus isolated Britain's vital interests from attack by the Continental military powers. Only in Canada and India did the Empire have vulnerable land frontiers. When Balfour listed areas of possible conflict for the British army in December 1903, he included only defense of India against Russia, police actions against Boer rebels in South Africa, "conceivably (but only barely conceivably)" defense of Canada against American invasion, and "small expeditions against the Naval Stations and Colonies of other Powers."[3] All other defense responsibilities rested on the Royal Navy.[4]

This strategy was successful only because British statesmen proved willing to limit their foreign policy objectives. This balancing of ends and means emerged clearly in the Fashoda crisis of 1898. Salisbury had shown no desire to dictate peace in the Hall of Mirrors at Versailles after bickering with his generals over how much of Normandy to annex. He asked only that France abandon its claim to the Sudan. Lord Kitchener's army did not have to parade through the Arc de Triomphe to achieve this goal. It simply had to remove seven isolated Frenchmen from an obscure

2. The best overall account of Balfour-Lansdowne foreign policy remains George Monger, *The End of Isolation* (London: Thomas Nelson and Sons, 1963), pp. 67–238. It should be supplemented by Zara S. Steiner, *Britain and the Origins of the First World War* (London: Macmillan, 1977), pp. 33–43. Alfred Gollin, *Balfour's Burden* (London: Anthony Blond, 1965), seriously underestimates Lansdowne's competence and influence. None of the Balfour or Lansdowne biographies contain much of value on foreign policy.

3. Balfour to Lord Kitchener (CIC, India), 3 Dec 03, Balfour Papers, AM 49726.

4. The best study of the Royal Navy in the predreadnought era remains Arthur J. Marder, *British Naval Policy, 1880–1905* (London: Putnam, 1940).

village on the Nile. The Royal Navy prevented France from bringing its overwhelming military power to bear. As long as British statesmen continued to define national interests in terms appropriate to their limited means of defense, as they had in 1898, the lesson of Fashoda remained valid.[5]

British reevaluation of maritime rights policy began in this strategic context. The Government and its advisers assumed that Britain would be neutral in wars between the Continental Great Powers. Any war that did involve Britain would be limited, primarily naval, and fought in defense of whatever part of the formal or informal empire was threatened. These assumptions shaped the attempt to modernize maritime rights policy in 1905 and continued to exercise a powerful influence throughout the next decade.

Traditional British policy had been formulated in an entirely different strategic context. Lord Castlereagh and his colleagues had sought to obliterate the French Revolution. They had assumed that Britain did have vital interests in Europe, especially maintenance of a balance of power, and had defended those interests by diplomatic, financial, and even military intervention. They stretched belligerent rights to the utmost, even at the cost of bringing new enemies into the war, in order to weaken France and thus bring closer the decisive military victory necessary to restore the Bourbons. Britain had abandoned this definition of national interests long before 1905, but had never repudiated the extreme claims of belligerent rights dictated by the earlier definition.

The problem the Balfour Government faced as it began preparations for the Second Hague Conference was to devise a new maritime rights policy appropriate for the Empire's modern foreign policy, particularly the retreat from Continental involvement. Britain did not approach this problem in the haphazard manner the United States had. Balfour had created the Commit-

---

5. On Fashoda, see ibid., pp. 320–340; Christopher Andrew, *Théophile Delcassé and the Making of the Entente Cordiale* (New York: St. Martin's Press, 1968), pp. 98–103; A. J. P. Taylor, *The Struggle for Mastery in Europe* (Oxford: Clarendon, 1954), p. 381; Paul M. Kennedy, *The Rise and Fall of British Naval Mastery* (New York: Charles Scribner's Sons, 1976), p. 207.

tee of Imperial Defence (CID) in 1902 to bring ministers and military leaders together to consider grand strategic questions in a systematic manner. The CID, therefore, was the natural body to provide a consistent definition of national interests and then determine the appropriate policy on maritime rights.[6]

CID Secretary Sir George Clarke formally raised the matter in a December 1904 memorandum. Noting the changed strategic context since the Napoleonic Wars, Clarke suggested that Britain would benefit from abolition of the doctrines of contraband and continuous voyage. After detailed analysis of possible wars, he concluded:

> The sea pressure that can be brought to bear on a Continental Power appears, therefore, to be far less effective now than formerly. If this be admitted, the advantage a belligerent State possesses from the right to capture contraband on the high seas, on the plea of "continuous voyage," must seem to be illusory. . . .
> The right to capture neutral vessels containing contraband . . . cannot confer any real advantage upon us in war with a European enemy; but it would give an enemy opportunities of injuring us as belligerents, and of hampering our trade or of driving us into war as neutrals.[7]

A month after Clarke circulated his memorandum, Lansdowne indicated that Britain would in fact "be found on the side of neutral rather than belligerent interests" in any international discussion of contraband.[8] The Admiralty also found Clarke's arguments convincing. Its leading expert on economic warfare, Captain Edmond Slade, wrote in June 1905 that "the amount of damage we could inflict on an enemy by interfering with his Trade carried on in neutral ships would probably be insignificant." The navy's primary means to exert economic pressure under modern conditions were capture of enemy ships and blockade. Unless "we are game to take the whole world on," Slade

6. On the origins of the CID see Monger, *End of Isolation*, pp. 93–94; W. J. McDermott, "The Immediate Origins of the Committee of Imperial Defence," *Canadian Journal of History*, 7 (1972):253–272; and d'Ombrain, *War Machinery*, pp. 27–73 and passim.

7. Clarke, "The Value to Great Britain as a Belligerent of the Right of Search and the Capture of Neutral Vessels," 12 Dec 04, CAB 4/1/41B.

8. Lansdowne to Balfour, 18 Jan 05, Balfour Papers, AM 49729.

concluded, Britain should seek limitation or even abolition of the doctrine of contraband.[9]

A consensus thus developed within the government during 1905. The CID accepted the Admiralty's principle that "sea com-. mand should be as far-reaching in its effects as is possible within reason." The navy recognized, however, that "Britain's enormous commerce compels her to insist upon the rights of neutrals within legitimate limits."[10] The problem was to balance the predominant interest in sea command with the secondary interest in freedom for neutral commerce. The solution the Balfour Government left to its Liberal successor in December 1905 was to retain the belligerent rights of blockade and capture of enemy ships, but to limit the right to capture contraband and the doctrine of continuous voyage.

The new policy abandoned the broad assertion of belligerent rights adopted for the all-out war against Napoleon in favor of a limited assertion. It thus reflected the limited objectives of Balfour's foreign policy. As Clarke and Slade had pointed out, the doctrine of contraband offered relatively minor military advantages in return for serious risk of trouble with neutrals. Such risks had been acceptable a century earlier when Britain had been fighting for survival, but they were not appropriate for a foreign policy of limited means and limited ends. Statesmen agreed with their professional advisers that limitation of the doctrine of contraband was the proper position for a nation committed to isolation from European Great Power conflicts.

Ironically, events were undermining this assumption of isolation at the very time that British maritime rights policy was being modernized. In 1914 Britain would plunge into Continental warfare on a scale unimaginable nine years earlier. This reversal resulted from a concatenation of complex events and was perceived only slowly and imperfectly by contemporaries. Nevertheless, by August 1914 Britain's position on belligerent rights would prove as incompatible with the requirements of British foreign policy as

9. Slade to Captain W. Nicholson (naval assistant secretary to CID), 9 Jun 05, CAB 17/85.
10. Adm to FO, 31 Dec 04, FO 372/38.

the traditional claim of broad belligerent rights had been incompatible with isolation.

The force that pulled Britain away from isolation and back into Continental involvement between 1905 and 1914 was the rise of Anglo-German hostility. The origins of this hostility remain confused and controversial, although there is general agreement that the first Moroccan crisis of 1905–1906 and formation of a Liberal Government in December 1905 were essential catalysts in the transformation of British policy.[11] In March 1905 Britain had one grand strategy: isolation from Europe. After August 6, 1914, it again had one grand strategy: military intervention on the Continent. Between those two dates Britain had two incompatible policies; isolationists and interventionists sought to implement their conflicting views. Without some understanding of this dichotomous policy making, there can be no understanding of British policy on maritime rights.

The existence of a split had become apparent in 1905, when a German challenge to growing French predominance in Morocco forced the British government to define more closely its vague promise of support in the Anglo-French Entente of April 1904. An agreement Lansdowne had signed in order to strengthen

---

11. There is no satisfactory analysis of the origins of Anglo-German hostility. Steiner, *Origins*, pp. 42–78, is the best modern study available, but the best overall summary remains that written by Lord Rosebery (Liberal prime minister, 1894–1895) to J. A. Spender (Liberal editor), 24 Jan 07, Spender Papers, AM 46387: "There is absolutely no reason for us to fight except that we dislike each other." Roosevelt reached a similar conclusion, arguing that mutual ignorance generated mutual suspicion, which in turn generated "wild manias of hatred" in both countries with but little relation to objective reality (Roosevelt to Reid, 19 Sep 05, Reid Papers, (M)179; cf. to Hay, 2 Apr 05, *TR Letters*, IV, 1157). Modern historians seem to have lost this appreciation for irrationality as a basic cause of international hostility. Explanations such as the rise of German naval power cited in Arthur J. Marder, *From the Dreadnought to Scapa Flow*, 5 vols (London: Oxford University Press, 1961–1970), I, 5–6, or the German threat to the European balance of power cited in Williamson, *Politics*, p. 21, confuse symptoms of hostility with root causes. Explanations based on economic or colonial rivalries have even less validity. The traditional methods of diplomatic history simply are inadequate to explain "wild manias of hatred" affecting both populations and leaders, and thus a satisfactory account of the origins of Anglo-German hostility awaits a historian with reliable techniques for understanding and evaluating the phenomenon of mass irrationality.

Britain's isolation[12] threatened to have the opposite effect. The Kaiser warned Prince Louis of Battenberg that "we know the road to Paris, and we will get there again if needs be."[13] The British promise to support France in Morocco, given in a colonial context, had acquired unanticipated European implications.

The exact nature of these implications remained unclear. Louis Mallet, one of the rising group of Germanophobes in the Foreign Office, argued that Britain must "fight if necessary" to prevent France from falling under German domination.[14] Admiral Sir John Fisher, the eccentric first sea lord, deliberately sought to use the crisis to provoke an Anglo-French attack on Germany. Although he assured Mallet that fears of a possible German naval base in Morocco were "all rot," Fisher warned Lansdowne that such a base would present an intolerable danger to Britain's maritime supremacy and thus a justifiable casus belli.[15] The prime minister and foreign secretary, who had been unmoved by Mallet's argument of European implications, responded immediately to Fisher's warning of a threat to imperial communications. Lansdowne telegraphed: "Germany may press France for a port on the Moorish coast. Admiralty think this fatal. May I advise French Govt. not to accede without giving us full opportunity conferring with them as to manner in which demand might be met."[16] With Balfour's approval, he then instructed Sir Francis Bertie, the British ambassador in Paris, to promise the French government "all the support we can" if it resisted German demands.[17]

12. Monger, *End of Isolation,* p. 159 and passim; Steiner, *Origins,* pp. 29–36. Perkins, *Great Rapprochement,* p. 258, is incorrect in saying that the Entente's authors "actually aimed to draw the two powers together in the face of a German threat." On the origins of the first Moroccan crisis, see Andrew, *Delcassé,* pp. 268–308.

13. Prince Louis, memo of conversation, 1 Apr 05, FO 800/130.

14. Mallet to Sandars, 20 Apr 05, Balfour Papers, AM 49747. On the Foreign Office Germanophobes, see Monger, *End of Isolation,* pp. 264–266 and passim; Zara S. Steiner, *The Foreign Office and Foreign Policy, 1898–1914* (Cambridge: Cambridge University Press, 1969), pp. 70–82 and passim; and C. J. Lowe and M. L. Dockrill, *The Mirage of Power,* 3 vols. (London: Routledge & Kegan Paul, 1972), I, 18–21.

15. Fisher to Lansdowne, 22 Apr 05, Fisher Papers, 149; Monger, *End of Isolation,* p. 189.

16. Lansdowne to Balfour, tel, 23 Apr 05, Balfour Papers, AM 49729.

17. Lansdowne to Bertie, tel, 23 [misdated 22] Apr 05, *British Documents,* II, 72–73.

This pledge committed the Balfour Government to aid France in a Continental war against Germany if the French would refuse to buy peace at the price of concessions dangerous to Britain's imperial interests. No one in the cabinet had more than the vaguest idea of what this commitment might require. Support for a Continental ally traditionally had meant ships and money. As the Kaiser pointed out, however, "no fleet can defend Paris."[18] The French premier complained that the Royal Navy "could not run on wheels."[19] For Lansdowne to promise support was easy enough, but for Britain to deliver effective support to France in a war against the German army was quite another matter.

Fisher, whose lie about the military value of a German naval base in Morocco had led to the Government's commitment, was not distressed because the Royal Navy could be of little direct assistance to France. The first sea lord was quite willing to fight to the last Frenchman to destroy German sea power. His letter to Lansdowne indicates precisely the sort of war he had in mind:

> This seems a golden opportunity for fighting the Germans in alliance with the French so I earnestly hope you may be able to bring this about. . . .
> All I hope is that you will send a telegram to Paris that the English and French fleets are *one*. We could have the German fleet, the Kiel Canal and Schleswig-Holstein within a fortnight.[20]

In Fisher's view, Britain's sole interest was to destroy the German navy and merchant marine and ensure that they could not be rebuilt. Whether the Franco-German fighting on the Continent ended in a Jena or a Sedan was significant only as an indication of Britain's next rival for maritime supremacy. The only support Britain could give to France was the Royal Navy, so Fisher saw no contradiction between Lansdowne's promise and continued isolation from European conflicts irrelevant to Britain's own national interests.

For Englishmen who agreed with Mallet that preservation of the Anglo-French Entente was itself a vital British interest, however, the strategic implications of the Moroccan crisis presented a

---

18. Prince Louis of Battenberg, memo of conversation, 1 Apr 05, FO 800/130.
19. Quoted in Taylor, *Struggle*, p. 437.
20. Fisher to Lansdowne, 22 Apr 05, Fisher Papers, 149.

problem rather than an opportunity. Russia was crippled by its war with Japan, leaving the French military situation worse than at any time since 1893. Mallet expressed confidence that "Germany would not fight both France and England,"[21] but his fellow diplomat and Germanophobe Cecil Spring Rice was less optimistic: "We *must not* encourage France to go to war in the present state of the Russian army & our own. It would be simply criminal. Germany has the cards—that is the army; horse foot & artillery. And what have we?"[22] Britain had its magnificent navy and an army smaller than those of many European Minor Powers. Even Mallet admitted that "Mr. Arnold Forster's Army cannot defend Paris."[23] The Continentalists found themselves in the embarrassing position of asserting that French security was essential to that of Britain while recognizing that they could do little to protect that security.

The French government did not formally request aid during 1905, so the Balfour Government never had to resolve the apparent contradiction between its promise to support France and its lack of means to provide effective military support. The Liberal Government of Sir Henry Campbell-Bannerman was not so fortunate. Balfour had resigned on December 4, and the new cabinet had taken office a week later. On January 10, two days before polling began in the general election, French Ambassador Paul Cambon asked "*the* question" of Lansdowne's successor, Sir Edward Grey: what aid would Britain give France in the event of a German attack?[24]

Cambon's question would have been difficult for any British foreign secretary to answer. It was particularly difficult for Grey. The Liberal party was a coalition united by little more than support of free trade and desire for office, at the end of a hard-fought campaign and facing a presumably close election.[25] Grey

21. Mallet to Sandars, 20 Apr 05, Balfour Papers, AM 49747.

22. Spring Rice to Lascelles, 2 May 05, FO 800/12.

23. Mallet to Sandars, 20 Apr 05, Balfour Papers, AM 49747. H. Arnold Forster was secretary of state for war.

24. Grey, memo of conversation, 10 Jan 06, CB Papers, AM 41218.

25. Wilson, *CB*, pp. 469–475; Rowland, *Last Liberal Governments*, I, 22–30; Keith Robbins, *Sir Edward Grey* (London: Cassell, 1971), pp. 140–141; José F. Harris and Cameron Hazlehurst, "Campbell-Bannerman as Prime Minister," *History*, 55 (1970):368, 371–375.

himself, despite the common historical view that he was "the obvious candidate for the Foreign Secretaryship,"[26] had been offered the position only after the refusal or incapacity of others had forced the prime minister to accept a man he neither liked nor trusted, but who had been parliamentary undersecretary at the Foreign Office under the last Liberal Government a decade earlier.[27] Given these circumstances, Grey had little choice but to give Cambon a vague answer and to lay the entire matter before Campbell-Bannerman in anticipation of "a Cabinet directly the elections are over to decide what I am to say."[28]

This official passivity was in marked contrast, however, with the new secretary of state's private opinions. Zara Steiner has written that "by the time Grey entered the Foreign Office, he had identified Germany as the enemy." Unlike Lansdowne, Grey was "convinced that the Germans were seeking to establish their control over the continent of Europe and that they were rapidly acquiring the means by which this could be accomplished."[29] His primary goal over the next decade would be to block this supposed drive for hegemony. In February 1906 Grey wrote that "an entente between Russia France & ourselves would be absolutely secure," able to "check Germany" if "necessary."[30] In his own mind, he already had abandoned isolation from the Continent in favor of an essentially unlimited commitment to a triple entente.[31]

This Continental definition of national interests forced Grey

26. Devlin, *Too Proud*, p. 146; cf. Williamson, *Politics*, p. 60.

27. Sir L. Harcourt (Liberal politician) to CB, 30 Nov 05, CB Papers, AM 52518; Wilson *CB*, pp. 423-458, 522; Robbins, *Grey*, pp. 120-128; Rowland, *Last Liberal Governments*, I, 15-18; Monger, *End of Isolation*, pp. 257-261; Steiner, *Origins*, pp. 37-39; and Harris and Hazlehurst, "Campbell-Bannerman," pp. 366-370.

28. Grey to CB, 10 Jan 06, CB Papers, AM 41218.

29. Steiner, *Origins*, pp. 41-42; cf. Monger, *End of Isolation*, pp. 280, 302, and passim.

30. Grey, memo, 20 Feb 06, FO 800/92.

31. Steiner, *Origins*, pp. 41-43 and passim; cf. Robbins, *Grey*, p. 154; and D. W. Sweet, "Great Britain and Germany, 1905-1911," in F. H. Hinsley, ed., *British Foreign Policy under Sir Edward Grey* (Cambridge: Cambridge University Press, 1977), p. 226. The picture of a passive Grey bobbing like a "cork" presented in Rowland, *Last Liberal Governments*, I, 171-172, is entirely unconvincing, while the statement that Grey's "policy abroad was genuinely pacific and non-provocative" in Lowe and Dockrill, *Mirage of Power*, I, 16, confuses Grey's own perception with the effects of his policy.

to confront the problem that had baffled Mallet nine months earlier: how could Britain ensure French security against Germany without a significant European military capability? In early January the foreign secretary had asked each service informally what aid it could give France in the event of a German attack. Fisher had replied that the navy could blockade the enemy coast and drive his flag from the high seas. This answer, while appropriate for an isolationist definition of British interests, failed to meet the requirements of Grey's Continentalist foreign policy. On January 8 Grey asked his friend and political ally, War Minister Richard B. Haldane, to prepare detailed plans for military operations in Europe in support of France.[32] The next day he learned that Clarke and Lord Esher of the CID, on their own authority and without the knowledge of anyone in the new Government, already had supervised preparation of detailed plans to land fifty thousand troops in the French Channel ports within two weeks of mobilization. Grey was "much pleased" with these preparations.[33] With the consent of Campbell-Bannerman and the cooperation of Haldane, he expanded Clarke's informal contacts with the French military attaché into formal talks between the British and French general staffs.[34]

These arrangements helped to reassure the French government, but they hardly resolved the basic problem of how to win a Continental war with an army shaped by decades of isolation. Britain ultimately found this problem impossible to resolve and abandoned the principle of a small professional army shortly after the outbreak of World War I in favor of a mass, and eventually conscripted, army on the Continental pattern. Nevertheless, from 1906 to 1914 Grey and many others who saw French security as essential to that of Britain believed that they had a solution which would be both militarily effective in wartime and politically feasi-

32. Grey to Haldane, 8 Jan 06, Haldane Papers, MS 5907.
33. Conference notes, 19 Dec 05, 6 Jan 06, CAB 18/24; Clarke to Esher, 1, 2, 9 Jan 06, Esher Papers, 10/38. Not all scholars of civil-military relations would agree with Williamson, *Politics*, p. 80, that it was "prudent and sensible" for a nonresponsible civil servant to make plans and promises in the name of the nation without the authority or even the knowledge of a single member of the Government.
34. The best source for the details of the staff talks is unquestionably Williamson, *Politics*, pp. 61–88. See also Monger, *End of Isolation*, pp. 236–256, and d'Ombrain, *War Machinery*, pp. 84–90.

ble in peacetime. Haldane came to the War Office determined to build "a highly-organized and well equipped striking force."[35] This British Expeditionary Force (BEF) remained small by French or German standards, but men desperate to believe that Britain could tip the Continental balance toward France convinced themselves that its training and sense of mission could make it a formidable factor. Although even Mallet had admitted that "Mr. Arnold Forster's Army cannot defend Paris," many of the Continentalists came to believe that Mr. Haldane's army could.[36]

Had Grey gone to the cabinet for an official answer to Cambon and sanction for the Anglo-French staff talks, the confusion between Continentalist and isolationist definitions of national interest probably would have been resolved early in 1906. With Campbell-Bannerman's consent, however, knowledge of the military preparations was not circulated within the Government, and the degree of British commitment to France remained uncertain. Grey and Haldane feared repudiation of their policies and were content to act without official sanction; Campbell-Bannerman and Lord Ripon, the lord privy seal and House of Lords leader, worried about "joint preparations" that seemed "very close to an honourable undertaking,"[37] but feared to split a cabinet so laboriously constructed from diverse party factions over an essentially hypothetical question; Lord Tweedmouth, the first lord of the Admiralty, rejected Grey's plea for naval cooperation with War Office plans but was not confident enough to bring before the

35. Haldane, "A Preliminary Memorandum on the present situation," 1 Jan 06, CB Papers, AM 41218.

36. John McDermott, "The Revolution in British Military Thinking from the Boer War to the Moroccan Crisis," *Canadian Journal of History*, 9 (1974):159–178, is a provocative analysis of the General Staff's shift from imperial to Continental focus, arguing that it originated partly as a response to the general anti-German atmosphere and partly as a justification for greater independence from the traditional demands of the navy and India. A. J. A. Morris, "Haldane's Army Reforms, 1906–8: The Deception of the Radicals," *History*, 56 (1971):17–34, amplified only slightly by the same author's *Radicalism against War, 1906–1914* (London: Longmans, 1972), pp. 70–96, is a useful account of the "selling" of the BEF in terms of Indian defense. The best brief summary of Haldane's reforms is Williamson, *Politics*, pp. 89–94.

37. CB to Ripon, 2 Feb 06, Ripon Papers, AM 43518; Monger, *End of Isolation*, p. 273.

cabinet a matter the other four preferred not to discuss.[38] The result was almost a decade of competitive chaos in British grand strategy, with the navy assuming that isolation from Europe remained national policy while the Foreign and War Offices proceeded on the diametrically opposed assumption of Continental military intervention.

Appreciation of this confusion is essential for an understanding of Liberal policy on maritime rights between 1906 and the outbreak of World War I. Despite occasional lapses into humanitarian rhetoric, there was general agreement that the national interest should dictate Britain's position on blockade, contraband, immunity, and other controversial issues. The Campbell-Bannerman Government had inherited a common definition of the national interest—isolation from the Continent— and a widely accepted maritime rights policy that reflected this definition—limitation or abolition of contraband and continuous voyage, but no compromise on blockade and capture of enemy ships. The Liberal failure to resolve the Continentalist challenge to isolation meant that British maritime rights policy after 1905 was built on a foundation that could shift at any time.

Grey decided in March 1906 to appoint an interdepartmental committee under Attorney General John Walton to prepare policy recommendations for the upcoming Hague Conference. He charged the committee to determine "whether it is to our advantage" to accept immunity, as well as other suggested changes in existing maritime law.[39] For the next year Walton and his colleagues from the Foreign Office, the Admiralty, the Board of Trade, and the Colonial Office studied and debated the implications of belligerent and neutral rights for British security with unprecedented thoroughness.

Fisher's Admiralty left no doubts about its position. In a formal memorandum for the committee it stated that "the right of capture of private property at sea is of great value to this country, and ought to be firmly maintained." The belligerent right of blockade, also vital to naval war planning, should be maintained as

---

38. Grey to Tweedmouth, 16 Jan 06, Tweedmouth Papers, Case A; Ottley to Clarke, 18 Jan 06, Esher Papers, 10/38.
39. Grey, n.d., minute on Board of Trade to FO, 7 Dec 05, CAB 17/85.

well. But "the abolition of the principle of 'conditional contraband' would be beneficial to the interests of Great Britain," and
"endeavour should be made to limit as far as possible and to
carefully define what are, and what are not, a belligerent's rights
in respect to contraband."[40] The first sea lord was especially ve-
hement in opposing immunity for private property at sea:

> We have a disquieting subject ahead in the new Hague Conference.
> All the world will be banded against us. Our great special anti-
> German weapon of smashing an enemy's commerce will be wrested
> from us. It's so very peculiar that providence has arranged England
> as a sort of huge breakwater against German commerce, which
> must all come either one side of the breakwater through the Straits
> of Dover, or the other side of the breakwater the north of Scotland.
> It's a unique position of advantage that we possess, and such is our
> naval superiority that on the day of war we "mop up" 800 German
> merchant steamers. Fancy the "knock-down" blow to German
> trade and finance! Worth Paris! These Hague Conferences want
> trade and commerce and going by train de luxe to Monte Carlo all
> to go on just as usual, only just the Fleet to fight! ROT!!!![41]

The Admiralty recommendations to the Walton Committee
were based directly on the existing naval war plans. These in turn
reflected Fisher's commitment to limited war for limited maritime
objectives. His primary, indeed almost sole, objective was destruction of German sea power. Fisher planned for his flotillas, operat-
ing in Heligoland Bight from bases he intended to seize on Heligoland and other offshore islands, to clamp a tight blockade on the
German North Sea coast. These light ships would intercept
enemy commerce raiders, enemy merchant vessels, and neutral
blockade runners attempting to leave or enter the blockaded
ports and would warn the battle fleet if the German High Seas
Fleet left its fortified bases. Behind this screen other British
squadrons would isolate German colonies in preparation for military occupation, protect British trade from any commerce raiders
that might run the blockade successfully, and support amphibious
operations against the enemy coast. Fisher had no delusion that
these measures would force the German government to accept

40. Adm, memo, 12 May 06, printed in CID Paper 75B, 15 May 06, CAB 4/2.
41. Fisher to S. Fortesque (Royal equerry), 14 Apr 06, Arthur J. Marder, ed.,
Fear God and Dread Nought, 3 vols. (London: Jonathan Cape, 1952–1959), II, 72.

terms similar to those imposed on France in 1871. He saw no reason, however, for Britain to annex provinces or demand vast indemnities. If the war ended with the German navy on the bottom of the sea, the German merchant marine under the British flag, and the complex shipbuilding, commercial, and insurance interest that supported *Marinepolitik* ruined beyond recovery—precisely what the war plans were designed to achieve—Fisher believed that Britain would have secured its primary national interest—maritime supremacy—at minimal cost.[42]

Seizure of contraband shipments to Germany under neutral flags played little role in these plans. There were two basic reasons for this omission. First was the danger that neutrals, angry at having their ships seized under questionable circumstances, would resist and perhaps widen a conflict the Admiralty believed must be limited. Fisher preferred to rely on blockade and capture of enemy ships, less controversial rights carrying less possibility of confrontation with neutrals.[43]

The second reason for the navy's decision to place little emphasis on capturing contraband was the general agreement among Admiralty strategists that "if we make War with Germany there is no doubt that we can do very little harm to her by capturing neutral Vessels carrying contraband."[44] Germany, with the world's greatest armaments industry, hardly would need to import absolute contraband. Potential conditional contraband destined for German North Sea ports could be seized for blockade running, thereby avoiding the requirement that the captor prove in prize court that the goods were intended for military use. Britain could theoretically claim a right to seize conditional contraband bound for unblockaded enemy or neutral ports, but only in the unlikely event the captor could prove ultimate destination to the German armed forces. Few neutral shippers presumably would be so stupid as to consign their goods openly to "Quartermaster General, Imperial German Army," so this proof was essentially impossible to obtain. With so much to lose in relations with

---

42. Fisher generally refused to reveal specific war plans for reasons of security, but for indications of his thinking see Adm 116/1043B.
43. Adm, memo, 12 May 06, printed in CID Paper 75B, 15 May 06, CAB 4/2; Adm, memo for Walton Committee, 4 Feb 07, CAB 37/86/14.
44. Slade to Nicholson, 20 Jun 05, CAB 17/85.

neutrals and so little to gain in economic harm to the enemy, Fisher's Admiralty concluded that the right to seize contraband was expendable under modern strategic conditions.

The Board of Trade concurred, offering the Walton Committee a third reason for recommending limitation or abolition of the doctrine of contraband. Although the navy asserted that it could "guarantee British commerce against all organized attack by the enemy's fleets" and prevent isolated commerce raiders from having "any serious effect,"[45] British commercial interests worried that future enemies could seize neutral ships carrying food and raw materials to Britain unless strict limits were placed on the definition of conditional contraband. The Board of Trade recommended that Britain try to restrict contraband to "munitions of war only," in effect abolishing conditional contraband entirely. If the British delegates could not win international approval for this reform, they should

> maintain the principle now generally accepted as a rule of international law on this subject, namely, that an article *ancipitis usus* is only contraband if it is intended for the direct furtherance of warlike operations, and that articles intended merely for the support of the civilian population of a belligerent country can in no circumstances be held to be contraband, even though the withholding of them from that population might tend powerfully to further the warlike operations of the captor by diminishing the resisting powers of the enemy.[46]

The Board of Trade's endorsement of the Admiralty opposition to immunity for private property[47] gave the Walton Committee a rare unanimity of bureaucratic opinion among the departments most immediately concerned with maritime rights. Clarke threw the weight of the CID secretariat behind the Admiralty position,[48] while Hardinge, who had recently replaced Sanderson as Foreign Office permanent undersecretary, warned his friend and sovereign Edward VII that if immunity were approved "the chief danger to Germany from a war with England will have been

45. Adm, memo for Walton Committee, 4 Feb 07, CAB 37/86/14.
46. Board of Trade, memo for Walton Committee, 22 Jan 06, printed in CID Paper 75B, 15 May 06, CAB 4/2.
47. Board of Trade to FO, 12 Mar 06, FO 372/38.
48. E.g., Clarke to CB, 26 May 06, CB Papers, AM 41213; Clarke, "The Capture of the Private Property of Belligerents at Sea," 14 May 06, CAB 4/2/73B.

removed."[49] The Walton Committee final report, submitted on March 21, 1907, endorsed the Admiralty recommendations in their entirety. After a year of study, the committee had concluded that British interests demanded retention of the belligerent rights of blockade and capture of enemy ships, but restriction or even abolition of the doctrine of contraband.[50]

At no time during the Walton Committee deliberations had the general willingness to offer concessions on contraband been challenged with the argument that Britain must retain the broadest possible belligerent rights in order to strangle Germany's economy and starve its industrial population. Nor did Grey or Haldane make this argument when the committee's recommendations came before the cabinet. The Continentalists simply did not believe that economic warfare would be a significant factor in a general European war. The War Office remained confident that such a war would be settled in a few weeks as the Anglo-French-Russian armies paraded down Unter der Linden while Entente diplomats dictated peace in Potsdam. From the Continentalist perspective, maritime rights were essentially irrelevant except in the unlikely event of an Anglo-German war in which the other Great Powers remained neutral. Grey and Haldane saw no contradiction between their commitment to French security and Fisher's advice to limit the doctrines of contraband and continuous voyage.

Ironically, the only significant opposition to the Walton Committee recommendations came not from those who opposed limitation of belligerent rights but from those who believed that further limitation was in Britain's interest. Lord Loreburn, the lord chancellor, had publicly advocated immunity for private property two months before formation of the Campbell-Bannerman government.[51] In December 1906, largely as a result of his efforts, 168 Members of Parliament had petitioned the prime minister to support immunity at The Hague.[52] Loreburn looked over Grey's

49. Hardinge to Edward VII, 26 Aug 06, quoted in Marder, *From the Dreadnought,* I, 381.

50. Walton, et al., "Report of the Inter-Departmental Committee," 21 Mar 07, CAB 37/87/42.

51. Loreburn, Letter to the Editor, *The Times,* 14 Oct 05, p. 4.

52. 168 M.P.s to CB, n.d., CAB 17/85. Morris, *Radicalism,* p. 117, mentions the agitation for immunity briefly and inaccurately. Asquith supported Grey, not Loreburn.

shoulder during appointment of the Walton Committee and was careful to ensure that Campbell-Bannerman received copies of all significant maritime rights documents.[53]

When the Walton Committee submitted its report, Loreburn and his supporters did not consider their defeat final. Commercial interests continued to lobby for immunity.[54] In a memo for the cabinet, the lord chancellor argued that his colleagues should consider the broad possibilities of the future and not simply the immediate situation. The report had justified rejection of immunity entirely in terms of strategic calculations in an Anglo-German war. The Admiralty had even admitted that immunity might be in Britain's interest in wars against other nations. Why, then, should the Government pass up the long-term advantages of immunity for British commerce solely to gain a temporary advantage against Germany? War with Germany had not been a serious concern five years in the past, probably would not be a serious concern five years in the future, and was not, in Loreburn's opinion, so serious a concern in the present as to justify a Liberal Government in opposing a major step toward limitation of the horrors of war.[55]

The cabinet met to consider the Walton Committee report and instructions to the Hague delegation on April 27, 1907, but could reach no agreement on immunity.[56] Campbell-Bannerman remarked to one of the delegates that "he had read both sides of the controversy, and at the end of each paper perused he found himself agreeing with the writer."[57] Tweedmouth and Grey led the fight against immunity, while Ripon and John Morley of the India Office supported Loreburn. Only in early June, after more than a month of wrangling, did the Government finally decide to insist on retaining the right of capture. The argument that ultimately seems to have persuaded the prime minister and enough other ministers to constitute a majority was stated by Grey in his draft instructions to the delegation:

53. Loreburn to Grey, 18 Mar 06, FO 800/99.
54. E.g., Manchester Chamber of Commerce to Grey, 22 Mar 07, FO 372/65.
55. Loreburn, "Immunity for Private Property at Sea in Time of War," n.d., CAB 37/88/58.
56. CB to Edward VII, cabinet letter, 26 Apr 07, CAB 41/31/16; John Burns (president, Local Government Board), diary entry, 26 Apr 07, Burns Papers, AM 46325.
57. Sir E. Satow, diary entry, 7 May 07, Satow Papers, PRO 30/33/16/10.

The British navy is the only offensive weapon which Great Britain has against Continental Powers. The latter have a double means of offence: they have their navies and they have their powerful armies. . . . Our army cannot be regarded as a means of offence against the mainland of a great Continental Power. For our ability to bring pressure to bear upon our enemies in war we have, therefore, to rely on the navy alone.[58]

Fisher's recommendations thus formed the basis of British policy at the Second Hague Conference. The rights of blockade and capture of enemy ships, essential to navy plans for a limited maritime war against Germany, had been retained. The right to seize contraband on neutral ships, which the Board of Trade believed would endanger British commerce and the Admiralty believed might enlarge a war Britain must limit, was to be restricted or abolished. The British delegates went to The Hague in 1907 instructed to establish the legal order the Admiralty had determined to be optimal for British naval interests.

Yet this sanction of Fisher's maritime rights advice should not be interpreted as endorsement of the basic strategic vision underlying that advice. Whereas Fisher and Loreburn would have agreed that the Royal Navy was Britain's only means of bringing pressure against a European Great Power, Grey certainly did not believe his own words. Either the foreign secretary who asserted that Britain needed to retain the right of capture because it possessed no Continental military capability had forgotten momentarily about the BEF and the Anglo-French staff talks or he was deliberately deceiving his colleagues. Fisher and Loreburn reached different conclusions on maritime rights from the same assumption of isolation from Continental Great Power conflicts. Grey reached the same conclusion as Fisher from the diametrically opposed premise that Britain did have a vital interest in maintaining a European balance of power against Germany. But at no time did he suggest that the cabinet consider the possibility of British intervention in a general European war or the implications of such intervention for the concessions the navy proposed to make in regard to contraband.

Only this complex pattern of political, personal, and interser-

58. Grey, draft instructions, 3 Jun 07, CAB 37/89/65; cf. Grey to Sir E. Fry (head of British delegation), 12 Jun 07, FO 800/69.

vice intrigue can explain the formulation of British maritime rights policy in 1907. The War Office and Admiralty planned for different and mutually exclusive wars. Neither was willing to co-ordinate its plans with its rival's. The navy was willing to abandon the right to seize contraband because it intended to fight a limited maritime war against German sea power. The army considered sea power irrelevant except as a means to transport troops who would block German hegemony in Europe. Grey followed a policy of Continental intervention, yet explicitly asserted in a cabinet document that Britain had no effective Continental military capability.

After the outbreak of war in 1914 the foreign secretary would be embarrassed by positions Britain had taken at The Hague and other international discussions of maritime rights. He would have been more embarrassed had he attempted in 1907 to explain to Campbell-Bannerman, Loreburn, Morley, Ripon, and other colleagues that Britain must retain belligerent rights the Admiralty was willing to surrender in order to bring maximum economic pressure against Germany and thus help defend the European balance of power. Fortunately for Grey's peace of mind, his confidence in Haldane's BEF allowed him to escape—until August 1914—consideration of the possibility that his policies might plunge Britain into a Continental war that would not be decided in a few weeks. The contradictions between the foreign secretary's ends and means, between the German army and the BEF, between a prolonged war that could only be won by dictating peace in Berlin and restrictions on Britain's belligerent right to seize contraband intended for Germany, seem obvious in retrospect. The measure of Sir Edward Grey's political skill, and also of his capability for self-delusion, is that he managed to conceal those contradictions until Britain was committed to a prolonged Continental war.

CHAPTER FIVE

✿

The Second Hague Peace Conference

The Second Hague Peace Conference convened on June 15, 1907. Its stated purpose was to prevent future wars and to limit those that could not be prevented. Because controversy between belligerents and neutrals as to their respective rights on the high seas in wartime had been an important source of international friction in recent years, the delegates assigned a high priority to establishing a common legal order. The Boer and Russo-Japanese Wars had given maritime law the urgency it had lacked at the First Hague Conference eight years before. The delegates who came to The Hague in 1907 believed that a comprehensive settlement was both necessary and attainable.

Discussion of maritime rights began on a positive note. Shortly after the conference opened, the chief German delegate, Baron Marschall von Bieberstein, announced that his government would not be satisfied with reform and codification of existing law. Germany proposed creation of an international prize court, with appellate jurisdiction over national courts, to enforce the new code the delegates would write. The British delegation, which had intended to introduce a similar resolution, and the American delegation expressed immediate support for this bold initiative.[1] With the three leading maritime powers apparently committed to the

---

1. James Brown Scott, ed., *The Proceedings of the Hague Peace Conferences* [*Proceedings*], 5 vols. (New York: Oxford University Press, 1920), II, 55.

broad principles of a settlement, only the details seemed left for negotiation.

This initial optimism soon dissolved, however, in a confusion of national rivalries and legal squabbles. France was willing to consider a prize court proposal if submitted by Britain, but refused to discuss "that of the Germans."[2] Britain was determined to block the American proposal for immunity, while the Americans rejected the British plan to abolish contraband. When the chief British delegate, the octogenarian Quaker jurist Sir Edward Fry, began to meet with Marschall informally in an effort to reconcile the British and German prize court drafts, his own political adviser, Foreign Office Germanophobe Eyre Crowe, warned William Tyrrell, Grey's private secretary, of the dangers implicit in even so limited an appearance of Anglo-German cooperation. The message soon reached the foreign minister.[3] He promptly warned Fry to beware of subtle German schemes to disrupt the Entente:

> It is possible that they [Germans] knew the French had difficulties about it [international prize court] and thought if it was proposed suddenly without our having time to consult with the French we might be separated from France upon it.
>
> I think you might explain to the French that our mercantile marine has suffered so much, especially of late years from the decisions of prize courts that almost any court of appeal would be a relief to us. It will I see be very necessary to avoid being drawn into an appearance of co-operation with Germany against France; the French are very sensitive at this moment; their internal troubles make them so and I am afraid of their thinking that we mean to throw them over & turn to Germany.[4]

Bound by Grey's instructions, the British delegates could only oppose everything the Germans suggested. The foreign secretary had offered no advice as to how his delegates could create an international prize court in cooperation with France, which opposed such a court, while not cooperating with Germany, which favored one. When Marschall presented the details of Germany's

2. Satow, diary entry, 20 Jun 07, PRO 30/33/16/10.
3. Crowe to Tyrrell, 17 Jun 07, and Tyrrell to Grey, 21 Jun 07, FO 800/69 and 92.
4. Grey to Fry, 22 Jun 07, FO 800/69.

prize court plan to the conference on July 4, Fry replied with an uncompromising and poorly reasoned negation that made a poor impression even on his own subordinates.[5] The Germans then proposed further informal negotiations aimed at resolving the differences between British and German drafts. Again, the French refused to discuss the German text, and Fry could only say no.[6] By early July the prize court proposal, which had seemed hopeful of success only two weeks before, was mired in Great Power rivalries.

This stalemate mirrored a similar failure to reach agreement on the specific provisions of the international code of maritime law. Choate made an eloquent appeal for immunity on June 28, arguing that capture of private property was both immoral and militarily ineffective: "Victory in naval battles is one thing, but ownership of the high seas is another." Was it not past time, he demanded, for the civilized world to abolish this practice "so abhorrent to every principle of justice and fair play?" Twenty-one nations agreed, but the eleven opposed included Britain, France, Russia, and Japan.[7] An agreement without four of the great naval powers would have been meaningless, so the conference moved on to other proposals.

British and French intransigence on immunity and the prize court angered Choate and produced a notable cooling in relations between the British and American delegations. In a bitter speech on July 11, which everyone recognized was aimed primarily at Britain and France, the chief American delegate assailed those nations whose refusal to compromise or even to discuss compromise was making the conference a mockery. Was the world to suffer an endless series of controversies and conflicts over maritime rights simply because a few selfish nations clung tenaciously to every point of national prize law? The maritime law of the United States, established by John Marshall, Joseph Story, and other internationally recognized legal giants, was second to none

---

5. *Proceedings,* III, 783–786; Satow, diary entry, 4 Jun 07, Satow Papers, PRO 30/33/16/10.

6. Satow, diary entry, 4 Jul 07, PRO 30/33/16/10.

7. *Proceedings,* IV, 752–767, 797–800; Fry to Grey, 17 Jun 07, FO 372/67; Davis, *Second Hague,* pp. 228–231.

in the world for authority and justice. Yet the American government and people were willing to submit this law to review by a
suitable international tribunal. "Better any court, however constituted, and with whatever powers, than no International Court at
all." The world would learn which nations worked for peace and
which blocked for selfish reasons all progress toward juridical
settlement of international disputes.[8]

Marschall followed Choate's lecture with the announcement
that Germany, in the interests of peace, was prepared to accept
the British draft article defining the law to be administered by the
international court.[9] At this point there could be little doubt that
Britain was the main obstacle to progress. The Government
found itself facing embarrassing questions about its attitude in the
House of Commons.[10] Lord Reay, one of the British delegates at
The Hague, complained to Campbell-Bannerman that Grey's instructions were unreasonable. Unless the Foreign Office allowed
the delegation more flexibility to negotiate, he warned, "our attitude at the Conference will be severely criticized in the House of
Commons on our own side."[11] The prime minister pointedly referred this letter to his foreign secretary.[12] Around the world,
even such confirmed Anglophiles as Andrew Carnegie complained of British intransigence.[13]

Although Grey indignantly denied that his instructions had
been unreasonable,[14] British policy at The Hague did become
more conciliatory. Crowe admitted, reluctantly, that Britain could
not continue to reject negotiation with Germany simply because
French feelings might be hurt.[15] Choate brought British and
German delegates together privately, and they quickly resolved
the differences between the two prize court drafts. By July 24 Fry
was able to report that "we hope without further difficulty to

8. *Proceedings,* III, 800–804.
9. Ibid., p. 805.
10. E.g., Ramsay MacDonald, Parliamentary Question, 11 Jul 07, FO 372/69.
11. Reay to CB, 21 Jul 07, CB Papers, AM 52514.
12. A. Ponsonby (CB's private secretary) to Grey, 25 Jul 07, ibid.
13. E.g., A. Carnegie to Morley, 30 Jul 07, Morley Papers, India Office Library, European Manuscripts D 573/66.
14. Grey to CB, n.d., CB Papers, AM 52514.
15. Crowe to Tyrrell, 18 Jul 07, FO 800/69.

establish complete agreement."[16] Grey then authorized the delegates to finalize the compromise settlement.[17]

The foreign secretary believed that the prize court would be of value to Britain primarily as a neutral:

> The appeals court is to be (I understand) for the use of neutrals aggrieved by the decision of the belligerent captor's court. Its interpretation of international law is bound to be not less favourable to the neutral than the interpretation of the captor's court. As a neutral we should therefore stand to gain. As a belligerent it is our present policy (e.g., by abolition of contraband) to interfere as little as possible with neutral shipping—we therefore stand to lose very little.[18]

When the Admiralty expressed concern that the new court might limit Britain's vital belligerent rights, Grey assured Tweedmouth that it would not have such powers. Only on relatively unimportant matters like contraband would the court exercise effective jurisdiction.[19]

As the conference moved to consider specific points of law, however, Admiralty concerns began to seem more realistic. The British draft article accepted by Germany and the United States authorized the justices to rule in accordance with existing bilateral or multilateral agreements signed by both parties to a particular dispute. But in the absence of such formal agreements, the court would apply "the rules of international law," or if no commonly accepted rule existed, "the general principles of justice and equity."[20] Discussion of contraband and blockade revealed substantially different interpretations of existing "rules," as well as of "general principles of justice and equity."

Several nations submitted reform proposals on contraband. Britain advocated total abolition, which France, Russia, the United States, and Germany immediately rejected. The British, who had expected American support and had hoped to persuade the French and Russian delegations, were stunned. Reay com-

---

16. Fry to Grey, 24 Jul 07, FO 372/70.
17. Grey to Fry, 25 Jul 07, FO 800/69.
18. Grey, n.d., minute on Fry to Grey, 22 Jul 07, FO 372/70.
19. Adm to FO, 16 Jul 07, FO 372/69; Grey to Tweedmouth, 26 Jul 07, FO 800/87.
20. *Proceedings*, III, 1060.

plained that the American attitude was inconsistent with Secretary of State William Marcy's position in 1856. Porter replied that his instructions came from Theodore Roosevelt, not from Franklin Pierce.[21] Grey offered to make a personal appeal to Ambassador Whitelaw Reid if the American delegates remained "unreasonable,"[22] but Choate and Porter refused to change their stand.

Unknown to the British, the American delegates at The Hague were acting under express instructions from the president when they rejected abolition of contraband. These orders stated that, although the United States favored "limitation of contraband by specific enumeration," or establishment of definite lists of absolute, conditional, and noncontraband goods, it believed that total abolition would "give rise to very serious and doubtful questions."[23] Already angry at the British for their role in defeating immunity, Choate took personal pleasure in carrying out his orders to defeat their proposal to abolish contraband.[24] In the final vote abolition received support from twenty-five nations, but Japan abstained and the United States, Russia, Germany, and France joined Montenegro in opposition.[25]

Failure of the British proposal because of the opposition of so many leading naval powers forced the conference to attempt codification of contraband law. Few nations appeared to agree on what the existing law of contraband was and fewer on what it should be. Russia, with French support, defended its prize regulations of 1904.[26] Germany and the United States agreed that contraband should be limited to goods intended for military use, but the Americans insisted on retaining the doctrine of continuous voyage, which the Germans refused to recognize.[27] France

21. Ibid., IV, 866.

22. Grey to Fry, 30 Jul 07, FO 800/69.

23. Roosevelt to Adee, 30 Jul 07, and Adee to Choate, tel, 30 Jul 07, SD/RG59/NF40/406; Roosevelt to Root, tel, 29 Jul 07, and Root to Roosevelt, tel, n.d., ibid. Cf. the misleading comment in Esthus, *TR*, p. 117, that "the American delegation therefore received no direction from Roosevelt, and it sided with Germany on a number of questions relating to neutral rights in maritime warfare."

24. E.g., F. Campbell (FO official) to Grey, 7 Sep 07, FO 372/73.

25. *Proceedings*, IV, 872; cf. Davis, *Second Hague*, pp. 233–238.

26. *Proceedings*, IV, 856–858, 1138–1139; Fry to Grey, 22 Aug 07, and C. J. B. Hurst (FO assistant legal adviser), "Contraband," 31 Aug 07, FO 372/72.

27. *Proceedings*, IV, 1136–1137, 1140.

agreed with Germany that continuous voyage could not be applied to contraband, while Britain agreed with the United States that it could. None of the Great Powers seemed willing to compromise on its own law.

Confronted with deadlock on contraband, the delegates turned to blockade. Here they found some common ground: all nations were willing to accept the Declaration of Paris rule that only effective blockades were legal. But no two nations seemed to agree on what constituted an "effective" blockade. When the debate appeared to be making some slight progress toward reducing differences, the British delegation ended the discussion by announcing that it had no authority to compromise a single point of national prize law on blockade. Unless all nations accepted British rules, there was no reason to continue negotiations that must ultimately prove fruitless.[28] The conference had reached yet another impasse.

By the end of August, eleven weeks of talks had produced only the draft international prize court convention. All the other bold proposals for reform and codification of maritime law had failed. Even the prize court achievement appeared insecure because the Admiralty continued to complain that the convention as approved by Grey endangered vital belligerent rights. Would not the justices from the Continental Powers rule in accordance with their national prize law in interpreting "the rules of international law" and "the general principles of justice and equity"? Would not Britain's one judge, even if supported by the American and Japanese judges, be consistently outvoted by the representatives of Germany, France, Austria-Hungary, Russia, and Italy? The Admiralty finally warned that it would appeal to the cabinet against the prize court convention unless Grey could modify it to provide a clear code of acceptable law.[29]

Although the foreign secretary told Tweedmouth to bring his complaints before the Government "if you think the matter of sufficient importance,"[30] he changed his position after Loreburn echoed the Admiralty argument that the court, without a specific

28. Ibid., pp. 953–954; Davis, *Second Hague*, p. 242.
29. Adm to FO, 15 Aug 07, FO 372/71.
30. Grey to Tweedmouth, 17 Aug 07, FO 800/87.

legal code to guide it, might rule contrary to British law and interests.[31] On August 26 Grey ordered Fry to "endeavour to secure recognition of British & American law" in the convention that would establish the prize court.[32] The obvious implication was that Britain would not ratify the convention without such recognition.

In the wake of this warning, the British delegation took the lead in the search for a compromise code of law for the new court to administer. Conversations between Admiral Sperry and the British delegates produced an Anglo-American proposal to retain the doctrine of contraband for a narrow list of arms and other articles of direct military use, but to abolish the principle of conditional contraband.[33] France, Russia, and Germany objected, but Grey persuaded the French government to reverse its position, and naval weakness after the Russo-Japanese War made Russia's objections academic for years to come.[34] An agreement seemed within reach if Germany could be persuaded to drop its opposition.

British and German delegates met informally throughout early September, and the outlines of a settlement gradually began to emerge. Britain sought to establish a legal order that would permit a strict blockade of Germany but would limit the rights under which German commerce raiders could attack neutral ships carrying goods to Britain. Germany, on the other hand, recognized that it could not blockade Britain and thus sought a code that would limit the effect of a British blockade while allowing maximum freedom for German commerce raiders. Both sides understood the strategic reasoning behind the other's position, giving their talks a note of stark reality often missing in Hague discussions.

One point of difference was the area within which ships could be seized for blockade running. Continental nations, more often

31. Loreburn to FO, 19 Aug 07, FO 372/71.
32. Grey to Fry, tel, 26 Aug 07, FO 800/87.
33. Sperry, memos, 11, 12, 21 Aug 07, Sperry Papers, 9; Satow, diary entry, 3 Aug 07, Satow Papers, PRO 30/33/16/10; *Proceedings*, IV, 1099–1100; Hurst, "Contraband," 31 Aug 07, FO 372/72.
34. Fry to Grey, 22 Aug 07, Grey to Bertie, 26 Aug 07, Bertie to Grey, 28 Aug 07, and Fry to Grey, 2 Sep 07, FO 372/72; Bertie to Grey, 28 Aug 07, FO 372/75.

blockaded than blockader, had argued for centuries that an effective blockade required a force of ships to be stationed directly off each blockaded port. Only these ships could legally capture a blockade runner. Britain and the United States maintained, on the other hand, that an effective blockade could be enforced anywhere on the high seas. As long as the blockader was able to create a substantial danger that a ship sailing with intent to run a blockade would be captured at some point during its voyage, the blockade was effective and therefore legal. In essence, Continental law required blockade runners to be captured in the act of entering a blockaded port, whereas Anglo-American law equated intent with the deed and authorized condemnation for both.

Another point in dispute was the doctrine of continuous voyage. Germany asserted, as it had during the Boer War, that neutral trade between neutral ports in neutral bottoms was free, whatever the ultimate destination of ship or cargo. Britain maintained that a neutral ship intending to run a blockade was guilty even if captured when bound for an intermediate neutral or unblockaded enemy port; that goods ultimately destined for the enemy armed forces were contraband, even when seized in transit to an intermediate neutral port; and that goods carried to a neutral port for overland transit to the enemy armed forces also were liable to seizure as contraband. Most of the Continental nations took the German view, while the United States shared the British interpretation.

A third point of dispute was the definition of contraband. Germany, backed by most of the Continent, argued that a belligerent had the right to declare contraband any article that might be valuable to the enemy war effort. Britain and the United States replied that only goods intended for direct military use could be considered contraband. The Anglo-Americans sought narrow and specific lists of absolute and conditional contraband, while the Continental Powers opposed such lists on the ground that it was impossible to determine in advance what imported articles might be vital to an enemy's war effort. Again, the difference seemed to be one of basic principle rather than specific detail.

Preliminary discussions among the delegates, and between the British and Germans in particular, demonstrated that none of these disputes could be settled in isolation. A general compromise, with concessions on one point traded for concessions by another nation on another point, seemed to offer the only possibility for agreement on a common code of law to guide the international prize court. Only after much talk did the outline of a settlement appear. Britain was to abandon its claim to seize blockade runners anywhere on the high seas, while Germany in return accepted the principle of an eight-hundred-mile *rayon d'action* around blockaded ports in which capture would be legal. Britain would abandon the doctrine of continuous voyage for cargoes bound to a neutral port for transshipment to a blockaded port, while Germany would recognize the liability of a ship that intended to call at a neutral port within the eight-hundred-mile radius of action from a blockaded port. Britain would abandon the doctrine of continuous voyage entirely for contraband, while Germany would accept specific lists of absolute and conditional contraband as well as a "free list" of goods that could never be declared contraband.[35] Although neither the British nor the German delegation was entirely satisfied with this compromise, it did seem to offer the only means to resolve the impasse and establish the international prize court while still protecting the vital interests of both nations.

Admiral Sir Charles Ottley, the former director of naval intelligence (DNI), who would assume the duties of secretary of the CID upon completion of his duties as Admiralty representative at The Hague, submitted with considerable trepidation the compromise he and his colleagues had worked out. Fisher had boasted that his private instructions had been so "stringent" that Ottley "would leave by the next train if our fighting interests are tampered with."[36] Now Ottley was recommending that Britain abandon the belligerent right to seize contraband under the doctrine of continuous voyage in return for a commitment that "British raw materials such as cotton, metallic ores and textile fabrics shall always be immune from seizure." Although Ottley

35. Crowe, "Memorandum showing the lines on which it is proposed to negotiate," 14 Sep 07, FO 372/73; Davis, *Second Hague*, pp. 239–242.
36. Fisher to Esher, 17 Oct 07, Esher Papers, 10/42.

himself was "strongly of opinion that such a compromise will be greatly to our interests,"[37] he was not certain that Fisher would share that opinion.

These fears proved groundless. Slade, Ottley's successor as DNI, wrote a strong endorsement of his predecessor's proposal. Under existing British prize law, he noted, goods intended for Germany but in transit to a neutral port under a neutral flag could be seized as contraband only if the British government could prove destination to the German armed forces. In practice "it would be almost impossible to bring this proof," and "most dangerous and impolitic" to try.

> The Dutch and Belgian ports are the feeders of such a vast region, a great deal of which would be neutral, that it would be practically impossible to prove anything against a vessel. Suspicion and presumption are not sufficient grounds to go on when dealing with a Court of Law, and it would be obviously impossible to check half the trade of Northern Europe because we considered that a small portion of it might be going to our enemy.[38]

Confronted by Slade's analysis, which none of the sea lords cared to contest, the Board of Admiralty formally endorsed Ottley's proposed compromise.[39]

Despite British approval, the Hague Conference ended before a comprehensive maritime code could be completed. Informal negotiations among the leading naval powers indicated that the remaining points could best be resolved at a separate conference limited to nations with powerful navies. Grey, who believed such a meeting would be more likely than the amorphous Hague conferences to produce a code acceptable to the Admiralty, agreed to serve as host.[40]

The Second Hague Conference adjourned on October 18, 1907. Its delegates had met for 126 days, talked enough to fill 2,951 pages of *Proceedings,* and consumed thousands of bottles of

37. Ottley to Admiral W. May (second sea lord), tel, 17 Sep 07, Tweedmouth Papers, Case B.
38. Slade, "Memorandum on 'Continuous Voyage,' and the probable result of abandoning the right," 18 Sep 07, ibid.
39. Adm to FO, 20 Sep 07, FO 372/73.
40. Grey to Fry, 28 Sep 07, ibid./74; David, *Second Hague,* p. 250.

vintage champagne in toasts to peace. More substantive achievements included thirteen conventions, one declaration, and a final act. The one significant agreement on maritime rights had been the International Prize Court Convention. Progress had been made toward a common code of law for the court to administer, although the conference closed without formal agreement on blockade, contraband, or continuous voyage.[41]

Three days before adjournment, Crowe wrote that "the net result of the Conference is practically nothing except the prize court convention. Whether that will be ratified by us, is another question."[42] The Admiralty continued to insist that recognition of British blockade law was a sine qua non for acceptance.[43] *The Times* mounted a public campaign against the court for the same reason.[44] Grey discovered that the Prize Court Convention would require changes in the structure of the British judiciary and that he therefore needed parliamentary sanction for changes in municipal law before he could ask the Crown to ratify.[45] Creation of the international court thus awaited the code the new conference of naval powers would draft during 1908.

British Germanophobes were not slow to draw general lessons from their perception of events at The Hague. Crowe saw the conference in retrospect as yet another example of Germany's insatiable appetite for European domination. Even Russia and the United States had been lured into the German web, the latter "most markedly in all naval questions, and often obviously in a sense quite opposed to their own interests."[46] Fisher echoed this analysis: "Choate tied with black and yellow [German colors] to Marschall's Chariot wheels would be a lovely picture!"[47] The first sea lord became so concerned by this supposed German influence

41. *Proceedings*, II, 599–696; Prize Court Convention on pp. 660–671.

42. Crowe to Sir C. Dilke (Liberal M.P.), 15 Oct 07, FO 800/243.

43. E.g., Adm to FO, 12 Sep 07, FO 372/73.

44. E.g., "The International Prize Court," *The Times*, 30 Sep 07, clippings with minutes by Davidson & Crowe, FO 372/74.

45. Grey, n.d., minutes on Adm to FO, 20 Sep 07, and on Fry to Grey, 24 Sep 07, ibid./73 & 74. On the complex legal issues involved, see G. Kenwick (FO assistant legal adviser), memo, 25 Oct 07, ibid./75; Grey, minute, n.d., ibid.

46. Crowe to Tyrrell, 11 Oct 07, FO 800/69.

47. Fisher to Tweedmouth, 14 Oct 07, Tweedmouth Papers, Case B.

in Washington that he ordered Slade to prepare detailed plans to repel a joint German-American attack on the British Isles.[48] In the twenty months after the Second Hague Conference there was a limited but serious reconsideration of the general British assumption that war with the United States was inconceivable.[49]

Roosevelt remained unaware of this chill.[50] The president had instructed the American delegates at The Hague to advocate immunity and oppose complete abolition of contraband, not for the purpose of siding with Germany against Britain, but because he believed those policies to be in the national interest of the United States. By the time the conference met, he had lost interest in it. Roosevelt admitted to Root early in July 1907 that "I have not followed things at The Hague," and asked, "Is there anything for me to do?"[51] The secretary of state replied that he saw no favorable opportunity for presidential intervention. With the Kaiser determined not to discuss limitation of land armaments and Grey equally determined not to discuss limitation of sea armaments, nothing worthwhile was likely to be accomplished.[52] A week later Roosevelt explained to Andrew Carnegie, America's most outspoken pacifist, "I am more concerned about keeping the peace with Japan than I am about advancing the cause of peace in The Hague just at the moment, for the former represents the 'instant need of things.'"[53] At the height of the Japanese crisis the president had little time for a conference the other Great Powers seemed determined to reduce to futility.

On one question Roosevelt might have been expected to take a more active role. Earlier in the year he had personally overruled

48. War Plans W.4 & W.5, n.d., Adm 116/1043B/1 & 2; Fisher, "War Plans and the Distribution of the Fleet," n.d., ibid.; Slade, "War with the United States—Germany unfriendly," n.d., Slade Papers, (M)3; Slade, diary entries, 22, 25 Jul and 16 Nov 08, ibid.

49. *Ibid.;* WO 106/40 and 46; CID, minutes, 14 May 08, CAB 2/2. On post-1900 British plans for war with the United States, see Bourne, *Britain and Balance of Power,* pp. 342–401.

50. E.g., Lee to Fisher, 30 Apr 08, Fisher Papers, 309, in which Lee passed on top secret information from the president on the status of the American Atlantic Fleet. American historians also have remained unaware of the chill in London resulting from the Second Hague Conference, as evidenced by Perkins, *Great Rapprochement,* p. 251.

51. Roosevelt to Root, 2 Jul 07, Root Papers, 163.

52. Root to Roosevelt, 8 Jul 07, Roosevelt Papers, (M)75.

53. Roosevelt to Carnegie, 15 Jul 07, Carnegie Papers, 143.

the advice of Root and Dewey to instruct the delegates to press immunity for private property. In September 1906 Carnegie had reported that "the President is keen on this point."[54] When Reid reported a month after the conference opened that the British were "extremely strong" against immunity, however, Roosevelt explained, "I hold to our traditional American view, but in a rather tepid fashion."[55] The president's initial "keen" interest in immunity, like his initial interest in the conference itself, grew "tepid" as he came to realize that the other powers would not accept the reforms he considered necessary for stable and peaceful international relations.

In April 1908 Root reported that the United States had accepted all the conventions its delegates had signed at The Hague except for the Prize Court Convention.[56] Until the British Parliament passed the necessary legislation Britain could not ratify that convention, and an international prize court without participation of the world's leading naval and mercantile power would be an absurdity. The future of the court thus rested on the ability of the nine naval powers Grey had invited to London to resolve their political and legal differences and to draft an acceptable code of maritime law.

54. Carnegie to Morley, 5 Sep 06, Morley Papers, Eur MSS D 573/66.

55. Reid to Roosevelt, 19 Jul 07, Roosevelt Papers, (M)75; Roosevelt to Reid, 29 Jul 07, ibid., (M)346. On Roosevelt's overall reaction to the Hague Conference, see Davis, *Second Hague,* p. 296; Beale, *Roosevelt and the Rise to World Powers,* pp. 337–352; Esthus, *TR,* pp. 113–117.

56. Root to Reid, 8 Apr 08, Reid Papers, (M)176; cf. Grey to Fry, 18 Jun 08, *British Documents,* VIII, 303–304.

CHAPTER SIX

✿

The Declaration of London: Negotiation, 1907–1909

Sir Edward Grey agreed to host the London Conference on maritime law for one reason: he hoped to secure a legal code so favorable to belligerent rights that the Admiralty would withdraw its objection to the international prize court. He admitted as much to the Dutch when they protested his failure to invite the host nation of the Hague conferences and the possessor of one of the world's largest mercantile fleets: "What we desired was to have an agreement with the great naval Powers which would safeguard a large Navy like ours from being unduly limited and crippled in its action in time of war. This was, therefore, a Conference rather for possible belligerents with large Navies than for neutrals with a mercantile marine."[1] The common historical assertion that the Declaration of London was drafted by a conference dominated by trading rather than naval interests[2] thus is incorrect. Although Grey later relented under German and American pressure and did invite the Netherlands,[3] the Dutch presence hardly changed the character of a conference in which the ten participants possessed more than 95 percent of the world's capital ship tonnage.[4]

1. Grey to E. Howard (British minister, the Netherlands), 23 Mar 08, *British Documents*, VIII, 315.
2. Cooper, *Page*, p. 290; cf. Tuchman, *Guns of August*, p. 333.
3. Root to Reid, tel, 17 Apr 08, SD/RG59/NF12655/1; Howard to Grey, 23 Mar 08, and Grey to Howard, 25 Jun 08, *British Documents*, VIII, 315, 318n; Davis, *Second Hague*, pp. 304–305.
4. Other nations participating were France, Russia, Austria-Hungary, Italy, Japan, and Spain. The total was ten, not eight as per Rowland, *Last Liberal Governments*, II, 40.

The conference was in fact dominated by the United States, Germany, and Britain, each of which sought an agreement favorable to its own national interests in possible—in the eyes of many, likely—future naval conflicts.

British preparations for the conference thus had been marked by an attitude of stark realism. The Admiralty, although willing to make some concessions, continued to insist on the broad interpretation of belligerent rights its war plans required. Commercial interests continued to press for safeguards to protect wartime trade. An embarrassing Commons debate in February 1908, in which one Liberal turned Campbell-Bannerman's famous "methods of barbarism" denunciation of Salisbury's South African policy against its author's maritime rights policy and another commended to the foreign secretary the Duke of Wellington's dictum that an army could fight or loot but could not do both, demonstrated that intransigent insistence on belligerent rights would meet substantial opposition from both sides of the House.[5] If the Government were to ratify the International Prize Court Convention, it needed the London Conference to produce a code of law acceptable to both the Admiralty and the proponents of commercial rights.

Grey, who coordinated preparations, left no doubt as to his own sympathies. Growth of Anglo-French cooperation and Anglo-German hostility convinced the foreign secretary that British neutrality in a future European war was becoming increasingly unlikely. The committee he appointed to prepare specific recommendations for the cabinet reflected this view. Its chairman was Lord Desart, the treasury solicitor. His colleagues were Crowe and Assistant Legal Adviser Cecil Hurst of the Foreign Office; Slade, now director of naval intelligence at the Admiralty; and Ottley, former DNI and present secretary of the CID. Unlike the Walton Committee, the Desart Committee included no representative of the Board of Trade to advise on what rules British merchants favored. It consisted of two senior naval officers to state the rules the Admiralty favored, two lawyers to cast those rules into acceptable legal terms, and a political adviser to ensure that the committee never lost sight of the German threat.

Primary responsibility for determining the details of British

5. *The Times*, 7 Feb 08, pp. 2, 12.

policy thus fell on Slade and Ottley. These two officers, under the first sea lord's supervision, had directed the drafting of every Admiralty war plan since 1905. Slade's reputation as the navy's leading authority on economic warfare may well have been a key factor in Fisher's decision to appoint him DNI when Ottley moved up to the CID. At the same time he was serving on the Desart Committee, Slade was directing development of the most detailed war plans in peacetime Admiralty history.[6] Although Fisher claimed to be too busy to advise the Desart Committee personally,[7] in Slade and Ottley it possessed two men whose knowledge of the existing plans to bring economic pressure against Germany was exceeded only by that of the first sea lord.

As the naval representatives explained to their colleagues, the essence of Fisher's strategy was to blockade the German North Sea coast. The orders to the commander in chief of the Channel Fleet, dated July 1, 1908, stated that "the principal object is to bring the main German fleet to decisive action, and all other operations are subsidiary to this end." War automatically would make all German merchantmen good prize. Neutral ships that approached the enemy's North Sea ports were to be seized as blockade runners; those attempting to enter the Baltic with contraband would be seized by a patrol at the entrance. This pressure would destroy Germany's overseas trade and ultimately force the German government to send the High Seas Fleet out to play its appointed role in a twentieth-century Trafalgar.[8]

Fisher, Ottley, and Slade did not delude themselves that these measures would press Imperial Germany as the Napoleonic War Orders in Council had pressed Imperial France.[9] The essence of Admiralty planning was application of measured force to achieve limited objectives. As the introduction to a set of draft plans circulated by the War College in 1907 stated,

> The first point to determine in constructing a war plan is the nature of the war in contemplation. We must decide whether it is a

6. Slade, diary entries, Mar–Dec 08, *passim,* Slade Papers, (M)3; Adm 116/1043B.

7. Slade, diary entry, 20 May 08, Slade Papers, (M)3.

8. "War Plan, Germany," n.d., enclosed in Adm to CIC, Channel Fleet, 1 Jul 08, Adm 116/1043B/2; "War with Germany: Attack on German Commerce," n.d., ibid./1.

9. E.g., War Plan W.3, n.d., Adm 116/1043B; minutes on naval attaché in Berlin, memo, 29 Jan 07, ibid.

limited or an unlimited war, that is, whether its object is the acquisition or defence of some particular piece of territory or other special and limited interest, or whether the object is to crush the fighting power of the enemy and generally reduce him to a state of inferiority and submission.[10]

In Fisher's Admiralty, the object of planning was the "special and limited interest" of forcing the Kaiser to abandon *Marinepolitik*. "It will be in no case the subjugation of Germany that we shall aim at, but merely that we wish to make her policy conform to our wishes."[11]

The obvious implication of this strategy was rejection of the Continentalist definition of British national interests. The 1907 plans had noted that "we shall be in a stronger position . . . without making the war general."[12] Fisher stated explicitly, "We are prepared to deal effectively with the 942 German mercantile vessels that cover the ocean. The one great drawback is that if France is our ally Germany may get her compensation on land for this slaughter of her commerce. So it is 'splendid isolation' that England wants."[13]

This grand strategic conception was the basis for Slade's recommendation that the Desart Committee endorse the Anglo-German compromise worked out in the final days at The Hague. The navy was willing to limit capture of blockade runners to either an eight-hundred-mile or an unspecified *rayon d'action* from a blockaded port because such a radius would include the entire North Sea. There was no reason to insist on maintaining the doctrine of continuous voyage for contraband landed in a neutral port for transshipment overland to the enemy because either a British or an international prize court would require an impossible degree of proof to authorize condemnation. Slade wanted aggressive action against enemy trade through capture of enemy ships and blockade, but warned that "there are very strong reasons why we should not interfere more than is absolutely necessary with neutral trade during a war. In the first place, we do

10. War College draft war plans, 1907, printed in P. K. Kemp, ed., *The Papers of Admiral Sir John Fisher*, vol. II, *Publications of the Navy Records Society*, CVI (London: Spottiswoode, Ballantyne, 1964), 318.
11. Ibid., p. 361.
12. Ibid.
13. Fisher, "War Plans and the Distribution of the Fleet," n.d., Adm 116/1043B/1.

not want to raise up fresh enemies."[14] The Admiralty recommended that Britain advocate rules that would permit the navy to inflict significant damage on the German economy while avoiding confrontation with neutrals which might widen a war Fisher believed must be strictly limited.

The Desart Committee approved Slade's proposal, but insisted on a formal, written Admiralty endorsement before submitting its report to the cabinet. Fisher made some general complaints against international conferences, but accepted the draft report without reservation. So did the first lord, Reginald McKenna, who had replaced Tweedmouth in April.[15] The committee recommendations thus had the explicit approval not only of Slade and Ottley, but of the responsible professional and political officials. The common belief that British policy at the London Conference was formulated without regard to the wishes of the Admiralty[16] is a myth.

Slade's recommendations, endorsed by the Desart Committee and the foreign secretary, now came before the cabinet. There they were attacked by Loreburn and Morley, who argued for a broad effort to limit belligerent rights in the interest of British commerce. Grey, with unexpected help from Local Government Board President John Burns, successfully resisted this proposal. The cabinet endorsed the Desart Committee's recommendations and specified that no further concessions on blockade be made without its express approval. It then appointed Desart, Crowe, Hurst, Slade, and Ottley to serve as the British delegation at the conference.[17]

The Admiralty policy incorporated in the Desart report had

14. Slade, "The proposed International Prize Court of Appeal: Its Effects on British Interests," n.d., Slade Papers, (M)1; Slade to Graham Greene (Admiralty secretary), 2 Oct 08, Adm 116/1070.

15. "Naval Conference Committee: Further Report," 26 Oct 08, CAB 37/95/132; Grey to Asquith, 30 Oct 08, FO 800/92; Fisher, 29 Oct 08, and McKenna, 18 Nov 08, minutes on Slade, "Naval Conference Committee: Memorandum by the Director of Naval Intelligence," 29 Sep 08, Adm 116/1079; Slade, diary entries, 20 May, 12 Nov 08, Slade Papers, (M)3.

16. E.g., Perkins, *Great Rapprochement*, p. 251.

17. Asquith to Edward VII, cabinet letter, 4 Nov 08, CAB 41/31/70; Burns, diary entry, 4 Nov 08, Burns Papers, AM 46326; Grey, pencil note, n.d., FO 800/92; Grey to Desart, 1 Dec 08, James Brown Scott, ed., *The Declaration of London* (New York: Oxford University Press, 1919), pp. 210-234.

survived its first test by winning cabinet approval. Ironically the only challenge had come from "Radicals" favoring greater concessions for commerce. No one had questioned the basic assumption of limited naval warfare. No one had argued that Britain must maximize belligerent rights in order to put all possible pressure on the German economy, whatever the cost in neutral opposition. No one had argued that Fisher's strategy, however appropriate to splendid isolation, offered little obstacle to a German hegemony in Europe incompatible with British security. Although the Desart Committee and cabinet deliberations coincided with a major effort by Haldane to win approval for closer military ties with France, neither Crowe nor Grey pointed out the contradiction between a navalist maritime rights policy and a Continentalist foreign policy.

Haldane's initiative, which should have made this contradiction impossible to ignore, was an attempt to take advantage of an improvement in the army's position relative to the navy to secure CID support for landing the BEF in France. Fisher's personal feud with Admiral Lord Charles Beresford had created anarchy within the navy and reduced its prestige.[18] At the same time Campbell-Bannerman's death and the succession of Herbert Henry Asquith, a friend and political ally of Grey and Haldane, in April 1908 had strengthened the Continentalists. When Ripon resigned in October, Loreburn lamented that the cabinet's internal balance had shifted dramatically since 1905.[19] The war minister hoped to take advantage of that difference to secure a major victory for the army. In the process, he offered yet another opportunity for a debate over British policies on maritime rights.

Asquith's succession to the premiership offered opportunity to Haldane, but War Office pressure for a decision between army and navy concepts of an Anglo-German war presented a delicate political problem for the prime minister. Demand for reductions in military spending had been growing since 1905. Asquith's suc-

18. Marder, *From the Dreadnought*, I, 76–104 and passim.
19. Loreburn to Ripon, 30 Oct 08, Ripon Papers, AM 43543. On Asquith's succession, see Roy Jenkins, *Asquith* (New York: Chilmark Press, 1964), pp. 177–193; Rowland, *Last Liberal Governments*, I, 142–154; and Cameron Hazlehurst, "Asquith as Prime Minister, 1908–1916," *English Historical Review*, 85 (1970):502–507.

cessor as chancellor of the exchequer, David Lloyd George, delighted in addressing Haldane as "The Minister of Slaughter" and
boasted of his determination to slash War Office estimates.[20]
Winston Churchill, the president of the Board of Trade, argued,

> It is therefore only in connection with minor emergencies that the
> scale of our land forces should be considered. Now that South
> Africa is out of the way, these may be reduced to four. First, the
> British invasion of Afghanistan; secondly, a mutiny of the Indian
> Army; thirdly, a rising of the civil population of India; and
> fourthly, a Turkish invasion of Egypt. . . . For all these the forces at
> our disposal are unnecessarily large.[21]

The primary Radical target was the BEF, the single most important element in the Grey-Haldane policy of Anglo-French rapprochement.

Asquith thus found Haldane pressing him for a definite decision to send the BEF to France in the event of war at the same
time that his Radical colleagues pressed for a reduction of the
force necessary to fight a Continental war. Grey had briefed the
prime minister on the Anglo-French staff agreements in July, but
Asquith's only comment had been "interesting."[22] In September
he reacted angrily when the French premier suggested enlarge-
ment of the BEF's Continental capabilities.[23] Certainly Asquith
was no more eager than Grey or Haldane to defend Continental
military intervention before Lloyd George, Churchill, Loreburn,
Morley, and the rest of the cabinet's anti-Continentalist majority.

Asquith's solution was to name a CID subcommittee to investigate the nation's military requirements. This political masterstroke postponed a cabinet confrontation over army estimates,
assured the Radicals that there would be a systematic review of
military needs and expenditures, and provided a safe forum for
Haldane to make his case for a BEF with Continental capability.
The only ministers the prime minister named to the subcommittee were himself, Haldane, Grey, McKenna, and Lord Crewe, the

20. E.g., Haldane to E. Haldane, 9 [?] Feb, 14 May 08, Haldane Papers, MS
6011.
21. Churchill, "A Note upon British Military Needs," 27 Jun 08, Lloyd George
Papers, C/18/3/6.
22. Asquith to Grey, 9 Jul 08, FO 800/100.
23. Asquith to Grey, 7 Sep 08, ibid.

colonial secretary. Aside from McKenna, all were members of the "Liberal Imperialist" wing of the party and generally sympathetic to Continentalist views. Campbell-Bannerman also had named subcommittees to investigate "the Military Needs of the Empire," so the unrepresented Radicals had no reason to suspect that the focus would not be on similar studies of Malta's dockyards or Singapore's fortifications, but on British aid to France in a war with Germany.[24]

Although the subcommittee did not issue its formal report until July 1909, after the Declaration of London had been signed, the height of the clash between navy and army grand strategies came in early December 1908. The day after the London Conference convened, Asquith directed the Admiralty to submit a detailed statement of "the financial and economic pressure that would result to Germany owing to the stoppage of her overseas trade, if she were at war with Great Britain & France."[25] Slade interrupted his duties at the conference to prepare the response.

The terms of the request put the Admiralty at an immediate disadvantage. Slade was not to explain how the navy could best defend British interests against Germany, but how the navy could help in a conflict in which Britain and France were allied against Germany. The DNI evaded this point in his paper. After a detailed analysis of the damage a British blockade would inflict on the German economy, he added lamely that "if France also is engaged in the war as an ally of Great Britain, Germany's trading loss would be intensified." He ignored the implications of a Franco-German land conflict.[26]

The Admiralty had explained its strategy to the Desart Committee, and Crowe had made no objection. Grey had submitted the committee's recommendations based on the navalist strategy to the cabinet with a favorable endorsement. The only opposition

24. CID, "Report of the Sub-Committee . . . on the Military Needs of the Empire," 24 Jul 09, CID Paper 109B, CAB 4/3. Grey substituted Hardinge for himself. On "Military Requirements of the Empire" subcommittees under Campbell-Bannerman, see d'Ombrain, *War Machinery*, pp. 88, 92–93. As Hazlehurst notes, Asquith also used cabinet subcommittees to defuse potentially dangerous issues ("Asquith as Prime Minister," p. 508).

25. Ottley to McKenna, 5 Dec 08, McKenna Papers, 3/7/1A.

26. Slade, "The Economic Effect of War on German Trade," 12 Dec 08, CID Paper E-4, CAB 16/5.

within the Government had come from those ministers who favored further limitation of belligerent rights. Even as the London Conference met, Asquith, Haldane, Crewe, the senior officers of the General Staff, and Hardinge (substituting for Grey) received Slade's detailed exposition of Admiralty policy. If any of the Continentalists had wished to challenge this policy, the first lord, the first sea lord, and two of the British delegates to the London Conference were present. Yet no one protested that British involvement in a Continental war would require enforcement of maritime rights on a Continental scale as had been done in the Napoleonic Wars. Haldane's subcommittee offered the advocates of European military intervention and balance of power a last, best opportunity to challenge the Admiralty analysis on which Britain was basing its maritime rights policies. Their silence speaks for itself. In that silence the British delegates moved to negotiate the Declaration of London.

British deliberation, however confused and contradictory its results, stands in marked contrast to the decidedly odd manner in which the United States government determined its position at the London Conference. Grey had proposed in February 1908 that each invited nation submit by August 1 a detailed statement of its interpretation of existing maritime law.[27] But when the State Department sought to draft a reply, the navy refused to cooperate. The General Board had persuaded Roosevelt in 1904 to withdraw the Naval War Code of 1900 lest the United States be at a disadvantage in a conflict with some less scrupulous nation.[28] In 1908 the navy was determined to avoid any statement that might be cited in the future to limit American claims of belligerent rights.[29] When the British chargé asked in September for a reply to Grey's request, the State Department informed him that the "practice and policy of the United States Government are well known and have not changed." He was then handed copies of the

27. Grey to Bertie et al., 27 Feb 08, *British Documents*, VIII, 306–307.
28. Naval War College, *International Law Discussions*, 1903, pp. 3, 89–91; George Wilson, speech, "The United States Naval War College and International Law," 25 Apr 08, Naval War College Archives, "International Law."
29. ND to SD, 27 Aug 08, SD/RG59/NF12655/23; Davis, *Second Hague*, pp. 306–307.

withdrawn War Code of 1900 and of the instructions to the American delegation to the Second Hague Conference.[30]

United States agreement to attend the London Conference meant that the navy eventually had to define some guidelines for the delegation. Two Naval War College study groups conducted thorough examinations of national interests on maritime rights under modern conditions. They reached directly contradictory conclusions,[31] a perfect example of the absence of any strategic consensus even within the navy. The president of the War College finally drew up a report recommending that the delegation press for adoption of the War Code of 1900, with strong confirmation of the American position on continuous voyage.[32] The secretary of the navy submitted this recommendation to the State Department, which considered it without urgency.[33]

This procrastination and confusion had unfortunate effects. Early in October, two months before the conference was to convene, Grey had proposed that, in light of "practical agreement between our two Governments as to most of the questions which are to be debated," American naval delegate Admiral Charles Stockton should meet with his British counterpart to plan strategy for the advancement of common Anglo-American interests.[34] Stockton as yet had no instructions from Washington, but he neglected to inform Slade and Ottley that he was speaking for himself and not for his government. The British officers pressed the Anglo-German compromise from The Hague, which involved the radius of action limitation on blockaders and some restriction of the doctrine of continuous voyage. Stockton made no objection, and the meeting ended in complete agreement. Slade privately described the American as "deaf & not very quick," but "very conciliatory."[35]

30. E. Howard to Grey, tel, 7 Sep 08, FO 372/119.
31. Committees, memos of 27, 31 Aug and 1, 3, 4 Sep 08, Naval War College Archives.
32. Admiral J. Merrill to ND, 29 Sep 08, ibid.
33. ND to SD, 1 Oct 08, SD/RG59/NF12655/42.
34. Grey to Reid, 6 Oct 08, *British Documents*, VIII, 330–331.
35. Stockton to Bureau of Navigation, ND, 18 Nov 08, Naval War College Archives; minutes, SD/RG59/NF12655/87; Slade, diary entries, 26, 28 Oct and 1 Dec 08, Slade Papers, (M)3.

The British concluded from these meetings with Stockton that the United States would "support our views throughout," a misunderstanding that would shape the entire course of the conference.[36] For the State Department was in the process of drafting instructions far different from those Stockton had expected to receive. Secretary Root seems to have had little personal interest in the conference, probably the result of disappointment with the Second Hague Conference and his imminent departure from office. He left the details of American policy in the hands of Scott, the department solicitor, who in turn relied heavily on his assistant, William Dennis. Scott's instructions to Stockton and his colleague, Professor George Wilson of Brown University and the Naval War College, followed closely the navy's recommendations. The delegates were to "endeavor, in your discretion, to secure as far as possible the adoption" of the Naval War Code of 1900. Any substantial deviation from the code was to be approved in advance by the State Department.[37]

When the London Conference convened on December 4, 1908, the preliminary discussions revealed that both Britain and Germany had decided to accept the compromise devised at The Hague the previous year. In return for British abandonment of the doctrine of continuous voyage for goods to be landed at a neutral port and acceptance of the *rayon d'action* principle for blockaders, Germany would accept three specific lists of absolute contraband, conditional contraband, and noncontraband. With these differences apparently settled, the conference gave every indication of being short and successful.[38]

Agreement between two, however, does not imply agreement among ten. American support for the compromise, which the British had taken for granted after the preliminary discussions

36. Slade, diary entry, 1 Dec 08, Slade Papers, (M)3.

37. Root to American delegation, 21 Nov 08, Scott, ed., *Declaration*, pp. 190–195; E. Stowell (secretary to American delegation) to Scott, 3 Dec 08, Stowell Papers, 6. "The vigorous presence of Admiral Mahan as chief American delegate" reported in Tuchman, *Guns of August*, p. 333, is interesting, since Mahan in fact was not present in either an official or an unofficial capacity.

38. Crowe, "Notes of Conversation with M. Kriege," 4 Dec 08, FO 371/794. Disputes that played no role in subsequent Anglo-American relations, such as transformation of merchantmen into warships on the high seas, are not included in this generalization.

with Stockton, evaporated when the American delegates received their instructions from Washington. The State Department would "certainly not consent to the surrender" of continuous voyage "unless there are very weighty reasons of which I am not now advised." That the conference might collapse and the international prize court never be established as a result did not seem a sufficiently "weighty" reason.[39]

Stockton and Wilson continued to press Washington for concessions during the Christmas recess and after the conference reconvened in January, but met only renewed rejection.[40] When Britain and Germany, in rare agreement proposed that continuous voyage be retained for absolute but abolished for conditional contraband, Washington thundered:

> It appears that the proposed compromises in the interest of unanimity are to be reached by the sacrifice on the part of the United States of cherished and well-known doctrines of its maritime jurisprudence.... Continental Powers at the Conference insist upon these sacrifices, but . . . have not offered to concede any doctrines of their own in return for concession. This seems to be surrender, not compromise.[41]

The State Department seemed oblivious to the fact that Britain, which was not a Continental Power and which had applied the doctrine of continuous voyage before the United States had existed, was an originator and proponent of the compromise in question.

With this attitude determining policy in Washington, there seemed little hope for a successful result to the conference. Scott condescended to offer abolition of continuous voyage for blockade in return for retention of the doctrine for all contraband, but Stockton and Wilson did not consider this suggestion worth raising.[42] On February 5 Slade noted in his diary that "the Ameri-

---

39. Stockton to Root, tels, 10, 15 Dec 08, and Root to Stockton, tels, 14 Dec 08 and 18 Jan 09, SD/RG59/NF12655/86, 88, 136; cf. similar correspondence elsewhere in the same file and in the Scott and Stowell Papers.

40. E.g., Root to Stockton, tels, 18, 20 Jan 09, SD/RG59/NF12655/136, 143.

41. Root to Stockton, tel, 22 Jan 09, ibid./144.

42. Root to Stockton, tel, 23 Jan 09, ibid./145; Slade, diary entry, 27 Jan 09, Slade Papers, (M)3.

cans are impossible and there is a strong probability of their wrecking everything."[43]

As the stalemate continued, the spirit of Anglo-American rapprochement vanished from the conference hall. Stockton warned the other delegates that he and Wilson would walk out unless more respect was shown for American views.[44] He was particularly delighted to block British proposals because he suspected that "the English Foreign Office has been intriguing in the American press to bring our Government and Delegation into line with its policies."[45] The British, meanwhile, despite some disagreements with other nations, agreed unanimously that "the Americans are the principal difficulty."[46] As the conference entered its third month, Grey's statement that there existed "practical agreement between our two Governments" had come to seem one of his less prescient remarks.

In a final vote on February 16, nine nations endorsed the rule that absolute contraband could be condemned only when the captor could provide absolute proof of enemy destination. The United States cast the sole negative vote. Stockton then announced that his government would not abandon its opposition despite the overwhelmingly favorable majority. Three days later the other delegates, too tired to resist such intransigence and unwilling to see the entire conference break up, yielded and struck out the draft article.[47] By threatening to walk out and by defying the will of the other nine nations represented, the United States had managed to defeat an important safeguard for neutral rights. Satisfied with this victory, the State Department finally agreed to abolition of continuous voyage for conditional contraband as long as the doctrine was maintained for absolute contraband and blockade. The United States joined the other nations

---

43. Slade, diary entry, 5 Feb 09, Slade Papers, (M)3.
44. Slade, diary entry, 6 Feb 09, ibid.
45. Stowell to Scott, 8 Feb 09, Stowell Papers, 6.
46. Slade, diary entry, 9 Feb 09, Slade Papers, (M)3.
47. Stockton to Bacon (secretary of state), tels, 17, 19 Feb 09, SD/RG59/ NF12655/233; article 9, draft declaration, 16 Feb 09, with minute "Withdrawn in deferrence to a strong protest by the Gov. of the U.S." by Slade, n.d., Adm 116/1079.

represented in signing the final document, the Declaration of London, on February 26.[48]

When submitting the declaration to the Admiralty, Slade asserted that "taking the draft as a whole the majority of the proposed rules follow our existing law." The belligerent right to seize conditional contraband under the doctrine of continuous voyage, which Britain had yielded, was "of no practical value as in most cases it would be impossible to obtain the requisite proof." Concession of the right to seize blockade runners outside the blockader's radius of action also was meaningless, the phrase *rayon d'action* being so vague as to admit any interpretation the Admiralty cared to give it. Other British concessions were equally unimportant, whereas the gains were substantial. Slade concluded that the declaration on the whole was a decisive victory for Britain.[49]

The British government shared this evaluation. The Board of Trade applauded the contraband regulations vital to British merchants.[50] Grey believed that he had secured an agreement acceptable to both the navy and those concerned with British commercial interests, and commended it to his colleagues along with the International Prize Court Convention. The cabinet agreed that the declaration protected British interests both as a belligerent and as a neutral, and gave it official approval.[51]

On the surface, British policy appears consistent and considered. But two anomalies demand explanation. Why did the Continentalists make no objection when Britain committed itself to a maritime rights agreement appropriate for an isolationist foreign policy but inadequate for a major European war in alliance with France? And why, even while the conference was meeting, had the Admiralty begun to express doubts about its own recommendation to make limited concessions on the doctrine of continuous voyage?

The second thoughts about continuous voyage had emerged

48. Scott, *Declaration*, pp. 144ff.
49. Slade, 18 Feb 09, minute on draft declaration, 16 Feb 09, Adm 116/1079.
50. Slade, diary entry, 4 Jan 09, Slade Papers, (M)3.
51. Grey to cabinet, 18 Feb 09, CAB 37/98/33.

when the British delegates met with Grey and McKenna to secure final approval of the Anglo-German compromise language. The first lord unexpectedly began to argue that Britain was giving up too much for too little advantage. Continuous voyage would

> give an opportunity of checking imports to a belligerent country through a neutral port inasmuch as any goods of a contraband nature found in a neutral ship bound to a neutral port in close connection with the enemy would form a good reason for detaining the vessel, if there was prima facie reason to presume the hostile destination of the contraband; and even if the detention did not result in the condemnation of the goods or ship, the cost of freights and insurance would at once rise against the belligerent affected and assist in causing a financial crisis.[52]

This argument stunned the first lord's listeners. Desart pointed out that his committee had considered the implications of continuous voyage in detail and had concluded, with the full agreement of Slade and Ottley, that Britain stood to lose far more than it stood to gain by such an assertion of the doctrine. Prize courts required evidence of enemy destination essentially impossible to obtain under the circumstances McKenna had outlined. Powerful neutrals were hardly likely to sit by while their ships were seized and detained without evidence in a flagrantly illegal effort to drive up the cost of enemy freights and insurance. The Admiralty might remember that its efforts to enforce continuous voyage against neutral ships during the Boer War had done no damage to the enemy, but had resulted in an expensive humiliation for the British government.

Grey was equally firm, if not so caustic. Creation of an international prize court was so important to Britain, he argued, that "certain concessions, not of vital importance, might be made in order to prevent the present Conference from coming to a barren conclusion." The Admiralty had indicated in the past that continuous voyage for conditional contraband was such a minor point. Now that the settlement had been negotiated, the navy could hardly expect to back out of it for such questionable considerations as those McKenna had advanced. Grey authorized the delegates to finalize the compromise with Germany.[53]

52. Greene, "Naval Conference," 15 Dec 08, FO 371/794.
53. Ibid.

McKenna was not yet ready to admit defeat. A week after this meeting, he circulated a memorandum arguing once again that continuous voyage was too important to be traded for German recognition of the three contraband lists alone. He admitted that Desart's objections "might be true," but asserted that the economic pressure against Germany generated by seizure of contraband intended for Dutch and Belgian ports "could not fail to be of the first importance to us in war.... In dealing with exigencies of naval warfare with a formidable opponent such as Germany, every legitimate weapon would have to be used." McKenna concluded that Britain should hold out for greater concessions before abandoning the potentially valuable right to apply the doctrine of continuous voyage to German contraband imports.[54]

The foreign secretary was not impressed. In a sharp reply, Grey stated flatly that he did not intend to see the London Conference fail and the international prize court be stillborn over continuous voyage. Any breakdown must be over "a point of first rate importance such as enemy's merchant ships or blockade." The net result of applying continuous voyage as the first lord proposed would be at best "some pretext for creating a scare about freights & insurance," the practical value of which "would be very slight." The foreign secretary, the responsible official, had authorized the delegation to accept the proposed compromise. "If the Admiralty do not agree to this I can see nothing for it except a Cabinet before the Conference reassembles."[55]

Confronted with the prospect of justifying the Admiralty change of face to colleagues suddenly recalled from their Christmas holidays, McKenna hastened to explain that he had "unintentionally misled" the foreign secretary. He had not meant to imply that Britain should not accept the proposed compromise, but only that it should bargain for better terms.[56] The Admiralty made no further objection. But the fact that it did suddenly reverse course on the importance of continuous voyage requires more of an explanation than McKenna gave Grey. Was the reversal simply a reflex action by a navy unwilling to part with any

54. McKenna, memo, 23 Dec 08, and Greene to Crowe, 23 Dec 08, ibid.

55. Grey, memo, 26 Dec 08, *ibid.;* see also Greene, memo of conversation with Crowe, 28 Dec 08, Adm 116/1079.

56. McKenna to Grey, 1 Jan 09, FO 800/87.

of its glorious past? Or did it represent a significant change in naval strategy?

The evidence available would seem to indicate that it was both reflex and calculation. The reflex undoubtedly came from Fisher, who bellowed periodically against conferences, law, or any limitation on British sea power.[57] The first sea lord told Crowe during the conference that he did not care what rules were made because Britain would throw them overboard in wartime anyway. Even the Declaration of Paris would not stand in the way of the Royal Navy's operations.[58] But Fisher punctuated these outbursts with approval of the specific concessions the British delegates made on belligerent rights. If he did not encourage an atmosphere conducive to a balanced view of maritime rights, neither did he take enough interest in the negotiations to attend the meeting with Grey on December 15. If rational calculation dictated Admiralty second thoughts on continuous voyage in December 1908, it did not come from Fisher.

The most likely source for such calculation, ironically, was Slade. The DNI's analysis of possible economic pressure for Asquith's CID subcommittee had forced him to reexamine the problem of attacking German trade. Two days after his memo for the subcommittee, he circulated another paper within the Admiralty in which he concluded that abandonment of continuous voyage remained desirable on the whole, but did have certain disadvantages previously overlooked:

> If we were belligerent, it would prevent our stopping the whole of the German trade by sea, as a blockade of the German coasts would not prevent a portion of it passing through Dutch and Belgian ports. If we could not even threaten to declare raw materials as contraband, nor threaten to stop contraband of any kind from going to these ports ... we lose a weapon which would be, to a certain extent, effective in forcing both freights and insurance up against the Germans.
>
> Still, we must remember that we have never declared raw materials as contraband, and we have invariably protested most strongly

---

57. E.g., minute, 29 Oct 08, on Slade, "Naval Conference Committee," 29 Sep 08, Adm 116/1079; Esher, diary entry, 6 Jan 09, Esher Papers, 2/12; Maurice, Lord Hankey, *The Supreme Command, 1914-1918*, 2 vols. (London: George Allen & Unwin, 1961), I, 99-100.

58. Crowe, "Record of meeting with Mr. McKenna," 24 Dec 08, FO 371/794.

when other nations have done so against us. Also we must not forget that we are not always belligerent. . . .

The value of the doctrine of "Continuous Voyage" to us, in its modern extended sense, is very doubtful. The difficulties of proof would be enormous, and the risk of becoming involved with powerful neutrals . . . is one to be carefully weighed.[59]

This memo seems to explain McKenna's abrupt shift during his meeting with Grey and the conference delegation the next day. The first lord obviously had been more impressed by Slade's description of the potential advantages from continuous voyage than by the DNI's warnings that these advantages were counterbalanced by "enormous" difficulties. McKenna withdrew his objection to the Anglo-German compromise as soon as he recognized that Grey was not willing to revise his instructions. The real significance of the 1908 incident was that Reginald McKenna had begun to doubt his admirals' advice on the value of continuous voyage. These doubts, driven away by the foreign secretary at the time, would return with considerable effect six years later.

The second anomaly in British maritime rights policy, the Continentalist failure to challenge the Admiralty's isolationist assumptions, is more difficult to explain. Again, as before the Second Hague Conference, the answer seems to lie in a combination of strategic ignorance, political calculation, and confidence in the BEF. The army continued to believe that Germany could be defeated only by the French and Russian armies, backed by the BEF. None of the Continentalists believed that sea power and its economic pressure could be decisive; most were of the opinion that it would not be a significant factor. Grey in particular tried to avoid recognizing the military implications of his commitment to France, as evidenced by his substitution of Hardinge on the Military Requirements subcommittee. The anti-Continentalist cabinet majority, weaker than in Campbell-Bannerman's day but still strong, remained an obstacle to any official reassessment of isolation. All of these factors combined to explain Continentalist silence while Britain adopted an isolationist maritime rights policy.

If British policy at the London Conference presents two anomalies, American policy is almost incomprehensible. The na-

59. Slade, "The Naval Conference," 14 Dec 08, Adm 116/1079.

tion that had gone to war in 1812 and had threatened war as
recently as 1904 in defense of neutral rights, the nation that had
consistently advocated immunity for private property at sea, suddenly appeared as the world's most intransigent upholder of belligerent rights. Even with Britain, Germany, and the other naval
powers united in accepting limitations on blockade, contraband,
and continuous voyage, the State Department had remained
adamantly opposed. Choate's 1907 denunciation of the selfish
blindness of nations that refused to compromise a single rule of
their national prize law seems particularly ironic in light of
American behavior eighteen months later.

The explanation for this extraordinary conduct seems to be
the poor timing of the conference rather than a drastic shift in
national policy. Roosevelt was preoccupied with preparations for
his African trip, while incoming President William Howard Taft
was concerned with politics and domestic affairs. Root resigned at
the end of January so his friend Assistant Secretary Robert Bacon
could be secretary of state for a month. The London Conference
as a result was left in the hands of military and civilian bureaucrats, men marked by the narrow view that often characterizes
middle-level government officials, men who believed it better to
break up an international conference than to compromise a single
established regulation.[60]

Insofar as American policy was not simply a product of
bureaucratic inertia, it reflected a ludicrously inaccurate perception of the American Civil War and the possible relation of that
conflict to future wars. Dennis wrote to the secretary of the
American delegation, "I hope you will come back without having
sacrificed the doctrine which contributed as much as any other
principle of law to winning the Civil War and which might be
equally valuable again in case we were in a war with Germany, or
for that matter, Japan."[61] He neglected to explain how the seizure
of a tiny number of cargoes under the doctrine of continuous
voyage had won the Civil War, or how the rule was to be enforced

60. Davis, *Second Hague*, p. 308; James Brown Scott, "Elihu Root" and "Robert
Bacon," in Samuel Flagg Bemis and Robert H. Ferrell, eds., *The American Secretaries of State and Their Diplomacy* (New York: Knopf, 1927 *et seq.*), IX, 276, 285,
296–297.
61. Dennis to Stowell, 21 Jan 09, Stowell Papers, 6.

effectively under modern conditions against enemies on the other side of a major ocean. The army and navy objected to any concessions, but neither appears to have given more than a cursory examination to Civil War precedents.[62] In the absence of presidential or secretarial guidance, no one conducted a systematic study of how the rules in question might be applied in a German-American or a Japanese-American war. Scott, oblivious to Stockton's repeated reports that the British naval delegates were among the strongest proponents of the suggested compromise, warned the British ambassador that the "Anglo-Americans" had been so badly outmaneuvered by the "Continentals" that the United States Senate was unlikely to ratify the declaration.[63]

The degree to which these State, Navy, and War Department bureaucrats were out of touch with reality became evident shortly after the American delegates returned to the United States. Naval officers sought out Stockton to congratulate him for negotiating an excellent agreement. Sperry was particularly enthusiastic about the culmination of his own work at The Hague. Root, who had ignored Scott's obstructionism while still secretary of state, described the declaration as "a most valuable agreement."[64] President Taft, in his Annual Message to Congress, praised it as "an eminently satisfactory code."[65] If American preparations for the Second Hague Conference seemed confused, the London Conference established a new standard for blind bureaucratic bungling. Scott and Dennis must bear primary responsibility for this fiasco, but Roosevelt and Root were hardly blameless. Perhaps the best that can be said is that the London Conference achieved its agreement despite the United States government.

The Declaration of London was a compromise. Each of the signatory powers had conceded certain of its national prize rules in order to reach unanimous agreement. No nation considered the declaration a perfect code. Each of the ten signatories considered it an acceptable code. Its ratification, together with that of

62. E.g., General Board to ND, 25 Jan, 17 Feb 09, General Board Letters, V, 389-390, 443-444; War Department to SD, 30 Jan 09, SD/RG59/NF12655/202.
63. Bryce to Grey, 26 Feb 09, FO 800/82.
64. Stowell to G. G. Wilson, 8 Apr 09, Stowell Papers, 1.
65. Taft, Annual Message to Congress, 7 Dec 09, *FRUS* 1909, p. xi.

the International Prize Court Convention, would create a juridical means to resolve controversies that in the past had been resolved by diplomatic confrontation or even war. President Taft was only one of many who hoped that creation of an international institution to settle maritime disputes would lead to similar institutions to settle other sources of international controversy. The International Prize Court Convention of 1907 and the Declaration of London of 1909 seemed to be substantial steps toward the ultimate goal of world peace through world law.

☆

The Declaration of London: Debate, 1909–1914

Two days before the signing of the Declaration of London, Eyre Crowe warned that it "would be made the subject of much criticism on the part of those people who are opposed to the establishment of the international prize court, and perhaps of discontented professors."[1] This prediction proved both an understatement and an inadequate evaluation of opposition motives. Attacks on the declaration began almost as soon as Grey released its text. Controversy mounted until December 1911, when the House of Lords rejected the Government's Naval Prize Bill and thereby blocked immediate ratification of either the declaration or the Prize Court Convention.

The pattern of debate was established in the House of Commons on April 7, 1909, when two Unionist backbenchers rose to denounce the declaration. Frederick Leverton Harris complained that the new code allowed potential enemies too much freedom to intercept British food shipments; Thomas Gibson Bowles complained that it placed intolerable restrictions on British enforcement of belligerent rights.[2] Although a *Times* editorial pointed out the absurdity of simultaneously criticizing the same agreement for allowing belligerents too many and too few rights to

---

1. Crowe, 24 Feb 09, minute on de Bunsen (British ambassador, Madrid) to Grey, 21 Feb 09, FO 371/794.
2. *The Times*, 8 Apr 09, pp. 6–7.

attack neutral commerce,[3] both themes were to appear frequently throughout the debate.

Despite this criticism, Grey initially believed that he could win the assent of Parliament with little difficulty. The most effective objection was raised by Leverton Harris, who argued that Article 34 contained potentially dangerous semantic ambiguities. Although the intent clearly had been to make conditional contraband liable to seizure only when consigned to the enemy government, to a military base, or to a known contractor for the armed forces, the text specified only consignment to "the enemy" or "to a fortified place." Harris warned that an unscrupulous enemy might take advantage of this sloppy drafting to claim that all British ports were fortified places because all had some defenses or that consignment to any British subject constituted "enemy" destination.[4] Grey considered this interpretation so strained that no belligerent would risk neutral wrath by advancing it, but admitted that to remove the ambiguity in peacetime was better than to tempt an enemy in wartime. He agreed to secure clarification of the language in question, which he believed would resolve the doubts of most critics.[5]

Effective opposition to the declaration already had ended in the United States. In September 1909 the General Board and Naval War College conducted an elaborate joint study of the agreement and gave it their endorsement.[6] The War College then revised the War Code to accord with the Declaration.[7] There was no more general review of the new rules because no institution existed to conduct such a study. The Joint Army and Navy Board created in 1903 had failed to provide effective coordination even between the two services.[8] Dewey claimed to favor a "Council of National Defense" equivalent to the British CID, but in practice vetoed cooperation with the War and State Departments in the

    3. *Ibid.*, editorial, 8 Apr 09, p. 9.
    4. E.g., Harris, Parliamentary Questions, 24 Mar 09, FO 371/795.
    5. Grey, 6 Apr 09, minute on A. Herbert, Parliamentary Question, 6 Apr 09, ibid.; Reid to Stowell, 17 Apr 09, Stowell Papers. 1.
    6. ND to SD, 11 Sep 09, SD/RG59/NF12655/375.
    7. Naval War College to ND, 31 Jan 12, General Board Papers, 28-12.
    8. Grenville and Young, *Politics*, pp. 300-301; Challener, *Admirals*, pp. 47-50.

drafting of war plans because naval officers should "rarely, if at all, be influenced by ulterior motives."[9] Taft, despite his reputation as an administrative reformer while secretary of war, made no effort to force the separate departments to cooperate in areas of common involvement.

Despite brief flurries of excitement during the Boer and Russo-Japanese Wars, the American public no longer exhibited in the first decade of the twentieth century the emotional attachment to freedom of the seas characteristic in the nineteenth century. On the other hand, few would have agreed with Dewey and Mahan that the United States should abandon isolation and expand belligerent rights. In the absence of either public pressure or strategic consensus, the Taft administration tended to treat maritime law as a technical legal matter, important mainly as a basis from which to encourage broader agreements for pacific settlement of international disputes. In February 1911 the Senate voted its unanimous advice and consent to the International Prize Court Convention.[10] The president completed the formalities of ratification a few days later.[11] The Senate unanimously approved the Declaration of London in April 1912, after some delay caused by difficulty in agreeing on a common Anglo-American English translation of the French text.[12] In neither case was there any opposition or debate. The staunchest legislative supporter of the two agreements, ironically, was the junior senator from New York, Elihu Root.

Sir Edward Grey undoubtedly envied the absence of rancor which characterized approval of the Prize Court Convention and the Declaration of London in the United States. Despite his hopes, debate in Britain did not end with his note clarifying the ambiguities of Article 34. Had the Government been able to intro-

9. Dewey to president, Naval War College, 19 Jun 12, General Board Papers, 65-12.

10. Senate, Executive Session, 15 Feb 11, U.S. Congress, Senate, *Journal of the Executive Proceedings of the Senate of the United States of America*, XLII, 61st Cong., 3d sess. (Washington: U.S. Government Printing Office, 1942), p. 205.

11. Scott to P. C. Knox (secretary of state), 31 Mar 11, Knox Papers, 14.

12. Senate, Executive Session, 24 Apr 12, *Journal of Executive Proceedings*, XLIV, 62d Cong., 2d sess. (Washington: U.S. Government Printing Office, 1946), p. 269.

duce a bill making the essential changes in British prize law in 1909 or even in 1910, the legislation almost certainly would have passed with much talk but little difficulty. The complexities of the issue and political distractions delayed presentation of the Naval Prize Bill until 1911, however, and thereby gave the opposition time to rally. The desultory objections of 1909 grew into an organized, essentially partisan, effort to defeat the Prize Bill and thereby kill both the declaration and the Prize Court Convention.

Two factors made rejection of the bill a practical possibility: Grey's failure to insist on unequivocal language to establish the immunity of neutral food shipments to the British civilian population and the decision of the Unionist party leadership to treat maritime rights as a partisan political issue. Although Ottley was a former Unionist candidate for Parliament and Desart generally sided with the Opposition majority in the House of Lords, the Government was unable to win bipartisan support for the agreement they had negotiated.[13] Nor was it able to ease the fears of those concerned about British commerical interests. When serious debate began in 1911, the Naval Prize Bill faced an organized opposition that, through contradictory paths, reached the common conclusion that national interests demanded rejection.

Discussion began on a subdued note in February, when Lansdowne, the Unionist leader in the House of Lords, expressed hope that "the representatives of the great commercial interests" would be consulted before the Government moved to ratify the Declaration of London. He emphasized that he was personally a strong supporter of the proposed international prize court and that he considered most of the criticism directed against the declaration to be unjustified. But the former foreign secretary wondered if fears that the new rules would increase the vulnerability of British food imports were "altogether unreasonable." The

13. On the efforts of Ottley and Desart to persuade the Unionist leadership to support the declaration, or at least not to oppose it as a partisan issue, see Ottley to Balfour, 17 Oct 10, Sandars Papers; Greene to Slade, 23 Jul 11, Slade Papers, (M)1. For political pressure on Balfour and Lansdowne to make opposition to the Prize Bill a party position, see Arthur Lee, *A Good Innings*, 3 vols. (Privately printed, 1939), I, 439; Walter Long (influential Unionist M.P.) to Balfour, 20 Jan 11, Balfour Papers, AM 49777; and Balfour, note, 10 Nov 10, with Sandars minute, Sandars Papers.

Government should not move to ratify the agreement, he argued, until no doubt existed on this vital point.[14]

Morley, speaking for the cabinet, thanked Lansdowne for the "certain caution" in his remarks and promised that there would be ample time for discussion of all aspects before the Government asked the Crown to ratify.[15] But this reasonable and respectful approach quickly evaporated in the heated political climate of 1911. In the year of the Parliament Bill which abolished the legislative veto of the Upper House, reasoned discourse across party lines proved essentially impossible. In March Lord Ellenborough, one of the more militant Unionist peers, attacked the declaration in a tone quite different from that of his leader the previous month:

> International lawyers appear to have forgotten two ancient Roman maxims that I first heard of when a boy at school: *Inter arma silent leges*, and *Salus populi suprema lex*. These two maxims have stood the test of hundreds of wars and of 2,000 years of time, and will continue to be acted upon so long as human nature remains what it is. They knock the bottom out of the whole of the Declaration.

If the Admiralty had approved the Naval Prize Bill, as the Government asserted, it was only because the sea lords "believe that the Declaration will be flung into the sea directly hostilities commence."[16]

The argument grew steadily hotter during the spring, as both sides tried to rally public opinion. Grey assured a delegation of merchants that the declaration in fact increased the security of British food imports because the United States and other powerful neutrals were sure to insist that such shipments go free in accordance with Article 24.[17] A Committee for Furthering the Ratification of the Declaration of London issued a series of pam-

14. Lansdowne, 6 Feb 11, Anonymous, ed., *Debates in the British Parliament, 1911–1912, on the Declaration of London and the Naval Prize Bill* [*Debates*]. (Washington: U.S. Government Printing Office, 1919), pp. 3–4.

15. Morley, 6 Feb 11, ibid., p. 4.

16. Ellenborough, 9 Mar 11, ibid., pp. 77–88. The Latin quotations mean "In time of war the laws are silent" and "The good of the people is the highest law," respectively.

17. Grey, memo of conversation with Corn Trade and Milling Associations, 9 Mar 11, FO 371/1279.

phlets.[18] Desart defended his agreement at the British Academy in May during a fierce debate against Gibson Bowles and Professor Holland.[19]

The first important test came in June, at the 1911 Imperial Conference. Australia, which already had complained that Britain should never have agreed to include food on the conditional contraband list "in view of the fact that so large a part of the trade of the Empire is in those articles,"[20] moved that the entire declaration be repudiated unless Article 24 was modified to exclude food from the contraband list. The other Dominions took the opposite view. After a vigorous and sometimes bitter debate, the conference passed a strong endorsement of the declaration with no opposition and only Australia abstaining.[21]

While the Government's attention was focused on the Imperial Conference, the opposition continued its public campaign and prepared for the coming debate in Parliament. Beresford staged a meeting at which 102 Royal Navy flag officers endorsed the statement that "the Declaration sacrifices those maritime rights which have preserved our Empire for centuries, and renders far more difficult the Navy's task of protecting the trade routes in time of war."[22] A representative of the militant Imperial Maritime League even suggested that the Unionists in the House of Lords turn from the Parliament Bill, "on which we stand to be beaten, to the question of the people's food, on which we stand to win."[23] An Opposition select committee under Arthur Lee met repeatedly to plan strategy.[24] By mid-June the Naval Prize Bill had become inextricably entangled with the Parliament Bill, the tariff question, the struggle for power within the Unionist party, and the general climate of political confrontation.

The political, although perhaps not the intellectual, high point

18. Committee, "Statement," n.d., FO 800/91; Grey, n.d., minute on L. Earle to E. Drummond, 6 Apr 11, ibid.; copies of pamphlets in FO 371/1279.

19. *The Times*, 1 Jun 11, p. 8.

20. Governor General of Australia to Harcourt (colonial secretary), tel, 24 Dec 10, FO 371/1278.

21. *The Times*, 2 Jun 11, pp. 5–6; 3 Jun 11, p. 8.

22. *Ibid.*, 26 Jun 11, p. 8; Beresford to Grey, 26 Jun 11, FO 800/87.

23. H. Wyatt to W. Short (Balfour's private secretary), 1 Jul 11, Balfour Papers, AM 49861.

24. E.g., *The Times*, 20 Jun 11, p. 12; 27 Jun 11, p. 8.

of the public debate came on June 27, when Arthur Balfour addressed a huge protest meeting in London. The Unionist leader and former prime minister faced a delicate problem. The co-sponsors of the gathering were the Imperial Maritime League and the London Chamber of Commerce, two groups that agreed on nothing except the desirability of defeating the Naval Prize Bill. Beresford and his fellow admirals would be satisfied only by a denunciation of the declaration as a dangerous surrender of Britain's belligerent rights. The merchants and shipowners, who only two months before had endorsed immunity for private property at sea,[25] would require a presumably contradictory denunciation of the declaration as a dangerous surrender of Britain's commercial rights.

Balfour resolved his dilemma with characteristic dexterity. He denounced the Declaration of London as both an unwise surrender and an unjustifiable extension of belligerent rights. The admirals cheered as he explained how "unquestionably and beyond any doubt the provisions of the Treaty of London do hamper the right of any Power which is exercising an effective blockade." The Chamber of Commerce people cheered as he expressed horror at the idea that any civilized nation would make food contraband and shock that a British Government had accepted such a travesty of international justice. The entire audience cheered at the end of the speech, each listener having heard what he wished to hear. *The Times*, which devoted more than a page to coverage of the meeting, praised the speech as "vigorous" and "closely reasoned."[26]

Balfour's public statement set the pattern for the Commons debate that began the next day. The first Government speaker pointed out that Opposition arguments were mutually contradictory: "I constantly find critics who attack us in the same document (1) because we have not secured absolute immunity for our own commerce, and (2) because we have not secured an absolutely free hand to deal with other people's commerce."[27] His point was well taken. Two of the first Unionist speakers were Sir Robert Finlay,

25. London Chamber of Commerce to Grey, 3 May 11, FO 371/1279.
26. *The Times*, 28 Jun 11, pp. 9–10.
27. T. McKinnon Wood (FO parliamentary undersecretary), 28 Jun 11. *Debates*, p. 171.

former attorney general, and Lord Charles Beresford, former commander of the Channel Fleet. The former complained that the declaration placed unprecedented and intolerable restrictions upon British commerce; the latter sneered that international maritime law should be dictated by the strongest navy, not by conferences.[28] During the three days of debate some Opposition speakers agreed with Finlay that the declaration abolished established neutral rights, while others supported Beresford's contention that it constituted a serious restraint on belligerent rights. Not a few used both arguments in the same speech.

The Commons debate culminated on July 3, when Balfour and Andrew Bonar Law confronted Grey and Asquith. The Unionist leader, who spoke first, repeated his argument that the new agreement surrendered both belligerent and neutral rights. His emphasis, however, was on the concessions to belligerents:

> Do you not suppose that when other nations came to consider the sort of prize law we had established in our courts they would say: "England has been the power of the sea for all these generations and the law which England has established will be tyrannical law, and let us mitigate it in favour of the neutral?" Has that been done? They have done just the reverse. They found our law ... so fair and favourable to neutrals that they have sought to modify it in the direction of making it more harsh to neutral powers, and, unfortuantely, they have found an ally in His Majesty's Government.

The declaration was "worse for us as belligerents, worse for us as neutrals, and ... certainly worse than the law which we have for so many years considered to administer in our prize courts." Balfour concluded that Britain had no choice but repudiation.[29]

Grey rose immediately. He agreed that Britain would be in a better position if all the world would accept British prize law than under the Declaration of London. This not being the case, however, the Government had to deal with the realities of international relations. Britain had made some concessions in the declaration, as had other nations. The responsible officers of the Admiralty advised that these concessions were of little significance,

28. Finlay, 28 Jun 11, and Beresford, 29 Jun 11, *Debates*, pp. 190–210, 300–312.

29. Balfour, 3 Jul 11, ibid., pp. 383–398.

while in return Britain had won international recognition of its own law in several areas of vital importance. "The most important point . . . as regards naval opinion in favour . . . is the effect the Declaration is likely to have on our rights of blockade when we are belligerent." The choice was not, as Balfour had implied, between the declaration and universal recognition of British prize law. The real alternative to the Naval Prize Bill was the lawless international strife advocated by Beresford, in which the strongest would rule. His Majesty's Government preferred law, especially when that law was as favorable to British interests as the Declaration of London.[30]

The foreign secretary, although generally considered the minister most respected by the Opposition, apparently changed no votes. Bonar Law continued the debate with a bitter attack on both Prize Bill and Government. His speech began with the admission that "when a party man claims that he is not wishing to deal with a question in a party spirit, such a claim is received with a certain amount of skepticism." He then amply justified such skepticism.

Bonar Law's major argument was that Britain gained nothing as a neutral and conceded much as a belligerent under the proposed regulations. The Admiralty may have advised the Government that the rules on blockade were all Britain could wish, as several of the bill's proponents had asserted, but it was wrong. Britain had secured its own blockade law only because the Continental Powers "held it to be of little or no value." But in return for this worthless concession on the obsolete doctrine of blockade, the Government had yielded the vital belligerent right to apply continuous voyage to conditional contraband. Under the new rules, "an American ship having tinned meats which were going straight to the German Army could pass through our Channel Fleet and we could not touch it" as long as the ship was bound for Antwerp or Rotterdam. Grey's arguments were simply "sloppy sentimentalism" and must be discarded in the interests of national security. Bonar Law concluded, as had Balfour, that the Declaration of London gave neutrals too many rights when Britain was belliger-

30. Grey, 3 Jul 11, ibid., pp. 398–415.

ent, gave belligerents too many rights when Britain was neutral,
and should be rejected in favor of traditional British prize law.[31]

Asquith responded with a sarcastic summary of the argument
against the declaration. Certain politicians had said, "in an airy
manner," that blockade was obsolete. The Board of Admiralty
disagreed, as did "every naval authority in the world." Politicians
complained that British food imports would be more vulnerable
under the new rules. The Board of Admiralty assured the Government that these fears were groundless. Under the circumstances, the cabinet preferred the advice of responsible admirals
to that of irresponsible politicians.[32] Amid cries of "Traitors!" the
Naval Prize Bill passed its second reading on what amounted to a
party vote.[33]

The declaration's opponents did not regard this vote as final
because the Unionists held a majority in the House of Lords. But
when the Prize Bill reached the Upper Chamber in December, it
lay in the shadow of the Parliament Act. Legislation approved by
the Commons could now become law without the assent of the
Lords. Nevertheless, the Opposition leaders decided to reject the
Naval Prize Bill.[34] Lansdowne explained their apparently futile
stand: "We are not now in the position of being able to destroy
any bill. All that we can do is to delay for a while a bill which in our
opinion has not yet been adequately considered either by the
whole community or by the classes whom it most affects."[35] Public
debate during the two years before 1911 had aroused considerable interest in the proposed changes in maritime law embodied in
the Declaration of London and the International Prize Court
Convention. The Unionist peers who rejected the Prize Bill could
only hope that further delay and discussion would force a change
in Government policy.

This strategy worked, rather to the surprise of its authors. The

31. Bonar Law, 3 Jul 11, ibid., pp. 445–454.
32. Asquith, 3 Jul 11, ibid., pp. 454–459.
33. *The Times,* 4 Jul 11, p. 14; cf. Churchill to George V, 4 Jul 11, in Randolph
S. Churchill and Martin Gilbert, *Winston S. Churchill* (Boston: Houghton Mifflin,
1966 *et seq.*), II, companion volumes, pt. 2, p. 1096.
34. Lansdowne to Bonar Law, 28 Nov 11, Bonar Law Papers, 24/4/87;
Lansdowne to Halsbury, 2 Dec 11, Halsbury Papers, AM 56372; Selborne to Lady
Selborne, 4 Dec 11, Selborne Papers, 102.
35. Lansdowne, 12 Dec 11, *Debates,* p. 684.

Asquith Government never reintroduced the Prize Bill, without which it could not ratify the Prize Court Convention. It never ratified the declaration, which it could have done without Parliament's assent. The Government seemed to back away at the last minute from the policy on maritime rights it had followed consistently since 1907.

An enormous mythology has grown up since 1911 to explain this shift. The common explanation, growing out of the World War I experience, has been that the Lords' negative vote was a defense of belligerent rights they believed to be threatened by an agreement that was overly favorable to neutrals.[36] The Government, forced by defeat to reconsider, recognized that the critics were correct and abandoned both the declaration and the Prize Court Convention.[37] By the time the United States proposed adoption of the declaration shortly after the outbreak of World War I, the British government had come to believe that its earlier policy represented a dangerous surrender of belligerent rights on which national security might well depend.[38]

Despite wide historical acceptance, very little of this interpretation is accurate. A few opponents of the declaration, the most notable of whom were Gibson Bowles, Ellenborough, and Beresford, did emphasize the supposed surrender of belligerent rights. Other critics, such as Balfour and Bonar Law, used the belligerent rights and neutral rights surrender arguments in the same speech. But a majority of the critics in Parliament, and an even greater majority in the country, opposed the declaration because they believed it extended belligerent rights in a manner dangerous to Britain's importation of food. Even the Imperial Maritime League, itself primarily concerned about limitation of British belligerent rights, recognized that public opinion could be rallied against the declaration only by emphasizing the food issue.[39] The Naval Prize Bill failed in the House of Lords not because the peers

---

36. E.g., Perkins, *Great Rapprochement*, p. 251; Devlin, *Too Proud*, pp. 166–167; Nils Orvik, *The Decline of Neutrality* (London: Frank Cass, 1953; 2d ed. 1971), p. 40; Smith, *Lansing*, p. 22.

37. Patrick, Lord Devlin, "The House of Lords and the Naval Prize Bill, 1911," *The Rede Lecture*, 1968 (Cambridge: Cambridge University Press, 1968); Tuchman, *Guns of August*, p. 333; Smith, *Great Departure*, p. 31.

38. E.g., Link, *Wilson*, III, 107–108.

39. R. Hunt to George V, 2 Nov 11, FO 371/1280; *The Times*, 4 Jul 11, p. 7.

were determined to preserve vital belligerent rights, but because they were predominantly Unionist and their party had decided to treat the bill as a partisan issue. The majority of Opposition speakers in the Lords, as in the Commons, emphasized the supposed threat to British food imports in justifying their negative votes.[40]

The Government's decision not to reintroduce the Prize Bill after its rejection in December 1911 also has been widely misunderstood. There was no sudden ministerial recognition that the Declaration of London would prevent Britain from bringing effective economic pressure to bear against Germany. The Government in fact remained both publicly and privately committed to the agreement until after the outbreak of war in 1914. Asquith announced in February 1912 that he intended to reintroduce the Prize Bill and force it through under the Parliament Act.[41] He delayed only because Grey had not yet completed the surprisingly complex negotiations needed to clarify the ambiguous language of Article 34.[42] The length of these negotiations was the sole reason for the failure to reintroduce the bill and force it thorough despite the Lords' opposition.[43] Liberal campaign literature drafted in June 1914 cited the Declaration of London and the International Prize Court Convention as major accomplishments in the search for world peace and order.[44] Asquith announced on June 29 that he hoped to reintroduce the Naval Prize Bill during the current session of Parliament.[45] On the next day, the British and German governments finally agreed on a definition of "base."[46] Grey directed that this clarification be submitted to the other signatory powers for their pro forma approval, after which "I will then press the matter in Parliament."[47] The date of this minute was on or about July 17, 1914.

40. E.g., Lansdowne, Selborne, and Lord Alverstone, 12 Dec 11, *Debates*, pp. 628–688.

41. Asquith, 21 Feb 12, ibid., p. 689; cf. James Bryce (British ambassador, Washington) to Knox, 4 Jan 12, SD 500.A2a/692.

42. See FO 371/1280, 1862 and 372/588 for details.

43. Lloyd George, 7 May 12; Asquith, 31 Jul 12; Lloyd George, 17 Oct 12; Grey, 5 Dec 12, *Debates*, pp. 689–690.

44. E.g., P. Illingworth (Liberal chief whip) to Grey, 15 Jun 14, FO 800/90.

45. Asquith, 29 Jun 14, response to Parliamentary Question, FO 372/588.

46. H. Rumbold (British chargé, Berlin) to Grey, 30 Jun 14, received 2 Jul 14, ibid.

47. Grey, n.d., minute, ibid.

With the advantage of hindsight, this continued commitment to the declaration seems inexplicably unrealistic. German merchantmen remained in harbor or in the Baltic during World War I, safe from capture, while German trade shifted to neutral bottoms. The Royal Navy found itself unable to impose an effective blockade on the German coast. Only by applying the doctrine of continuous voyage to contraband, and especially to conditional contraband, was Britain able to generate serious economic pressure. Bonar Law's 1911 complaint that the declaration preserved obsolete and unenforceable belligerent rights while conceding rights vital for future conflicts proved well founded in 1914. Wartime experiences convinced many that the Asquith Government's prewar maritime rights policy had been a deliberate sellout of national interests directed by a traitorous pro-German conspiracy.[48] Lloyd George expressed a similar conspiratorial theory in 1918, although he implied that Grey and his subordinates had been dupes rather than traitors.[49] Subsequent attempts to explain the contradiction between prewar policy and wartime actions have been less romantic, but no more accurate.[50]

The real explanation for British prewar policy on maritime rights is that the statesmen and naval officers who negotiated and supported the International Prize Court Convention and the Declaration of London lacked one advantage of their post-1914 critics: hindsight. No one foresaw the stalemate of World War I. The Admiralty expected a limited naval war in which economic pressure would inflict measured damage on Germany while avoiding friction with neutrals. The War Office expected a brief conflict settled by a few great land battles before economic pressure could become a significant factor. Each service planned for its own vision of war and maneuvered to impose that vision on the Government. Neither succeeded before the outbreak of war in August 1914.

Only Maurice Hankey, a Fisher protégé who served as naval assistant secretary to the CID in 1911 and would succeed Ottley as secretary the next year, gave serious consideration to what might happen if neither the navy's concept of limited maritime war nor

48. E.g., clippings and letters in FO 800/243.
49. "Notes of a conversation at Colonel House's Residence," 3 Nov 18, House Papers.
50. E.g., Williamson, *Politics,* p. 241.

the army's concept of quick military victory proved accurate. In a series of memos written during February and March 1911, Hankey pointed out that Asquith's charge to the Military Requirements subcommittee in 1908 had seemed to imply military intervention in Europe. If such intervention took place, and if the Anglo-French armies failed to defeat the German army, Britain would find itself in a full-scale European war. In such a prolonged conflict, economic pressure might well prove the decisive factor. Yet current policy called for abandonment of many of the belligerent rights Britain would require to conduct an effective economic campaign on a Continental scale. Hankey recommended that the Government repudiate the Declaration of London and withdraw the Naval Prize Bill immediately. The navy then would be free to bring decisive economic pressure against Germany in the event of war by declaring all German imports absolute contraband, by blockading the entrace to the Baltic, and by enforcing the doctrine of continuous voyage against neutral trade with the enemy through the presumably neutral ports of Antwerp and Rotterdam.[51]

Hankey's memos led to a conference with Ottley and McKenna, in which the first lord freely admitted that there was a contradiction between the navy's ability to bring decisive economic pressure against Germany in a general European war and present policy on maritime rights. The contradiction was not with the Declaration of London, however, but with the Declaration of Paris. No peacetime Government could repudiate the agreement that had formed the basis of international maritime law since 1856. Ratification of the Declaration of London would make little practical difference, therefore, to Britain's capability to wage an economic campaign. Present Admiralty plans called for limited use of sea pressure to achieve limited political objectives. If some future Government determined that more stringent economic pressure was necessary, as in the case of a prolonged Continental war such as Hankey had posited, "international treaties are easily evaded in wartime." McKenna freely predicted that involvement in a general European war would cause

51. Hankey, "The Effect of the Declaration of London: Great Britain's Belligerent Rights," n.d., Hankey Papers, Churchill College, 7/5; cf. drafts in CAB 17/85.

Britain to throw the Declaration of Paris overboard, drowning the Declaration of London in its splash. But until that circumstance arose, the Admiralty would continue to base its policy on the twin goals of mounting effective economic pressure without giving offense to powerful neutrals.[52] Hankey's objections and McKenna's cynical defense of current policy, prophetic as they were to prove three years later, never circulated beyond the first lord's office.

Responsibility for the failure to consider the issues Hankey raised in their larger context rests on the Admiralty, with its myopic concern for limited maritime war, on the War Office, with its equally myopic concern for a short European war, and especially on the cabinet for its decade of failure to define national objectives or to coordinate diverse and sometimes contradictory goals with national means. The CID Military Requirements sub-committee had concluded in July 1909 that both the army and the navy strategies for war with Germany were viable options that should remain available to future Governments.[53] It authorized each service to continue developing its own plan, but made no effort to enforce cooperation.[54] This remained the official position until August 1914.

Many historians have argued that this interservice contradiction was finally resolved in the army's favor during the second Moroccan crisis in 1911. Zara Steiner, a recent proponent of this view, asserts, "At the famous C.I.D. Meeting of 23 August 1911 [General Henry] Wilson's almost completed plans received official

52. Hankey, memo of conversation, 23 Feb 11, CAB 17/87; cf. statement by Fisher quoted in Hankey, *Supreme Command*, I, 99–100.
53. CID, Subcommittee on Military Requirements of the Empire, Report, 24 Jul 09, CID Paper 109B, CAB 4/3.
54. Ibid.; d'Ombrain, *War Machinery*, pp. 93–99. Williamson, *Politics*, pp. 109–112, is also a most useful discussion, although both Williamson (p. 108) and Steiner (*Origins*, p. 196) give a misleading impression by referring to the subcommittee on "the military needs of the Empire as influenced by the Continent." While a fair statement of Asquith's purpose in creating the group, this description implies that the Continental focus was so well known as to be stated in its title. The report of "a joint meeting of the C.I.D. and the Cabinet on 3 December 1908" in which the Government agreed to send the BEF to France contained in Marder, *From the Dreadnought*, I, 387, carries this confusion further. The majority of the cabinet did not know in 1908–1909 that the subcommittee was concerned primarily with military intervention in Europe and certainly never gave its approval to landing a single British soldier in France.

sanction and the earlier decision in favour of a continental strategy was reaffirmed."[55] Despite common acceptance, however, this interpretation is supported neither by the minutes of the meeting nor by subsequent events.

The CID meeting of August 23, 1911, originated with an attempt by Haldane to take advantage of certain favorable circumstances to win final approval of the War Office plan for Continental intervention by the BEF. Fisher had resigned as first sea lord as a consequence of the Beresford feud,[56] and his successor, Admiral Arthur Wilson, was a fine sailor but a poor bureaucratic politician.[57] Haldane meanwhile had brought in General Henry Wilson, the army's leading proponent of Continental operations, most polished staff officer, and most effective bureaucratic infighter, to serve as director of military operations (DMO).[58] Careful wooing had persuaded Lloyd George and Churchill that preservation of the Anglo-French Entente was a vital national interest that could best be protected by sending the BEF to the Continent in the event of war.[59] The Admiralty's apparent nonchalance at the height of the second Moroccan crisis had left several ministers with doubts as to its basic competence.[60] When Haldane persuaded Asquith on August 15 to call a special CID meeting,[61] the

55. Steiner, *Origins,* p. 200. Michael G. Fry, *Lloyd George and Foreign Policy,* vol. I, *The Education of a Statesman, 1890–1916* (Montreal: McGill-Queen's University Press, 1977), 143, also sees the 23 Aug 11 meeting as having reached a decision. Williamson, *Politics,* pp. 193–204, argues that the meeting itself was not decisive but the consequent replacement of McKenna with Churchill was. D'Ombrain comes closest to the truth in stating that the real result of the meeting was confusion, further strategic fragmentation, and the final destruction of the CID as a significant body in the shaping of British grand strategy (*War Machinery,* pp. 102–114).

56. Marder, *From the Dreadnought,* I, 204–207.

57. Ibid., pp. 211–214.

58. There is no satisfactory biography of Henry Wilson. His diary, available on microfilm in the Imperial War Museum, remains the best source on his personality and his role in preparing the BEF for war. It should be supplemented by Williamson, *Politics,* pp. 167–169 and passim, and d'Ombrain, *War Machinery,* pp. 147–149 and passim.

59. E.g., A. Law (FO official) to Bertie, 8 Apr 08, FO 800/165; Haldane to M. Haldane, 8 Sep 09, Haldane Papers, MS 5982. See also Fry, *Lloyd George,* pp. 82–83 and passim. Hazlehurst's statement ("Asquith as Prime Minister," p. 510) that "Lloyd George and Churchill did not learn about the controversial Anglo-French military conversations until the whole Cabinet was informed in 1911" clearly is wrong.

60. Marder, *From the Dreadnought,* I, 242–244.

61. H. Wilson, diary entry, 15 Aug 11, H. Wilson Papers, (M)4.

war minister was confident he would receive the endorsement Steiner and others believe he did receive.

Haldane had caught the Admiralty unaware, as he had planned. The War Office submitted a strong statement of the Continentalist position, emphasizing Britain's vital interest in the balance of power, the potentially decisive effect of BEF intervention, and the improbability of sea power alone preventing German victory over France. The description of the consequences of failure to dispatch the BEF was stark: "If we once allow Germany to defeat France our expeditionary force would be valueless and the duration of our naval predominance could be measured by years." The Admiralty responded with its traditional argument that "the primary object in a war with a great maritime Power from a naval point of view must be the destruction of the enemy's fleet, and naval opinion on any proposed action by the Army must be determined mainly by the extent to which it helps or hinders that object." The proper role for the BEF was to support the British navy, not the French army.[62] In contrast to the army memo, the navy's was poorly written and argued. Churchill characterized it, with some justice, as "quite childish."[63]

The contrast was even more marked when the CID met on August 23. Lord Esher, a strong anti-Continentalist not invited to attend, later called it "that imprudent summoning of a packed Defence Committee."[64] Hankey used similar language.[65] Asquith, Haldane, Grey, Lloyd George, and Churchill represented the cabinet's five Continentalist ministers. McKenna represented the other fourteen ministers, most if not all of whom opposed military intervention in Europe.[66] Any naval hopes of a fair hearing which might have survived a look at the invitation list were dispelled by

62. General Staff, "The Military Aspect of the Continental Problem," 15 Aug 11, and A. Wilson, "Remarks by the Admiralty," n.d., CAB 4/3.

63. A. Grant Duff (army assistant secretary, CID), diary entry, 21 Aug 11, Grant Duff Papers, (M).

64. Esher, diary entry, 24 Nov 11, Esher Papers, 2/12. Other uninvited anti-Continentalists included Morley, Harcourt, and Fisher, as well as Crewe, whom Hankey believed likely to support the navalist position.

65. Marder, *From the Dreadnought*, I, 392.

66. Not present were Harcourt (Colonies), Crewe (Privy Seal and India), Loreburn (lord chancellor), Morley (president of the Council), Sinclair (Scotland), Pease (Duchy), Buxton (Board of Trade), Burns (Local Government Board), Carrington (Agriculture), Runciman (Education), Birrell (Ireland), Samuel (postmaster general), and Beauchamp (commissioner of works).

Asquith's opening remarks. The discussion was limited to the best means of "giving armed aid to the French." The navy's argument that British interests were best defended by a limited maritime war to destroy German sea power was out of order.

After some preliminary sparring, Henry Wilson presented the War Office case. In his best Staff College lecture style, complete with visual aids, the DMO spent almost two hours explaining how "it was quite likely that our six divisions might prove to be the deciding factor" in a general European war. Arthur Wilson then attempted to present the Admiralty case. In contrast to his rival's polished persuasiveness, the first sea lord seemed "all adrift."[67] He tried to explain that the planned naval operations, though primarily designed to destroy German sea power, would actually help relieve military pressure on France by forcing diversion of German troops to coast defense. Before he could finish, the chief of the Imperial General Staff politely described this strategy as "madness." Grey considered it irrelevant: "The problem which they had to solve was how to employ the Army so as to inflict the greatest possible amount of damage upon the Germans . . . the struggle on land would be the decisive one." The Admiralty debacle was so bad that even Henry Wilson felt pity for his rival.[68]

There can be no doubt that a vote of the cabinet members present at the August 23 meeting would have been five to one in favor of the army. But contrary to the impression given by Steiner's account, six ministers had no authority to give "official sanction" without consulting the more than two-thirds of the Government not present. Hankey was quite correct in writing that "no decision was arrived at" on August 23.[69] The five ministers who entered the meeting convinced that the Continentalist strategy was correct had their conviction strengthened; the one who went in committed to the naval view was forced to recognize that Arthur Wilson was not an effective advocate. The majority of the Government was unmoved by the navy's failure to present an adequate case because they had not been present. Lewis Har-

67. Fisher to Hankey, n.d., Hankey Papers, 5/2.
68. CID, minutes, 23 Aug 11, CAB 2/2; cf. Grant Duff, diary entry, 25 Aug 11, Grant Duff Papers, (M), and H. Wilson, diary entry, 23 Aug 11, H. Wilson Papers, (M)4.
69. Marder, *From the Dreadnought*, I, 393.

court, the colonial secretary, left no doubt of his position when he wrote on August 26 that he would have "retired to a back bench" long before the cabinet approved the "criminal folly" of sending the BEF to France.[70]

The degree of opposition to Haldane's military plans and Grey's commitment to French security became evident in the months after the August 1911 CID meeting. The war minister, in an effort to formalize his victory, threatened to resign unless Asquith replaced McKenna with a Continentalist committed to full cooperation with the War Office. The prime minister agreed that Admiralty plans were "puerile" and that "in principle, the General Staff scheme is the only alternative."[71] On October 10 Asquith informed McKenna that he was to exchange the Admiralty for Churchill's Home Office.[72]

This blatant attempt to establish Continentalist control over the navy, followed by the forced retirement of Arthur Wilson and the installment of a first sea lord whose cooperative attitude pleased even Henry Wilson,[73] precipitated the cabinet confrontation that had been delayed since the beginning of the Anglo-French staff talks. McKenna, with strong support from Harcourt, Morley, and Loreburn, complained that a small group of ministers had taken upon themselves authority properly reserved for the entire cabinet. Asquith attempted to justify the shift of Churchill to the Admiralty as an administrative reform, going so far as to claim that both he and the new first lord opposed sending the BEF to the Continent.[74] These statements, which can only be considered deliberate attempts to deceive fellow ministers, persuaded no one. The angry debate spilled from the privacy of the cabinet room, and Liberal backbenchers and editors rallied

70. Steiner, *Origins,* p. 76.
71. Asquith to Haldane, 31 Aug 11, Haldane Papers, MS 5909; cf. Steiner, *Origins,* p. 208.
72. Asquith to McKenna, 10 Oct 11, McKenna Papers, 4/1.
73. H. Wilson, diary entry, 17 Jan 12, H. Wilson Papers, (M)5; Marder, *From the Dreadnought,* I, 255–258.
74. McKenna, "Notes of a Conversation at Archerfield," 20 Oct 11, McKenna Papers, 4/2; Asquith to Crewe, 7 Oct 11, Crewe Papers, C/40; K. M. Wilson, "The War Office, Churchill and the Belgian Option: August to December 1911," *Bulletin of the Institute of Historical Research,* 50 (1977):255. On the McKenna switch with Churchill, see also Morris, *Radicalism,* pp. 291–293, and Rowland, *Last Liberal Governments,* II, 121–127.

behind the attack.[75] Jack Sandars, Balfour's canny political secretary, warned Lansdowne in November that "the Government has been on the very edge of busting up."[76]

Despite the heat and excitement, the main effects of the political crisis were negative. The cabinet's antiContinentalist majority laid down definite restricitons on the Anglo-French staff talks, which Henry Wilson evaded with little difficulty.[77] Churchill remained at the Admiralty, but closely watched by his colleagues. The majority considered Grey's "revival of the old Palmerstonian policy of the Balance of Power" to be "rotten to the core," but were unwilling to pay the political price—breakup of the Government—which removing the foreign secretary entailed. As Loreburn soon realized, twenty busy men, most with their own departmental responsibilities, could neither define a foreign policy in the abstract nor supervise its implementation in detail. Frustrated in spirit and sick in body, the lord chancellor resigned in June 1912,[78] to be replaced, ironically, by Haldane.

The net result was a continuation of the contradiction and confusion that had characterized British grand strategic planning

75. E.g., Loreburn to Grey, 26 Aug 11, FO 800/99; Asquith to George V, cabinet letter, 2 Nov 11, CAB 41/33/28; C. E. Hobhouse (chancellor, Duchy of Lancaster), diary entry, 16 Nov 11, Edward David, ed., *Inside Asquith's Cabinet* (London: John Murray, 1977), pp. 107–108; Manchester Liberal Federation to Grey, 12 Jan 12, FO 800/109. Useful secondary accounts of the revolt against Grey's foreign policy in late 1911 include Howard S. Weinroth, "The British Radicals and the Balance of Power, 1902–1914," *Historical Journal*, 13 (1970):677; Morris, *Radicalism*, pp. 259–281, 295–306; Robbins, *Grey*, pp. 246–254; Fry, *Lloyd George*, pp. 148–153; Rowland, *Last Liberal Governments*, II, 127–142; Lowe and Dockrill, *Mirage of Power*, I, 46–47; and Williamson, *Politics*, pp. 198–204. It should be noted that the 1911 dispute was not between realistic interventionists and "faint-hearted" isolationists, as pictured in Dockrill, "British Policy during the Agadir Crisis of 1911," Hinsley, ed., *British Foreign Policy*, p. 285, but between men honestly holding different strategic views. Different definitions of national interest, and not different degrees of personal courage, distinguished Grey and Loreburn.

76. Sandars to Lansdowne, 24 Nov 11, Sandars Papers.

77. Wilson, diary entry, 17 Nov 11, Wilson Papers, (M)4; Haldane to M. Haldane, 16 Nov 11, Haldane Papers, MS 6011. See Williamson, *Politics*, pp. 199–201.

78. Quotations are from C. P. Scott (Liberal editor, *Manchester Guardian*), diary entries, 14 Sep, 2 Dec 11, and 22 Jan 12, Scott Papers, AM 50901; see also Rowland, *Last Liberal Governments*, II, 168. Note that Loreburn did not resign in 1913, as per Steiner, *Origins*, p. 147, and certainly not in August 1914, as per V. H. Rothwell, *British War Aims and Peace Diplomacy, 1914–1918* (Oxford: Clarendon, 1971), p. 37.

since the Liberals took office. The Continentalists continued to plan for military intervention in Europe, although aware that the cabinet majority, whose support was necessary to implement any plan, opposed such intervention. The majority rejected the balance of power definition of national interests, but was unable to impose its will on the Foreign and War Offices. Neither faction was prepared to seek a resolution of these contradictions by breaking up the Government over what remained a hypothetical question until August 1914.

This continued strategic confusion does much to explain Britain's continued commitment to the policy of limited belligerent rights represented in the Declaration of London during the three years before the outbreak of World War I. Although Churchill blustered both before and after becoming first lord about the need to blockade neutral Dutch and Belgian ports as well as the German coast,[79] he offered no objection in 1913 when the Admiralty adopted the Declaration of London as the basis of its new prize manual.[80] In 1914 he horrified his staff by toying with acceptance of immunity for private property.[81] The new first lord may not have gone as far as Henry Wilson, who sneered that the Royal Navy was worth less than a single battalion of infantry to the French,[82] but he did share the general Continentalist view that the land campaigns, not any economic campaign, would be the decisive weapon to defeat Germany. Busy with problems of materiel and personnel, and with the plans for transport and convoy of the BEF to France, Churchill devoted little time to economic warfare.[83] In the absence of any Continentalist challenge, the navy's maritime rights policies remained unchanged and Hankey's questions remained unanswered.

---

79. Churchill to Henry Wilson, 29 Aug 11, FO 800/88; Churchill to Lloyd George, 31 Aug 11, Lloyd George Papers, C/3/15/7; CID, minutes, 6 Dec 12, CAB 2/3/1.

80. Adm to FO, 15 Aug 13, FO 371/1862.

81. E.g., Churchill to Asquith, 8 Sep 13, and Churchill, cabinet memo, 5 Dec 13, Churchill and Gilbert, *Churchill*, II, companion volumes, pt. 3, pp. 1770–1771. 1818–1824; cf. response by Admiral H. Jackson, 16 Jan 14, Adm 116/2314.

82. Wilson, diary entry, 14 Feb 13, Wilson Papers, (M)5.

83. On Churchill at the Admiralty, see Marder, *From the Dreadnought*, I, 252–271 and passim. For the argument that Churchill did act to strengthen belligerent rights, see Devlin, "House of Lords."

Yet another opportunity for systematic reconsideration of the Declaration of London came in 1912, when a CID subcommittee under Desart conducted an elaborate study of British municipal laws against trading with an enemy. Its report concluded that even with the German coasts under blockade, the enemy would be able to continue his vital trade through adjacent neutrals. Not only was Britain unable to prevent such trade, but it could not prevent British goods from reaching the enemy through neutral middlemen. Considerable doubt existed, in fact, as to whether in the complex web of international commerce and insurance a stoppage of Anglo-German trade would hurt the enemy worse than it would hurt Britain. The subcommittee's report concluded that a British blockade of the German coasts combined with a rigorous effort to prevent British goods from reaching Germany would inflict some injury on the enemy, but by no combination of measures could Britain hope to cut off Germany entirely from overseas commerce.[84]

This conclusion, although the product of exhaustive research and supported by elaborate analysis, did not satisfy the chancellor of the exchequer. When the full CID met in December 1912 to consider its subcommittee's report, Lloyd George argued that to bring severe economic pressure against Germany was "essential." He demanded, with Churchill's support, that Britain extend the blockade of Germany to include Belgium and the Netherlands. Either these presumed neutrals must be "entirely friendly to this country, in which case we should limit their oversea trade" in order to block reexport to the enemy, or they must be "definitely hostile, in which case we should extend the blockade to their ports." Although Asquith warned that to blockade a neutral port was by definition an act of war, certain to raise up new enemies and alienate neutrals not directly affected, the CID approved the chancellor's resolution as well as the contradictory conclusions of the Desart subcommittee.[85] A day earlier Grey, who did not bother to attend the CID meeting, had announced to the House

84. CID, Subcommittee on trading with the enemy, Report, Sep 12, CID Paper 160B, CAB 2/3/1.
85. CID, minutes, 6 Dec 12, ibid.; Fry, *Lloyd George*, pp. 165–166, discusses this meeting briefly, but neglects to mention that the CID approved the Desart subcommittee report as well as the Chancellor's contradictory proposal.

of Commons that the Government remained committed to the Declaration of London and intended to reintroduce the Naval Prize Bill as soon as possible.[86]

Despite this intrigue, confusion, ignorance, and contradiction —or perhaps because of them—British policy on maritime rights did not change significantly from 1905 to August 1914. The Admiralty continued to plan for a limited economic campaign enforced through capture of German ships, blockade of the enemy's North Sea coast, and a restricted application of the doctrine of contraband. The Continentalists occasionally bellowed about the need to blockade neutral coasts, but generally considered economic warfare of little value in a conflict they believed would be settled by a few great land battles within weeks after mobilization. Although they challenged the navy's concept of limited maritime war, they made no systematic challenge to its policy of restricting enforcement of belligerent rights against neutral shipping. A few critics of the Declaration of London argued that Britain was surrendering essential belligerent rights, but most emphasized the argument that sloppy wording in Article 34 could expose British food imports to enemy attack. Britain ultimately failed to adopt a peacetime maritime rights policy appropriate for a prolonged Continental war against Germany because, with the exception of Hankey, no one was able to foresee or willing to admit that such a war was possible.

---

86. Grey, 5 Dec 11, *Debates*, p. 690. Sir Arthur Nicolson, Grey's permanent undersecretary, attended the CID meeting but took no part in the discussion.

✿

Origins of the British Blockade of Germany, August to September 1914

On the morning of August 5, 1914, only hours after the British declaration of war on Germany, Winston Churchill remarked to an Admiralty staff officer, "Now we have our war. The next thing is to decide how we are going to carry it on."[1] The point was well taken. The British government had proved unable to resolve the contradictions among its strategic policies during the decade before the outbreak of war. The Continentalists had undermined isolation, but the cabinet had neither formally abandoned the old definition of national interests nor endorsed a new one. Now, under the urgent pressure of war, the Government had to resolve the questions it had left unanswered in peacetime.

In theory, the means by which a nation wages war are determined by its military capabilities and its political objectives. But Britain, in practice, went to war in 1914 with no common objective except victory and little recognition that its means of waging effective war against Germany were severely limited. Steiner's conclusion that "Britain entered the war because she feared a German victory in western Europe which would threaten her safety and her Empire"[2] was true for Grey and a few of his colleagues, but not for a majority of the nineteen men who made the decision. Two ministers, John Morley and John Burns, resigned rather than agree to actions they believed likely to lead to an unjustified

1. Sir Herbert Richmond, diary entry, 5 Aug 14, Richmond Papers, 1/9.
2. Steiner, *Origins*, p. 242.

war. Seventeen ministers remained, although two submitted resignations which they were persuaded to withdraw and joined in advising the Crown to declare war. Yet each of the seventeen had his own justification for the decision.

Cabinet opinion during the last days of peace ranged from the carefree bellicosity of the first lord of the Admiralty to the anguished pacifism of the attorney general. Churchill saw war as a convenient escape from the perils of "bloody peace" in general and Irish Home Rule in particular.[3] Asquith, Grey, and Haldane would fight to preserve the European balance of power from German hegemony, although the prime minister was determined not to be drawn into a war to advance Russian ambitions in the Balkans.[4] Several other ministers, led by Lloyd George and Harcourt, explicitly rejected the Continental balance as a justifiable casus belli but were prepared, with varying degrees of willingness, to resist a German invasion of Belgium. Had Grey pressed for a declaration of war solely to block German hegemony on the Continent, several more members of the Government would have resigned.[5] Britain could have entered the war only under a coalition of Liberal and Conservative Continentalists, in the face of a hostile Liberal-Labour-Irish majority and a divided nation. Such disintegration was avoided only by the German invasion of Belgium, which caused a relieved Asquith to note that "this simplifies

3. Asquith to Venetia Stanley (personal confidante), 28 Jul 14, Stanley Papers; Hobhouse, diary entry, n.d. [ca. 6 Aug 14], David, ed., *Inside Asquith's Cabinet,* p. 179; cf. Churchill and Gilbert, *Churchill,* II, 706–722, and III, 1–31.

4. Asquith to Stanley, 26 Jul, 2 Aug 14, Stanley Papers.

5. An enormous amount of documentation and an even greater number of secondary accounts are available on the British decision for war in 1914. The most valuable of the former are: Asquith to Stanley, 29, 31 Jul and 2, 4 Aug 14, Stanley Papers; C. P. Scott, diary entries, Aug–Dec 14 (based on conversations with Lloyd George and other participants), Scott Papers, AM 50901; Harcourt to Lloyd George, n.d., and other cabinet notes, Lloyd George Papers, C13/1; Esher, diary entry, 3 Aug 14, Esher Papers 2/13; and Hobhouse, diary entry, n.d., David, ed., *Inside Asquith's Cabinet,* pp. 179–181. The best secondary account is Fry, *Lloyd George,* pp. 183–213, which emphasizes the complexity and even contradiction of individual motives. Morris, *Radicalism,* pp. 386–402, and Cameron Hazlehurst, *Politicians at War* (New York: Knopf, 1971), pp. 49–102, picture the group against a balance of power war, and especially Lloyd George, as more concerned with saving face than with staying out of the conflict. Other worthwhile accounts include Lowe and Dockrill, *Mirage of Power,* I, 146–151; Robbins, *Grey,* pp. 294–297; Peter Rowland, *Lloyd George* (London: Barrie & Jenkins, 1975), pp. 280–284; Steiner, *Origins,* pp. 230–241; and Williamson, *Politics,* pp. 243–272.

matters."[6] Ministers might have different justifications for war, but they agreed it could not be avoided.

Failure to agree on national war aims before entering the conflict left Britain with no common objective but victory to guide its strategic planning. A majority of the cabinet would fight for Belgium, but not for the Continental balance. A minority was determined to check the supposed German drive for hegemony and considered the Low Countries pawns to be used, and if need be sacrificed, in pursuit of British interests.[7] Because any attempt to resolve these differences would renew the split within the Government, consideration of war aims was postponed by mutual consent until after Germany had been defeated.

This absence of political guidance left British strategists in a vacuum. Cabinet opposition to British military operations in Europe had been even more pronounced than opposition to a war fought to preserve the European balance of power. On August 2 the Government had decided that it would not send the BEF to France in accordance with the Anglo-French staff agreements.[8] Grey warned the French and Russian ambassadors that British military intervention on the Continent was most unlikely and spoke to the House of Commons of a war in which Britain's contribution would be almost exclusively naval: "For us, with a powerful Fleet, which we believe able to protect our commerce, to protect our shores, and to protect our interests, if we are engaged in war, we shall suffer but little more than we shall suffer even if we stand aside."[9] For a brief moment Fisher, retired and seemingly discredited, appeared to have won his long battle against the War Office.

This navalist triumph proved short-lived, however. The cabinet Continentalists appear to have deliberately led their colleagues to believe that they had abandoned the Anglo-French

6. Asquith to Stanley, 4 Aug 14, Stanley Papers.

7. E.g., Churchill's plan to seize Dutch offshore islands as advanced bases and to divide the Dutch East Indies with Japan, discussed in Richmond, diary entry, 9 Aug 14, Richmond Papers, 1/9.

8. Asquith to Stanley, 2 Aug 14, Stanley Papers; Grey to Bertie, tel, 2 Aug 14, FO 371/2160.

9. Taylor, *Struggle*, p. 526; Grey, House of Commons speech, 3 Aug 14, Great Britain, 5 *Parliamentary Debates* (Commons), LXV (1914), 1823. Note that this vital statement was made on 3 Aug, not 4 Aug as per Steiner, *Origins*, p. 210.

staff agreements in order to ease a united Government into war. Once Britain was committed to the conflict, Asquith and Haldane set out immediately to undermine the decision not to send the BEF to France. At a carefully packed war council on August 5 the Empire's most famous and respected military leaders endorsed the Anglo-French plan. The Admiralty, effectively silenced by the 1911 purge, had no opportunity to make the case for the sort of limited naval war Grey had spoken of only two days before.[10] Committed to the war and confronted by the seemingly unanimous advice of the responsible professional strategists of both services, the cabinet reversed itself on August 6 and authorized dispatch of the BEF to France "with much less demur" than Asquith had expected.[11]

This decision, the most important political act of a British Government during the entire war, was made with little consideration for its political consequences. During the war council on August 5 the BEF's commander-designate, Field Marshal John French, had suggested that his force be sent to Antwerp rather than to France. The cabinet majority, which had gone to war in defense of Belgium, was not represented at the council and thus had no opportunity to state the political arguments for limiting British military operations to that country. Churchill and the General Staff vetoed Antwerp on purely military grounds.[12] Field Marshal Lord Kitchener, the new secretary of state for war, also dodged the political implications in his formal instructions to French dated August 9. These stated that the BEF was to land in France and cooperate with the French armies to liberate Belgium and to preserve the balance of power in Europe.[13] Political default rather than deliberation ultimately committed Britain to the Continental war.

The War Office had won its decade-long struggle with the

10. Hankey, War Council minutes, 5 Aug 14, CAB 22/1; Haldane to E. Haldane, 5 Aug 14, Haldane Papers, MS 6012.
11. Asquith to Stanley, 6 Aug 14, Stanley Papers.
12. Hankey, War Council minutes, 5 Aug 14, CAB 22/1; Wilson, diary entry, 5 Aug 14, H. Wilson Papers, (M)5; Sir Douglas Haig, diary entry, 5 Aug 14, Haig Papers, Accession 3155/98.
13. Kitchener, "Instructions for the General Officer Commanding the Expeditionary Force proceeding to France," 9 Aug 14, WO 106/298; Asquith to Stanley, 8 Aug 14, Stanley Papers.

Admiralty. Yet Grey, Haldane, Asquith, Churchill, Henry Wilson, and the others responsible for the Continental commitment had as yet no conception of the grim years of decimation to come. They believed that dispatch of the BEF to France had ensured a quick, decisive Entente victory. The General Staff departed en masse for the field, convinced that a few great battles in the next few weeks would settle the conflict. On August 12 the BEF's chief of staff predicted that "the war will last three months if everything goes well, and perhaps eight months if things do not go so satisfactorily."[14] He was generally regarded as a pessimist.

Only one of the Government's military advisers warned that the fighting in France might be neither brief nor decisive. Lord Kitchener had learned in South Africa the power of resistance available to a modern nation fighting for survival. The cabinet having established no war aim more specific than victory, the war minister defined his mission as decisive military victory at any cost. He considered Wilson's plan for the French and Russian armies and seven British divisions to vanquish Germany in three months a dangerous illusion. Years and millions of trained British soldiers, Kitchener believed, would be needed to grind Germany and its army to defeat. From his first day in office, over the protests of French and Wilson, he sought to build the mass armies he considered essential to victory in a general European war.[15]

While the BEF marched off to pursue victory in a short Continental war and Kitchener began preparing for a long Continental war, the Admiralty confronted the problem of how to wage a war its best strategists believed should never be fought. Fisher denounced the dispatch of the BEF as "criminal folly,"[16] but the very fact that he and Arthur Wilson were languishing in retirement discouraged active officers from renewing the conflict with the War Office. The option of a limited war in which Britain pursued its maritime and imperial interests while allowing France, Russia,

14. General Sir Archibald Murray, quoted in Esher, diary entry, 13 Aug 14, Esher Papers, 2/13.

15. George H. Cassar, *Kitchener* (London: William Kimber, 1977), pp. 184–189, 195–212, and passim; B. H. Liddell Hart, *The Real War, 1914–1918* (Boston: Little, Brown, 1930), pp. 68–69. On opposition to the Kitchener armies at BEF headquarters, see Wilson, diary entries, 12 Aug 14 and passim, H. Wilson Papers, (M)5.

16. Marder, *From the Dreadnought*, II, 192.

and Germany to determine their own relationship was dead. Yet the Admiralty had no alternate strategic plan to establish its mission and priorities for a war in which British power was committed to the Continent.

The last peacetime naval war plan, dated July 3, 1914, had established command of the North Sea and English Channel and destruction of the High Seas Fleet as primary objectives.[17] Neither was of offensive value in a Continental war, although command of the Channel was essential to transport, supply, and reinforce the BEF. Germany had ordered its merchant marine to run for friendly or neutral ports when war became imminent, so few of Fisher's vaunted "942 German mercantile vessels" were exposed to capture.[18] Although the war plan asserted that "continual movement in the North Sea of a fleet superior in all classes to that of the enemy will cut off German shipping from direct oceanic trade, and will as time passes inflict a steadily increasing degree of injury on German interests and credit sufficient to cause serious economic and social consequences,"[19] no one in the Admiralty believed that any economic pressure the navy could bring to bear in a few months would force the enemy to accept peace on terms acceptable to the Allies.[20]

Thus the decision to fight a Continental war seemed to have reduced the Royal Navy to a secondary role. If the war could be won only on land, as the men dominating British strategic planning in August 1914 assumed, then the fleet's primary mission must be to secure the sea-lanes vital to the nation's ability to survive and wage war, to protect the BEF's communications, and to defend the British Isles from invasion so every available soldier could be sent to France. Destruction of the High Seas Fleet, which

17. Ibid., I, 382.
18. Marion Siney, *The Allied Blockade of Germany, 1914–1916* (Ann Arbor: University of Michigan Press, 1957), p. 20; quotation from Fisher, "War Plans and the Distribution of the Fleet," n.d., Adm 116/1043B/1.
19. Quoted in Marder, *From the Dreadnought*, I, 382.
20. See chapter 6 at notes 6–13 and chapter 7 at notes 51–52 and 84. Esher and Slade noted separately that if Germany won a decisive land victory, Britain would have to fall back on the traditional maritime strategy to win what Esher described as "a Napoleonic war, going on for years." Esher to M. Brett, 12 Aug 14, Esher Papers, 7/27; Slade, 14 Aug 14, minute on Adm to CIC, Devonport, tel, 13 Aug 14, Adm 137/988.

Fisher, Arthur Wilson, and the July 3 war plan had defined as the highest priority, now seemed less important. Economic pressure, which the Admiralty believed could be effective only in a long and limited war and the War Office considered worthless in any war, seemed destined for the lowest priority of all.

British strategists during the first week of fighting continued to assume that any action taken against enemy trade would be within either customary law or the Declaration of London. The Foreign Office assured shippers that the declaration "probably will be observed by the belligerents in the present war."[21] On August 11 the Admiralty formally advised Grey that it wished the order in council under which the fleet would enforce belligerent rights to be based on the official naval prize manual of 1913, itself based directly on the declaration.[22] After discussing possible political opposition to such de facto acceptance of the controversial agreement with the attorney general, Sir John Simon, the foreign secretary directed Hurst to draft an order embodying the "instructions already issued to naval officers."[23]

Had this defensive conception of the navy's mission and acceptance of established maritime law remained the basis of British thinking, the blockade of Germany could not have developed, American neutrality probably would not have been tested by differences over maritime rights, and the Allies almost certainly would have lost the war. Both assumptions did break down, however, within the first two months of fighting. By the end of September many of the same British leaders who had discounted economic pressure early in August had come to see a campaign against enemy imports as a potentially decisive weapon to weaken and ultimately shatter Germany's ability to make war.

This sudden reversal had its origin in two factors that often influence wartime policy making: unsubstantiated rumor and the

21. E.g., FO to J. W. Baird & Co., 9 Aug 14, FO 372/600.
22. Adm to FO, 11 Aug 14, ibid./588. Slade and Chief of Staff Sir Doveton Sturdee recommended formal acceptance of the declaration, but Graham Greene persuaded the first sea lord, Prince Louis of Battenberg, that the prize manual would be easier for naval officers to interpret than the technical legal language of the agreement itself. Minutes, 7, 8, 9 Aug 14, on FO to Adm, 7 Aug 14, Adm 116/1233.
23. Hurst, memo, 10 Aug 14, with minutes by Simon and Grey, n.d., FO 372/588.

desire of politicians to share in military glory. Almost from the first day of the conflict, the British press had carried accounts of German food shortages. On August 9, for example, *The Times* printed a sensational story on mass starvation among enemy forces in Belgium. Because "few or no arrangements have been made for feeding" the armies, "many Germans, including officers," had "surrendered for bread."[24] These accounts contained little or no truth, the German army's quartermaster department being perhaps the world's most efficient, but the rumors did influence both public and official perceptions in Britain.

Evidence of this effect emerged on August 12, when the chancellor of the exchequer informed his colleagues that exceptionally large wheat shipments were in transit from New York to Rotterdam. Although he had no direct proof, Lloyd George concluded that in light of the enemy's supposed food shortage these shipments "undoubtedly" had "as their ulterior destination the German market."[25] Grey, who had received independent French reports of the vulnerability of German food supply,[26] had to reconsider the policy of acting under the existing prize manual. The next day he proposed to the cabinet that the German North Sea coast be placed under formal blockade and all food consigned to Rotterdam be seized as conditional contraband "unless it was not destined, directly or indirectly, for the German armies."[27]

The Government spent considerable time during the next week trying to resolve what Asquith called the "difficult questions of law and policy" raised by Grey's proposal.[28] The Admiralty quickly disposed of the suggested blockade, which it considered suicidal under modern conditions. To be legitimate, a blockade had to be effective and enforced equally against ships of all nations. A distant blockade could not prevent Dutch or Scandinavian ships from entering the German North Sea ports; a close blockade would be decimated by mines, submarines, and other modern

24. *The Times,* 9 Aug 14, p. 1; cf. 12 Aug 14.
25. Asquith to George V, cabinet letter, 12 Aug 14, CAB 41/35/28.
26. E.g., Bertie to Grey, tel, 3 Aug 14, FO 800/166.
27. Asquith to George V, cabinet letter, 13 Aug 14, CAB 41/35/29; see also Hobhouse, diary entry, 14 Aug 14, David, ed., *Inside Asquith's Cabinet,* p. 182. Hobhouse recorded that Grey was "the fiercest of us all to destroy her [Germany] once and for all."
28. Asquith to George V, cabinet letter, 13 Aug 14, 41/35/29.

weapons. The navy vetoed Grey's blockade proposal and continued to veto similar suggestions throughout the war. Although the term "blockade" is commonly used to describe the British economic campaign, in the technical sense there never was a blockade of Germany during World War I.[29]

Grey's proposal to apply the doctrine of continuous voyage to food shipments consigned to Rotterdam also met with serious difficulties. British law had been stated only fifteen years before by Lord Salisbury: food was conditional contraband, and its capture was justified only when the captor could prove destination to the enemy armed forces. The Declaration of London expanded this principle slightly by authorizing seizure if the captor could prove consignment to the enemy government, but stated explicitly that the doctrine of continuous voyage could not be applied to conditional contraband. Customary British law did permit capture of food shipped to a neutral port, but only if the government could prove enemy military destination. Because no exporter presumably would be stupid enough to consign his food shipments through Rotterdam to "The Quartermaster General, Imperial German Army," the cabinet majority could see no way to intercept such shipments without blatant violation of international law.

Despite these difficulties, Grey, Lloyd George, and Churchill argued that some way must be found to deny the enemy his supposedly vital grain cargoes. After considerable discussion with Hurst on the legal implications, the foreign secretary submitted a draft order in council for Admiralty comment on August 14. This proposal consisted of the Declaration of London with five changes. Four were technical points necessary for agreement with the official prize manual. The fifth was application of the doctrine of continuous voyage to conditional contraband.[30]

Slade, the first officer at the Admiralty to comment on the draft order, found little good in it.

> The provisions of this article will enable us to capture neutral ships carrying conditional contraband to Dutch Ports. This appears to be

---

29. Marder, *From the Dreadnought*, I, 373–377, and II, 372–377.
30. Hurst, draft order in council, 14 Aug 14, FO 372/588; Simon, memo, 14 Aug 14, FO 800/89.

most satisfactory but practically it is almost impossible to apply it as the Courts will never condemn, except on the clearest evidence, which is always very difficult to obtain.

Goods which come under the heading of conditional contraband cannot be condemned unless the destination can be proved to be without question the armed forces of the enemy, a fortified place or some person who is supplying the enemy Government with such articles. This is no new rule, but it is part of the customary law which will be administered in our Courts. Unless the vessels are condemned and declared to be good prize, heavy compensation has to be paid and neutral Powers are needlessly irritated.[31]

Slade, who had spent much of the previous decade studying possible economic warfare against Germany, thus remained convinced on August 15 that application of the doctrine of continuous voyage to conditional contraband offered little advantage and raised serious dangers. Admiral Doveton Sturdee, the chief of staff, and Admiral Prince Louis of Battenberg, the first sea lord, agreed.[32]

With professional opinion at the Admiralty unanimously against Grey's proposed modification of the Declaration of London, the draft order in council presumably would have had little support in a cabinet already concerned with its legal implications. The prime minister and foreign secretary in particular prided themselves on deferring to professional judgment on strategic questions.[33] Yet the cabinet never learned of the opposition to the draft order within the Admiralty. The first lord saw no reason to bother his colleagues with opinions contrary to his own. Rumor had played its role by producing Grey's draft order. Churchill's desire for military glory now became a major factor in pushing it through the cabinet.

The first lord did not question his subordinates' conclusion that application of continuous voyage to conditional contraband

31. Slade, 15 Aug 14, minute on draft order in council, 14 Aug 14, Adm 116/1233.

32. Sturdee and Battenberg, 16 Aug 14, minutes, ibid.

33. J. A. Spender and Cyril Asquith, *The Life of Herbert Henry Asquith, Lord Oxford and Asquith*, 2 vols. (London: Hutchinson, 1932), II, 120–123; Sir Edward Grey, *Twenty-Five Years, 1892–1916*, 2 vols. (New York: Frederick A. Stokes, 1925), II, 73–78; Paul Guinn, *British Strategy and Politics, 1914–1918* (Oxford: Clarendon, 1965), pp. 181–183. Cassar, *Kitchener*, pp. 190, 253–255, is too harsh on Asquith.

would be ineffective in denying necessary supplies to the enemy. Nor did he question their warnings of danger from neutrals. But during the week of cabinet debate on maritime rights, Churchill's attention had been focused on the clash of armies on the Continent. Much of his time had been spent organizing naval personnel into units for land service, designing uniforms, and studying the land campaign for an opportunity to intervene at the head of his troops.[34]

Had the first lord's thirst for military glory led only to Antwerp and command of a battalion on the Western Front, it would have had little relevance to the origins of the blockade. But Churchill's preoccupation with the land fighting convinced him that the invading enemy armies were dependent on supplies imported through Dutch ports. He had believed since 1911 that Henry Wilson's predictions might prove too optimistic and that the Allies might be defeated in the initial battles, fall back to regroup, and finally win the war only after several months of attrition.[35] In such a war, cutting off supplies to the German forces in Belgium and northern France even for a brief time could be decisive. On August 17 he urged his admirals not to dismiss Grey's proposal on continuous voyage out of hand. If French and Wilson won the war within a few weeks as they predicted, the question would become academic. If they did not, and Britain found itself in a longer war, the admitted disadvantages of seizing conditional contraband bound for neutral ports would have to be weighed against "the vital importance of preventing Rotterdam from becoming effectively a base for the enemy's supplies."[36]

The cabinet met again that afternoon. Churchill did not inform his colleagues that professional opinion at the Admiralty unanimously opposed Grey's draft order. Instead he threw the weight of the navy behind the proposal. Grey and Lloyd George joined in arguing that the potential military benefits should, in the current emergency, outweigh the admitted diplomatic and com-

---

34. Richmond, diary entries, 14, 20 Aug 14 and passim, Richmond Papers, 1/9; Balfour to Sandars, 22 Sep 14, Sandars Papers.

35. Churchill, "Military Aspects of the Continental Problem," 13 Aug 11, CID Paper 132B, CAB 4/3.

36. Churchill, 17 Aug 14, minute on draft order in council, 14 Aug 14, Adm 116/1233.

mercial disadvantages. Simon led the opposition, stating that the order was legally indefensible and certain to alienate neutrals. Prolonged debate revealed that the majority sympathized with Grey's objectives, but were not willing to disregard international law so flagrantly so soon after the invasion of Belgium had blackened Germany's reputation. Alternatives to assertion of continuous voyage were suggested and discussed, including plans for the Allies to charter all neutral ships that might otherwise carry food to Germany and to trade a guaranteed supply of British coal for a Dutch government embargo on food exports to Germany. The cabinet finally adjourned, deeply split and without a final decision.[37]

Grey and Churchill convened a special conference two days later to consider the entire economic warfare question and, if possible, to agree on a common recommendation to the Government. Kitchener indicated his opinion of the value of the meeting and of economic warfare in general by failing to attend or to send a War Office representative. Those who were present agreed that "all possible steps" should be taken to prevent food from reaching Germany "whether directly or through Dutch ports," but seemed unable to accomplish this goal within the rules of established law. There seemed no way around the embarrassingly clear statement by Lord Salisbury: "Foodstuffs with a hostile destination can be considered contraband of war only if they are supplies for the enemy's forces. It is not sufficient that they are capable of being so used. It must be shown that this was in fact their destination at the time of seizure." Lansdowne had repeated this rule in his notes to Russia in 1904. British delegates had asserted it at The Hague in 1907 and in London in 1909. Asquith and Grey had cited it publicly as established law during the Naval Prize Bill debate of 1911.[38] If there was one principle to which the British government seemed inextricably committed, it was that food could be

---

37. Hurst to Greene, n.d., Adm 116/1234; Grey and Slade, n.d., minutes on Hurst, memo, n.d., ibid./1233; Asquith to Stanley, 17 Aug 14, Stanley Papers; Asquith to George V, Cabinet letter, 17 Aug 14, CAB 41/35/31.

38. Quotation from Salisbury to Choate, 10 Jan 00, *FRUS*, 1900, pp. 549-550; see also Lansdowne to Hardinge, tel, 13 Aug 04, FO 46/628; Grey, Instructions to Fry, 3 Jun 07, CAB 37/89/65; Grey to Desart, 1 Dec 08, Scott, ed., *Declaration*, pp. 210-234; Grey, memo of conversation with Corn Trade and Milling Associations, 9 Mar 11, FO 371/1279; Grey and Asquith, House of Commons speeches, 3 Jul 11, *Debates*, pp. 398-415, 454-459.

seized as conditional contraband only when the captor could prove destination to the enemy armed forces.

It was, ironically, the home secretary who pointed the way out of this dilemma. Three years earlier Reginald McKenna had predicted that international law could be "easily evaded in wartime."[39] He now pointed out that although British prize law did not permit seizure of food as contraband without proof essentially impossible to obtain under existing circumstances, the Declaration of London authorized capture of any conditional contraband destined to "a government department of the enemy State." Because "the German Government (according to reliable reports) had taken over the whole of the foodstuffs in Germany," all food imports could be considered destined de facto for the enemy government. The Declaration of London could be used to justify capture on grounds unacceptable under traditional British law; national prize law then could be used to justify application of continuous voyage to conditional contraband, an action explicitly forbidden in the declaration. By taking the most favorable rules from both legal systems, McKenna argued, Britain could provide a plausible legal justification for intercepting the supposedly vital German food shipments.

This suggestion seemed to resolve the difficulties the Government had wrestled with over the past week. The August 19 conference endorsed Grey's draft, now given the necessary appearance of legitimacy by McKenna's ingenious interpretation.[40] The cabinet formally approved the Order in Council of August 20 the next day.[41] At 3:15 that morning the Admiralty issued orders that "a neutral ship is to be detained for carrying conditional contraband although she is proceeding to a Dutch Port." Food was explicitly listed as contraband.[42] The fleet immediately began to intercept neutral ships sailing to neutral ports.[43]

39. See Chapter 7 at n. 52.
40. Minutes of meeting, 19 Aug 14, FO 372/588.
41. Asquith to George V, cabinet letter, 20 Aug 14, CAB 41/35/34.
42. Adm to All Ships, etc., 20 Aug 14, Adm 116/1233.
43. CIC, the Nore, to Adm, tel, 21 Aug 14, ibid.; Devlin, *Too Proud,* p. 192; Archibald C. Bell, *The Blockade of the Central Empires, 1914–1918* (London: His Majesty's Stationery Office, 1937), unnumbered volume in series Great Britain, Committee of Imperial Defence, Historical Section, ed., *Official History of the War* (London: His Majesty's Stationery Office, 1920–1961), pp. 43–46 and passim.

On August 22 Crowe informed the American ambassador that Britain had considered a United States proposal for general adoption of the Declaration of London for the duration of the present war. The government had decided to "adopt generally the rules of the Declaration in question subject to certain modifications and additions which they judge indispensable to the efficient conduct of their naval operations." The most important of these changes were paragraph 5, which extended the doctrine of continuous voyage to conditional contraband, and paragraph 3, which authorized British prize courts to condemn contraband "on any sufficient evidence." Both "modifications" repudiated explicit provisions of the declaration. Both also repudiated the maritime rights policy the Admiralty had advocated since 1904.[44]

Grey and Churchill had won again. Between August 2 and August 6 Britain had decided to intervene militarily in a Continental war. Two weeks later it replaced the Declaration of London, an agreement deliberately tailored by Admirals Slade and Ottley to permit effective economic pressure against Germany, with a new maritime rights policy the responsible professional advisers unanimously considered militarily ineffective and diplomatically dangerous. The question must be: why?

The answer is that Britain had plunged into a Continental war fought on a scale Europe had not seen since the days of Napoleon. Only Kitchener in August 1914 recognized the awesome task ahead. The cabinet had abdicated its responsibility to define political ends or strategic means for the nation's war effort. Nowhere was this confusion more apparent than in maritime rights policy. Grey proposed application of the doctrine of continuous voyage to conditional contraband because he had the vague hope that intercepting food imports might somehow defeat Germany. This hope was encouraged by Churchill, whose detailed study of the military campaign convinced him that the German armies in Belgium and northern France might gain a decisive tactical advantage by using Rotterdam as a secure logistical base. Battenberg, Slade, and Sturdee continued to think in terms of the limited naval war that might have been rather than the grim Continental

---

44. Crowe to Page, 22 Aug 14, Savage, II, 194–195; Order in Council, 20 Aug 14, ibid., pp. 195–197.

struggle that was beginning.[45] The cabinet grasped any plan that seemed to promise quick and easy victory. Much as during "Black Week" fifteen years before, a British government had decided to enforce broad belligerent rights without any real conception of what it hoped to accomplish and without systematic consideration of neutral reaction.

The confusion of British maritime policy emerged clearly as the government sought to enforce the Order in Council of August 20. Two days after the Order went into effect, the Dutch minister protested. Grey "thought" that the Royal Navy had "not stopped a single neutral ship bound for Rotterdam."[46] Churchill confirmed that "the only restraint we are putting on wheat shipments to Holland is the prevention of traffic of enemy's ships and the diversion of British-owned grain-carrying ships."[47] Only the next day did the Admiralty casually inform the Foreign Office that the fleet had been ordered on August 20 to seize all neutral ships carrying conditional contraband, including food, to Dutch ports.[48] Whether deliberately or not, the Admiralty had misled the Foreign Office and Grey had misled neutrals as to the rules Britain was enforcing on the high seas.

There was no room for misunderstanding on August 25, however, when Grey warned the Dutch minister that Britain intended to "capture all food stuffs consigned to Rotterdam unless accompanied by a definite guarantee from the Dutch government not only that they will be consumed in the country, but that they will not release for Germany equivalent supplies of foodstuffs in Holland at the time."[49] Stripped of rhetorical embellishment, this statement announced Britain's intention to starve the Netherlands until the Dutch government agreed to trade its established neutral rights for survival. In 1904 Lansdowne had been prepared to go to war rather than accept Russian seizures of food

45. E.g., Slade, Sturdee, and Battenberg, 15, 16 Aug 14, minutes on draft order in council, 14 Aug 14, Adm 116/1233.

46. Grey to Johnstone (British minister, The Hague), 22 Aug 14, CAB 37/120/101.

47. Churchill, 22 Aug 14, minute on Nicolson to Grey, 21 Aug 14, FO 368/1026.

48. Adm to FO, 23 Aug 14, FO 372/600.

49. Grey to Johnstone, tel, 25 Aug 14, FO 368/1026; minutes of conference, 27 Aug 14, CAB 17/88B.

destined for the civilian population of Japan. A decade later Grey threatened to seize the food a neutral state needed for its own subsistence on the vague hope that by doing so he might hurt Germany. The initial suggestion of trading British coal for a Dutch embargo had given way to naked force.

By August 30 fifty-two ships carrying grain to either Germany or the Netherlands had been detained in British ports.[50] When the procurator general asked what evidence he should cite in court to justify these captures, Grey ignored the request for a month and then lamely suggested that the Crown should claim "the condemnation of all foodstuffs where there is evidence that the ultimate destination is Germany." The procurator general was to cite German nationalization of food supplies, although the foreign secretary admitted that "the evidence at present in his hands is not sufficient to be utilizable in Prize Court Proceedings." Grey did promise to begin gathering evidence to support this assertion "directly."[51]

The evidence under which Britain had captured more than fifty ships on the high seas thus consisted of a report, based on rumor and wishful thinking, that Germany had nationalized its food supplies. The McKenna interpretation of the Declaration of London, under which this provision had been justified to the cabinet, was itself admittedly contrary to customary British law. Yet the declaration stated that it must be enforced as a whole or not at all. Britain had detained neutral ships in its ports for more than a month before the Foreign Office began to seek evidence against them, although the Law Officers had stated in 1899 that detention of a neutral ship without sufficient evidence to justify immediate prize court proceeding was a gross violation of international law, entitling the neutral to substantial damages. Britain had paid such damages in 1900 and had been prepared to go to war in 1904 to defend the principle that neutral ships could not be seized without immediate prize proceedings. Under these circum-

---

50. Esher, diary entry, 31 Aug 14, Esher Papers, 2/13.
51. Procurator general to FO, 26 Aug 14, FO 372/600; FO to procurator general, 29 Sep 14, ibid./601. Siney's statement (*Allied Blockade*, p. 25) that the British had made "no attempt" to intercept "imports intended for the German civilian population" under the Order of 20 Aug 14 clearly is incorrect in light of the documentation now available.

stances, the procurator general's reluctance to go to court in autumn 1914 is both understandable and the measure of the British government's own opinion of its legal case.

Although the campaign of economic warfare initiated under the Order in Council of August 20 far exceeded the limits of international law, it did not satisfy the British public. The press demanded that a Germany supposedly on the verge of starvation not be permitted to "feed herself through Holland," whatever the law said.[52] Esher complained that the Foreign Office should be placed "under the Admiralty," if not "scrapped" altogether for the duration.[53] Newspapers reported vast shipments of vital supplies reaching the enemy under Britain's nose.[54] As early as September 4, this public pressure led Asquith to defend the Government's policy by asserting that measures already implemented had "largely curtailed" German food imports.[55]

This demand for stronger action against German trade reflected a general hardening of attitudes during September. Despite continued optimism at BEF headquarters, London was coming to accept Kitchener's prediction of a long and bloody war. On August 29 the cabinet had authorized an army of one million men.[56] Allied victory on the Marne in September raised brief hopes of imminent German collapse,[57] but they were smothered in blood and mud at Ypres. Well before Christmas trench warfare had transformed the Western Front into the static meatgrinder that would decimate a generation of British, French, Belgian, and German manhood.

As casualty lists grew, so did determination to redeem the immense sacrifices by total victory. Nations lost sight of the essentially defensive reasons for which they had gone to war and came to see the struggle as one between good and evil. This tendency was especially marked in Britain, where the cabinet's failure to

52. *The Times,* 26 Aug 14, p. 9; cf. *The Morning Post,* 28 Aug 14, clippings in FO 372/588.
53. Esher, diary entry, 31 Aug 14, Esher Papers, 2/13.
54. E.g., *The Times,* 2 Sep 14, p. 5.
55. Asquith, speech, 4 Sep 14, *The Times,* 5 Sep 14, p. 10.
56. Asquith to George V, cabinet letter, 29 Aug 14, CAB 41/35/37.
57. E.g., *The Times,* 2 Oct 14, p. 7.

define specific war aims left the public free to provide its own objectives. Militant orators were quick to tell the nation what terms it should demand. On September 10 a Glasgow crowd cheered widely as Lord Curzon exclaimed: "I should like to see the lances of the Bengal Lancers fluttering down the streets of Berlin."[58] A *Times* editorial four days later entitled "The Retreat of the New Attila" thundered that "there will never again be any safety in Europe until peace is signed in the very heart of Berlin."[59] Eyre Crowe struck the word "standpoint" from a draft message because it was "a German and not a good English expression."[60] In such an impassioned atmosphere, with "the freedom of the world" at stake in a conflict between "civilized right and conscienceless might,"[61] apparently abstract concepts like international maritime law commanded little respect from the British public.

As the people became more determined to win a total victory during September, the British government became more willing to employ whatever weapons might be necessary to smash Germany to its knees. The War Office continued to emphasize the need to break the German armies on the Western Front. But London, shocked by the casualty lists, turned increasingly to economic warfare as a relatively bloodless path to victory. The most vigorous proponent of striking at Germany through its imports was the Committee on the Restriction of Enemy Supplies, chaired by Sir Francis Hopwood of the Admiralty.[62] During August this group, which included Hurst and Slade, had advised against a broad assertion of the doctrine of continuous voyage.[63] On August 29, however, it reversed course and recommended that the campaign against food shipments launched under the Order in Council of August 20 "be vigorously followed up" and "extended and made

58. Curzon, speech, 10 Sep 14, *The Times,* 11 Sep 14, p. 7; cf. F. E. Smith, speech, 11 Sep 14, *The Times,* 12 Sep 14, p. 10.

59. *The Times,* 14 Sep 14, p. 9.

60. Crowe, emendation, n.d., on Grey to Cambon, draft note, 24 Sep 14, FO 372/600.

61. Editorial, *The Times,* 19 Sep 14, p. 9.

62. CID, "List of Committees," 20 Aug 14, CID Paper 195B, CAB 4/5; Adm, memo, 12 Dec 16, Adm 137/2737.

63. CRES, Report 2, 21 Aug 14, and Report 3, 25 Aug 14, Adm 137/2988.

to apply to certain other commodities of value to the enemy, particularly petroleum."[64]

Seizure of tankers carrying oil to a neutral port was impossible under the Declaration of London and could be justified under British law only if the captor could establish enemy military destination. The Hopwood Committee admitted that the possibility of obtaining such proof was "very remote." Nevertheless, it recommended on September 9 the "immediate and drastic action" of capturing "one or more of the largest" tankers carrying American oil to Rotterdam. The committee had little hope that the ship or its cargo would be condemned, but believed a lengthy and costly detention would discourage oil shipments in the future. "A certain outcry in the United States" should be expected, but the military advantage of cutting off or slowing down the flow of oil to the enemy was "worth it."[65]

The Hopwood Committee's recommendation on petroleum brought to a head the general debate within the government over treatment of raw materials. Grey pressed for adding such metals as zinc, copper, and nickel to the contraband list. Hurst warned that this action would be "a substantial departure from the rules of international law," but the foreign secretary was more concerned with casualty lists and political pressure than with legal abstractions. A committee under his sponsorship recommended that several types of metals and metallic ores be made conditional contraband.[66] The cabinet approved this list, with the addition of rubber, on September 17.[67] Four days later Britain issued the broadest list of contraband raw materials in its history.[68]

During the next week the Royal Navy seized several neutral ships loaded with oil and other supplies, all bound for neutral European ports. The Hopwood Committee applauded capture of a Dutch tanker carrying American oil to the Netherlands and called for similar treatment of other tankers.[69] The fleet

64. CRES, Report 4, 29 Aug 14, ibid.

65. CRES, Report 6, 9 Sep 14, ibid.; Hurst, memo, 8 Sep 14, FO 372/600.

66. Greene to Hankey, 14 Sep 14, CAB 17/104; Hurst to Grey, n.d., FO 372/600; cf. Bertie to Grey, 12, 18 Sep 14, ibid.

67. Hurst, 17 Sep 14, minute on Hurst to Grey, n.d., FO 372/600.

68. Skinner (American consul-general, London) to Bryan (secretary of state), tel, 22 Sep 14, SD(M)M-367/188.

69. CRES, Report 9, 22 Sep 14, Adm 137/2988.

obliged.[70] Hopwood then urged that speculative seizure be applied to copper as well as to food and petroleum.[71] The expansion of economic warfare, from the restricted campaign conducted under established law in early August, through the food interceptions of late August, and finally to the broad attack on raw materials of late September, seemed both a military and a political masterstroke. Even *The Times* expressed satisfaction with the latest measures to "suffocate" the enemy.[72]

By the end of September the Admiralty's limited plans for economic warfare had evolved into what history has called "the blockade" of Germany. This name was technically inaccurate because Britain never proclaimed a formal blockade. Nevertheless, expansion of the doctrines of contraband and continuous voyage were beginning to achieve the effects of blockade by other means. Britain had succeeded in cutting off most trade with Germany from overseas.[73] The chaos of August had given way to a coherent plan, spearheaded by Grey and the Hopwood Committee, to deny the enemy vital raw materials for his industry and food for his industrial population. Many in the British government had come to believe that the economic campaign could squeeze Germany until it cracked, bringing victory sooner and with fewer British crosses left in the mud of Flanders.

Only one flaw threatened to block development of the economic weapon's full potential. The blockade struck not only at Germany, but at the neutral nations whose shipping carried enemy imports. McKenna's ingeniousness could not hide the fact that Britain was enforcing measures that violated established international law. Some case could be made for the Order in Council of August 20. No case could be made for British methods of

70. E.g., "Grand Fleet Narrative," entry, 27 Sep 14, Admiral Sir John Jellicoe (CIC, Grand Fleet) Papers, AM 48995.
71. CRES, Report 11, 29 Sep 14, Adm 137/2988.
72. Editorial, *The Times,* 23 Sep 14, p. 9.
73. Bell, *Blockade,* pp. 43–46, 51–53, 61–117, 124–125, and passim. Bell's effort to distinguish between "arrest" of neutral ships, which was relatively rare, and "detention" of neutral ships, which was the common procedure, should not be allowed to disguise the degree to which Britain was in fact interfering with neutral commerce. The difference was that an "arrested" ship could be defended in prize court, whereas a "detained" ship was simply held because the British government lacked evidence to bring charges.

enforcing it. There could be no justification in existing law for Grey's threat to starve the Netherlands, for speculative seizures without prize court evidence, or for other British actions. Such measures constituted a direct challenge to each neutral they affected.

At least one minister continued to remind his colleagues that economic warfare had its risks as well as its rewards. Asquith reported his attorney general "in a very disgruntled mood: in trouble about his soul; and talks about shouldering a musket & going to the front!"[74] Simon had warned that the neutrals injured by the obviously illegal aspects of the blockade could be expected to protest, and perhaps to act, in defense of their rights. These warnings had been disregarded in the government's new-found enthusiasm for the economic weapon. Simon was troubled in September 1914, but less for "his soul" than for his country.

74. Asquith to Stanley, 27 Aug 14, Stanley Papers.

CHAPTER NINE

The United States and the Blockade, August to October *1914*

The quasi-legal smokescreen devised by McKenna and others could not long conceal the reality of British actions. The Netherlands and other European neutrals protested vigorously and often.[1] But only one neutral possessed the power to command respect for its rights in London. Joseph Chamberlain had written in 1899 that "it hardly seems wise for us to be the first to make food-stuffs contraband, as in any European war we should expect that the United States would help us by protesting against any such practice on the part of a foreign nation."[2] Fifteen years later the European war had become a reality, but Britain, not its enemy, was seizing American food shipments. The expectation of American protest had become a threat rather than an assurance.

British leaders had demonstrated some awareness since the beginning of the war that the United States must be a major factor in any economic campaign against Germany. On August 13 Grey had ordered that ships entering Rotterdam be reported in three categories: those under the enemy flag, those that had sailed from American ports, and all others.[3] The Admiralty warned the fleet four days later that "great care is to be taken in the diversion of neutral ships with neutral cargo. It is of prime importance to keep

---

1. E.g., W. Stewart (FO official), 20 Aug 14, minute on Johnstone to Grey, 20 Aug 14, FO 372/600; Grey to Johnstone, 22 Aug 14, CAB 37/120/101.
2. Chamberlain to Milner, 6 Dec 99, Milner Papers, 17.
3. Grey to Maxse, 13 Aug 14, FO 368/1026.

the United States of America as a friendly neutral."[4] Grey tried to ease the way for American acceptance of the Order in Council of August 20 by assuring the American ambassador that Britain would be as lenient as possible with his nation's ships and cargoes and would buy rather than confiscate "comparatively innocent contraband, such as foodstuffs."[5] Most British leaders believed by the end of September 1914 that economic pressure might help win the war. Few questioned that a conflict with the United States could lose it.

Ultimate responsibility for determining the American government's response to the blockade rested on the president of the United States, Woodrow Wilson. Wilson was an uncertain factor in British calculations. Few British leaders had met the president, and none had the close relationship with him that several had enjoyed with Roosevelt. Outgoing British Ambassador James Bryce had characterized Wilson as "an able man, with a will of his own" and added that "I should fully expect him to be friendly to England."[6] The president's actions in the Panama Canal tolls controversy had demonstrated both the will and the friendship.[7] In that case, however, international law had supported Britain's position. The fate of the blockade, and perhaps the outcome of the war, would depend on how Wilson reacted when international law did not support Britain.

British statesmen attempting to predict American responses to the economic campaign thus faced a peculiarly difficult task. Not only was the president little known personally, but he and his advisers had given little indication of their views on foreign affairs. Wilson himself had remarked shortly before his inauguration that "it would be the irony of fate if my administration had to deal chiefly with foreign affairs," his interest and training having been focused almost exclusively on domestic reform.[8] Secretary of

4. Adm to "All Cruisers," 17 Aug 14, Adm 137/982.
5. Grey to Spring Rice (ambassador, Washington), 29 Aug 14, FO 372/600.
6. Bryce to Grey, 30 Oct 12, FO 800/83.
7. Link, *Wilson*, II, 304–314.
8. Quotation from Link, *Wilson the Diplomatist* (Baltimore: The Johns Hopkins Press, 1957), p. 5. On Wilson's overall background in foreign affairs, see ibid., pp. 4–21; Link, *Wilson*, II, 277–280; Devlin, *Too Proud*, pp. 108–131; Smith, *Great Departure*, pp. 24–27; and the dated but still useful Harvey Notter, *The Origins of*

State William Jennings Bryan was a political appointee without diplomatic experience, and the little Englishmen knew of him was not favorable.[9] The only member of the incoming administration who had foreign affairs training and experience, State Department Counselor John Bassett Moore, had resigned before the outbreak of war. His replacement, Robert Lansing, was a less imposing figure little known abroad.[10] A magazine editor who had hoped to be named secretary of agriculture became ambassador to London, while a Tammany politician went to Berlin.[11] British leaders were not alone in believing that almost anything might be expected from the Wilson administration in foreign affairs. Mahan spoke for many Americans when he warned a British friend in November 1913, "With two green hands at the head of external affairs, both, I think, more of less faddists, there is cause for anxiety as to where we will fetch up. . . . As they are both opinionated, and I fancy don't esteem law as highly as they do their own ideas, I am a little afraid of consequences at once serious and preposterous."[12]

These words were to prove prophetic. Yet the administration's public reaction to the outbreak of war gave no indication that it would behave differently from earlier Americans who had faced similar problems. The president's formal neutrality proclamation, dated August 4, might have been issued by George Washington or

---

the Foreign Policy of Woodrow Wilson (Baltimore: The Johns Hopkins Press, 1937). The recent argument that Wilson was not so unprepared to deal with foreign affairs, advanced in John Milton Cooper, "'An Irony of Fate': Woodrow Wilson's Pre-World War I Diplomacy," *Diplomatic History*, 3 (1979):425-437, is far from convincing. For British prewar views of Wilson, see Perkins, *Great Rapprochement*, pp. 289-292.

9. Rachel West, *The Department of State on the Eve of the First World War* (Athens: University of Georgia Press, 1978), pp. 24-37 and passim; Smith, *Great Departure*, pp. 15-18; Richard Challener, "William Jennings Bryan," in Norman Graebner, ed., *An Uncertain Tradition* (New York: McGraw-Hill, 1961), pp. 79-88; Perkins, *Great Rapprochement*, pp. 20-26, 100-101, 292.

10. Smith, *Lansing*, pp. 1-9, and *Great Departure*, pp. 18-21; West, *Department of State*, pp. 47-49, 56-63.

11. West, *Department of State*, pp. 77-92; Cooper, *Page*, pp. 243-248; Ross Gregory, *Walter Hines Page* (Lexington: University of Kentucky Press, 1970), pp. 22-26. There is no solid scholarly study of the ambassador to Berlin, but see James Gerard, *My Four Years in Germany* (New York: George H. Doran, 1917), for colorful but unreliable memoirs.

12. Mahan to Admiral W. Henderson, 7 Nov 13, Henderson Papers, 1/16.

Thomas Jefferson.[13] When Wilson urged Americans two weeks later to be "neutral in fact as well as in name" and "impartial in thought as well as in action,"[14] his words echoed Washington's Farewell Address. History and law offered the United States a clear definition of neutrality. If Wilson followed that definition, as his public statements promised, Simon had ample justification for his fear that the blockade would lead to confrontation.

Several issues were to test American neutrality during the first months of war, including loans to belligerents, purchase of belligerent merchant ships, and construction of warships for belligerents. The record of the Wilson administration on these questions was complex and sometimes contradictory.[15] But the key test of American neutrality was the administration's response to the British blockade. Neutral businessmen had the right under "well-recognized principles of international law," as the State Department noted publicly on August 15, to trade with both belligerent camps.[16] Germany and the European neutrals had been important prewar customers for American exports.[17] The British blockade established under the Order in Council of August 20 constituted a direct, seemingly inescapable, challenge to this profitable trade with Germany, to continued commerce with the European neutrals, and to those "well-recognized principles" of law. How the administration met this challenge would shape the entire pattern of American neutrality.

Neither Wilson nor Bryan was familiar with maritime law, so

13. Wilson, Neutrality Proclamation, 4 Aug 14, Ray Stannard Baker and William E. Dodd, eds., *The Public Papers of Woodrow Wilson*, 6 vols. (New York: Harper, 1925-1927), III, 151-156.

14. Presidential statement, 18 Aug 14, *The New York Times*, 19 Aug 14, p. 4; cf. Wilson, message to the Senate, 19 Aug 14, Baker and Dodd, eds., *Public Papers*, III, 157-159.

15. On warships built for belligerents, see Gaddis Smith, *Britain's Clandestine Submarines, 1914-1915* (New Haven: Yale University Press, 1964); on the ship purchase controversy, see Jeffrey J. Safford, *Wilsonian Maritime Diplomacy, 1913-1921* (New Brunswick, N.J.: Rutgers University Press, 1978), pp. 35-65; on loans, see Smith, *Great Departure*, pp. 34-38; May, *World War*, pp. 45-47; and Savage, II, 44-46.

16. State Department, circular, 15 Aug 14, Savage, II, 189-193.

17. The United States exported $332 million worth of goods to Germany in 1913 and $352 million in 1914. Exports to Norway, Denmark, Sweden, and the Netherlands totaled $165 million in 1913 and $151 million in 1914 (statistics from Jessup, *Neutrality*, III, 221).

the burden of recommending specific policies fell mainly on Lansing. The counselor already had tried to defuse the potential for conflict by proposing general adoption of the Declaration of London for the war's duration.[18] When Britain vetoed this initiative and issued its Order in Council,[19] Lansing turned to two of the nation's leading experts on maritime law, former State Department Solicitor James Brown Scott and Harvard Law Professor Eugene Wambaugh. During the first two weeks of September, these three men wrestled with the problems the British blockade posed for American neutrality.

Scott, Wambaugh, and Lansing agreed with Slade and Simon that the Order in Council of August 20 could not be enforced effectively within existing international law. None expressed doubt that British actions did constitute a violation of American neutral rights or that failure to oppose such a violation would constitute "non-neutrality toward Germany" and "a manifest failure to safeguard the interests of United States citizens engaged in perfectly legitimate business." Wambaugh went so far as to state that Britain's policy was "so injurious to neutral commerce and so inconsistent with general International Law as to bring it wholly within the legal rights of a neutral . . . to protect its commerce by war." Although the three men recommended initial recourse to public rejection of the Order in Council and an appeal for negotiations, Wambaugh's mention of war indicates the seriousness with which a sober international lawyer regarded the challenge posed by the blockade.[20]

Lansing commissioned Scott, who had returned to government service shortly after the outbreak of war as chairman of the interdepartmental Joint Neutrality Board,[21] to prepare a protest note. As submitted on September 17, this draft emphasized the illegality and unacceptability of British attempts to use the Declaration of London to justify expansion of belligerent rights while

---

18. Bryan to W. Page (American ambassador, London) and other ambassadors, circular tel, 6 Aug 14, *FRUS*, 1914, Supplement: The World War, p. 216.

19. Crowe to Page, 22 Aug 14, Savage, II, 194–195.

20. Quotations from Joint Neutrality Board (signature by Scott) to Lansing, 5 Sep 14, SD(M)M-367/172, and Wambaugh to Lansing, 9 Sep 14, ibid./188; cf. Wambaugh to Lansing, 2, 8 Sep 14, ibid.

21. Scott to Lansing, 10 Aug 14, Lansing Papers, 3; Smith, *Lansing*, p. 20.

ignoring the safeguards that agreement provided for neutrals. The declaration, Scott noted, had been written at Britain's insistence by a conference dominated by strong naval powers. In the American view, it "stretches a point in the interests of belligerents." Nevertheless, in order to provide a common code and reduce the danger of international friction, the American government had offered to accept the agreement for the duration of the current war. But it had made that offer subject to acceptance by all belligerents. The United States certainly would not consider itself bound by the declaration if Britain continued to expand already inflated belligerent rights. Scott offered the British a clear choice: accept the declaration in toto, with its safeguards for neutrals as well as its rights for belligerents, or abandon the declaration entirely and expect the United States to insist on all neutral rights sanctioned by customary maritime law.[22]

Lansing revised Scott's draft, casting it into less legalistic language, and as acting secretary of state submitted it to the president on September 27. Its message and purpose were stated succinctly in the covering note:

> I cannot but feel that the action of the British Government calls for unqualified refusal of this Government to acquiesce in its legality and that our objections should be clearly and firmly stated.
> The British Order in Council will suggest to you, I think, the obnoxious Orders in Council of the Napoleonic Wars, and will, if its provisions are called to public attention in this country, cause severe criticism in the press.[23]

On the evening of September 27, therefore, responsibility for preservation of American neutrality rested squarely on Woodrow Wilson. The State Department had warned him that the British blockade was legally indefensible and had proposed a formal protest to London. Lansing had warned that failure to make some effective response to the blockade might well have unfortunate political consequences for the administration. The president hardly wanted "severe criticism in the press" six weeks before midterm elections vital to his legislative program. But neither, as

22. Scott to Lansing, 17 Sep 14, SD(M)M-367/188; draft note, n.d., SD 763.72112/135½.

23. Lansing to Wilson, 27 Sep 14, *FRUS,* The Lansing Papers, I, 247–248; for text of draft note as revised by Lansing, see Savage, II, 197–205.

his confidant and adviser Colonel Edward House warned, did the president want a major controversy with Britain. House considered the tone of the note "exceedingly undiplomatic" and more likely to provoke than to resolve differences. A private accommodation between the two governments, he argued, might well resolve the problems discussed in the note without either unfavorable publicity or formal diplomatic confrontation. If agreement could not be reached, then Lansing's note could be sent to London with nothing lost except a little time. By such arguments, House persuaded Wilson to delay dispatching any protest pending informal discussions with Sir Cecil Spring Rice, the British ambassador.[24]

The colonel's meeting with Spring Rice the next morning seemed to confirm the wisdom of the informal approach. House recorded that the ambassador was "thoroughly alarmed" at the draft note, exclaiming that one paragraph "amounted almost to a declaration of war." Why, he demanded, had the State Department said nothing for two months and then confronted Britain with an utterly unexpected crisis? The British government appreciated American friendship and would be as conciliatory as the necessities of war allowed. But to present such a note without any previous effort to discuss the matter in a gentlemanly fashion was to question the good faith of His Majesty's Government and to slap Britain's outstretched hand of friendship. An obviously embarrassed House said that he understood and quite agreed. As long as the British government was willing to hold serious discussions of the issues raised in Lansing's note, there was no need for a formal diplomatic confrontation that would be in the interest of neither nation. The colonel returned to the White House congratulating himself for averting the worst crisis in Anglo-American relations since 1896 and persuaded Wilson that informal talks, held in London away from the prying American press, offered the best chance of resolving the maritime differences without unwanted public controversy.[25] That same afternoon, on the president's orders, Lansing instructed Ambassador Walter

24. House, diary entry, 27 Sep 14, House Papers. Smith, *Great Departure*, pp. 21–24, is the best brief sketch of House and his influence.
25. House, diary entry, 28 Sep 14, House Papers.

Hines Page to seek a private accommodation with Sir Edward Grey.[26]

This decision, although criticized by several revisionist historians,[27] was legally unimpeachable. Scott, who had been hired for his legal expertise, had stated the case against the British blockade in legal terms. Lansing, also a lawyer but with the wider duties of counselor and acting secretary of state, recognized the legal issues but emphasized the political implications of a failure to protest. Wilson and House chose to rely on informal talks rather than direct protest because they honestly believed such an approach offered the best chance of resolving Anglo-American differences while minimizing political and diplomatic risks. The United States had an obligation to Germany and to its own citizens, as Scott had pointed out, to defend its neutral rights against British violations. But the government was free to select its own method of defense and certainly was under no obligation to rush into confrontation or conflict. The ideal solution from Washington's point of view would have been for the entire question of maritime rights simply to go away. Given the still common expectation of a short war, such a painless resolution may not have seemed unlikely to Wilson and House in September 1914. If the war did drag on, on the other hand, there would be ample time to make the American position clear by whatever means ultimately proved necessary.

Although the basic decision to pursue an informal accommodation was fully compatible with American obligations under international law, the Wilson administration's implementation of that decision made a mockery of neutrality. During a series of meetings over the next few days, House, Lansing, Page, and Wilson seemed to compete with one another in expressing the most fervent pro-Allied sympathies and in undermining the talks they had initiated. These conversations confused and irritated British leaders, thereby substantially reducing the levels of mutual trust and confidence between the two governments. Ironically, the ad-

26. Lansing to Page, tel, 28 Sep 14, Savage, II, 205–206. Smith, *Great Departure*, p. 31, overestimates the role of Lansing and House and underestimates the importance of Wilson's personal intervention, as does Gregory, *Origins*, p. 33.

27. E.g., Charles Callan Tansill, *America Goes to War* (Boston: Little, Brown, 1938), pp. 141–150; Walter Millis, *Road to War* (Boston: Houghton Mifflin, 1935), pp. 87–88.

ministration's attempt to settle the maritime rights difficulties while maintaining good relations with London resulted in a tightened blockade even more violative of American neutrality and a growing contempt for the president within the British government.

This self-undermining process began on the evening of September 28. While Lansing was conveying Wilson's decision in favor of informal negotiations to Page, House called again on the British ambassador to report that he had been successful in persuading Wilson to authorize private talks in London. The American government would have to insist on revocation of the most objectionable sections of the Order in Council of August 20, but otherwise had no desire to place obstacles in the path of Britain's economic campaign. House emphasized the administration's eagerness to maintain friendly relations and hinted that London would receive the benefit of any possible legal doubts in the upcoming negotiations. He noted that the real need of both governments was to avoid public confrontation on such a sensitive issue and expressed confidence that Page and Grey could work out a satisfactory accommodation.[28]

House's comments had been within the letter of neutrality law, although certainly not within the spirit. Lansing, who called on Spring Rice shortly after the colonel left, was both more specific and more overtly unneutral. The acting secretary of state indicated that the administration's primary concern was to avoid agitation in the press which might force an Anglo-American confrontation over neutral rights that neither government wished. He pointed to British seizure of American food shipments as a blatant violation of international law with enormous potential for embarrassing the administration and arousing popular hostility in the United States. Spring Rice agreed that his government was treating food "practically" as absolute contraband, "contrary to the British traditional policy as well as to that of the United States." He suggested that if the American government would take a liberal policy toward addition of raw materials such as oil and copper to the contraband lists, London might well agree to

28. Spring Rice to Grey, tel, 28 Sep 14, FO 800/84; House, diary entry, 28 Sep 14, House Papers.

stop interfering with food shipments. Lansing replied that such an arrangement might be possible, although he had no authority to commit his government. But the ambassador was missing the point. The administration was not particularly interested in whether American exporters were able to ship food to Germany. It was interested in avoiding public controversy, which it considered inevitable if the Royal Navy continued to seize American food shipments. If the British government succeeded in "getting" the Dutch government to impose an embargo on reexport, thus denying Germany American food by indirect means, Washington was not likely to object.[29]

Lansing's message was clear: the administration had no objection to the British blockade per se, even if it hurt American trade and violated American rights. The counselor had emphasized throughout the conversation that his real objective was an accommodation that would allow Britain to intercept German imports while not provoking a public outcry in the United States. International law had hardly been mentioned, in marked contrast to the draft note Lansing had submitted to Wilson only the day before. In essence, the acting secretary of state was offering the administration's services as mediator between the British blockade and American public opinion.

Why had Lansing changed overnight from the defense attorney for American neutrality to mediator between a foreign government and his own countrymen? The only plausible answer is that in submitting the Scott-Lansing note he was representing his own views, whereas in his conversation with Spring Rice he was representing the views of the president. Despite public calls for neutrality "in thought as well as in action," Wilson had been making private pro-Allied statements almost since the outbreak of war. He had told House in August that "if Germany won it would change the course of our civilization and make the United States a military nation."[30] A few days later he assured the British ambassador that "every thing that I love most in the world is at stake" and restated his fear that German victory in Europe would mean

29. Lansing, 29 Sep 14, memo of conversation on 28 Sep 14, Savage, II, 206–208.
30. House, diary entry, 30 Aug 14, House Papers.

inevitable militarization in the United States. The president did not regard these statements as unneutral in any way, and indeed in the same conversation with Spring Rice described his policy as "absolute neutrality."[31] But when the events of late September forced Wilson to make some response to the blockade, his personal pro-British, anti-German attitudes came into direct conflict with the legal requirements of neutrality.

As Wambaugh, Scott, and Lansing had agreed, the United States could retain its claim to the legal status of neutral only if it defended its maritime rights against all violators, including Britain. The president had authorized discussions intended to reach an accommodation with London on the disputed matters. But, as Lansing's September 28 conversation with Spring Rice indicates, the American objective in negotiating was not defense of neutral rights, of noncontraband trade with Germany, or even of trade with the European neutrals. The acting secretary of state emphasized that he did not wish to hinder the British economic campaign, but only to ensure that its enforcement did not embarrass the administration in the eyes of the American people. Twenty-four hours earlier Lansing had recommended a formal protest on legal grounds. He still believed on September 28 that only such a protest could be effective in preserving American neutrality.[32] Yet he hardly mentioned law to Spring Rice, while implying American acceptance of measures clearly violative of established neutral rights. The president, who instructed his subordinate before the meeting with the British ambassador and reviewed the record of their discussion afterward,[33] must bear responsibility for this shift from neutrality under law to pursuit of an accommodation that would preserve the appearance of neutrality while offering no real obstacle to systematic British violation.

In a conversation with House on September 30, Wilson explained why he had refused to insist on real protection for American rights or trade. He drew a detailed analogy between the pre-

---

31. Spring Rice to Grey, tel, 3 Sep 14, FO 800/84; cf. Spring Rice to Grey, 8 Sep 14, ibid.
32. Lansing to Wilson, 28 Sep 14, SD(M)M-367/189.
33. Wilson to Bryan, 1 Oct 14, ibid./241.

sent situation and an event he had treated in his 1902 textbook, *History of the American People:* "The War of 1812 was started in exactly the same way as this controversy is opening up." James Madison, with whom Wilson felt close identification as "the only two Princeton men that have become President," had been a "peaceloving" man. He had nevertheless been forced into war with Britain by "popular feeling" aroused by violation of American neutral rights. Neither president nor people, in Wilson's view, had realized that they were making a dreadful mistake:

> Napoleon was the enemy of the civilized world.... England was fighting him almost alone, all Europe thrown into his scale and hers almost kicking the beam; and now America had joined the forces of Napoleon, in fact, if not in intention, as he had subtilely planned.... It was a tragical but natural accident that the war should be against England, not against France.[34]

This passage, which Wilson read to House on September 30 with the comment that "the circumstances of the War of 1812 and now run parallel," is essential for an understanding of American maritime rights policy during World War I. In 1812 Napoleonic France had been the nation seeking to dominate the "civilized world"; in 1914 it was Wilhelmine Germany. In both cases, despite flaws of which Wilson was well aware, Britain represented the cause of civilization. The president thus considered the War of 1812 an unnecessary conflict, forced on the United States by an unsophisticated public more concerned by relatively minor British abuses than by the overwhelming threat Napoleon represented. Wilson based his maritime rights policy in 1914 on the three fundamental assumptions reflected in this historical analogy: that American national security would be endangered by a German victory, as a century earlier it would have been endangered by a French victory; that neither trade nor legal rights was of sufficient importance to the United States to justify a break with Britain; and that public opinion must not undermine presidential leadership as it had under Madison to force the United States to side with the enemies of civilization.

The historian, with his advantage of hindsight, can identify

---

34. Final, extracted quotation from Woodrow Wilson, *History of the American People*, 5 vols. (New York: Harper, 1902), III, 216–217; quotations in the paragraph from House, diary entry, 30 Sep 14, House Papers.

these three assumptions as the roots of a consistent pattern of American unneutrality on maritime rights. Yet to Woodrow Wilson, struggling during the last months of 1914 with the normal duties of his office, the extraordinary demands created by the war, and the personal trauma of his wife's death on August 6,[35] these same assumptions appeared to offer the surest, safest guidelines to true neutrality. The president believed passionately that the United States must remain above the madness and carnage which had engulfed Europe.[36] Until the German submarine warfare proclamation of February 1915, the gravest danger of American involvement seemed to lie in the potential conflict with Britain over maritime rights. In Wilson's view, an accommodation with London that defused this explosive potential would strengthen rather than undermine American neutrality. He failed to realize that to bend the law of nations to avoid confrontation with one belligerent invited confrontation with the other. He failed to understand that "neutrality" was a state of law in contemporary international relations, not a state of presidential sincerity or even conscience.

The chasm between administration actions and the legal requirements of neutrality emerged clearly in the wake of the decision not to present the Scott-Lansing draft note to the British government as a formal protest. The president's September 28 instructions to Lansing, intended to accommodate Britain's economic campaign without arousing American public opinion, already had compromised Washington's position. His decision to remove the detailed negotiations from under the eyes of the American press corps by entrusting them to his ambassador to London, Walter Hines Page, represented another pro-Allied step. In an administration in which the ambassador to Berlin supplied secret intelligence to the British navy and the chairman of the Joint Neutrality Board described Germany as an aggressor he hoped to see punished,[37] in an administration in which the presi-

---

35. See Link, *Wilson* III, 5, 57, and Devlin, *Too Proud*, pp. 225–228, for the best insight into the pressures on Wilson at this time.

36. The best summary of Wilson's complex reaction to the war is Link, *Wilson* III, 49–56.

37. Fisher to Jellicoe, n.d. [ca. 29 Dec 14], Jellicoe Papers, AM 49006; Scott to P. Fauchille, 10 Aug 14, Scott Papers (cf. Scott to Bryce, 10 Oct 14, Bryce Papers, USA/18).

dent himself assured the British ambassador that he hoped for Allied victory,[38] the ambassador to London was unquestionably the least neutral in attitude or in action.

When Page called on Grey on September 29 to begin the talks ordered by the president, he was not inclined to place obstacles in the path of British economic warfare. On the contrary, he seemed determined to remove those London still recognized. The American ambassador assured the foreign secretary that his government had no desire to press the case "of people who traded deliberately & direct with Germany." Its only concern was to protect the well-established trade of the United States with the European neutrals. Grey quickly explained that there was then no reason for controversy because the British government sought only "to prevent the enemy from receiving food and materials for military use and nothing more." He pointed to two neutral "vessels full of copper consigned direct to Krupp" as examples of the American trade he wished to block. Page hastened to agree that "no objection could be taken" by the United States if Britain seized such ships. On this basis—protection of American trade legitimately intended for the European neutrals and interception of direct or indirect trade with Germany—Page and Grey agreed to negotiate the detailed agreement defining American and British maritime rights for the duration of the war.[39]

The ambassador considered this conversation a satisfactory solution to a potentially troubling Anglo-American dispute. Grey's feelings can hardly be imagined. Even Jay's Treaty, which Britain had all but dictated to the United States, had not defined all American trade with France as contraband. Yet in a single meeting Page had withdrawn the protection of the American flag from all commerce with Germany. He had recognized an unprecedented application of the doctrine of continuous voyage. The American ambassador, charged by the president with defense of his nation's neutrality, had made the greatest surrender of neutral rights in the history of the republic. Page had conceded every point raised in the Scott-Lansing draft note, had essentially ig-

38. Spring Rice to Grey, tel, 3 Sep 14, FO 800/84.
39. Page to Bryan, tel, 29 Sep 14, SD(M)M-367/189; Grey to Spring Rice, tel, 29 Sep 14, FO 372/601.

nored the telegram of instructions that Wilson and Lansing had sent, and had gratuitously recognized belligerent rights the British government had not as yet claimed.

Grey was now thoroughly confused as to the American position. He had noted Spring Rice's reports of Wilson's pro-British attitude, which had led the ambassador to conclude that "I am sure we can at the right moment depend on an understanding heart here."[40] The foreign secretary had read Spring Rice's report on the Scott-Lansing note and his warning that the American press showed "signs" of having been "tuned" by German propagandists to exploit Anglo-American blockade differences.[41] Did these indications that Washington was breaking its two-month silence on maritime rights mean that Britain must choose between limitations on the blockade and confrontation with the United States? Apparently not; House and Lansing both had implied that the administration's real objective was to quiet American public opinion rather than maintain established rights and trade. But then Page, whom the president had named chief American negotiator, had offered his assurance that Britain need not worry about American reaction as long as there was no interference with legitimate trade with the European neutrals. This statement contradicted the warnings from Washington that continued American acquiescence in the blockade depended on certain changes in the justification and enforcement, although not the result, of current measures. With the acting secretary of state and Wilson's closest friend taking one position and claiming to speak for the president, while the ambassador to London took a contradictory position yet also claimed to speak for the president, the British could only conclude that the administration was not sure itself what its policy was.

After sorting through this confusion, Grey decided that Page's remarks had reflected the ambassador's pro-English attitude and ignorance of law rather than his instructions. When the two met again on September 30, the foreign secretary explained that Britain would prefer to use the Lansing–Spring Rice talks on Sep-

40. Spring Rice to Grey, 8 Sep 14, FO 800/84.
41. Spring Rice to Grey, tel, 28 Sep 14, FO 372/601; Spring Rice to Grey, tel and letter, 28 Sep 14, FO 800/84.

tember 28 as the basis for the detailed agreement. The British government was prepared to draft a new order in council along the lines of Lansing's suggestions, which it hoped would meet American desires. The new rules would add copper and other raw materials to the absolute contraband list, but would permit American food to go unmolested to the Netherlands as long as the Dutch government banned its reexport to Germany. Food shipments currently detained would be released at once, which Page considered "an important concession in our favor." Grey even promised to submit the new order to the American government before publication, thereby hopefully avoiding the type of misunderstanding which had occurred concerning the Order of August 20.

Page concluded his report to Bryan by stating that this conversation demonstrated a "desire to meet our wishes so far as the most relentless war ever waged will permit."[42] Once again the ambassador either had not understood or had not wished to understand the real nature of Grey's proposals. The additions to the contraband list were goods not recognized as conditional contraband, much less absolute contraband, under Anglo-American prize law. To permit American merchants to export food to the Netherlands as long as the Dutch government provided a guarantee against reexport, which Page considered a major British concession, in fact would have recognized that a belligerent had the right to seize shipments of conditional contraband in transit between two neutrals unless the merchant could provide ironclad guarantees of neutral consumption. Such a belligerent right was not only unprecedented in law, but had never before been advanced in theory. The release of neutral ships carrying American food to Dutch ports, which Page claimed as another British concession, was in fact, as the correspondence between the Foreign Office and procurator general proves,[43] the release without compensation of ships Britain had had no legal right to seize in the first place. The proposed order actually extended rather than restricted belligerent rights.

42. Page to Bryan, tel, 30 Sep 14, SD(M)M-367/189; Grey to Spring Rice, tel, 30 Sep 14, with covering note by Spring Rice, ibid./188.
43. See Chapter 8, following n.50.

If Page's report on his conversation with Grey was overly optimistic and misleading, the State Department's response can only be characterized as wishful thinking. Bryan wired that he was "gratified by disposition of British Government to remove possible causes of irritation by promulgation of new order in council to remove all orders which have been issued modifying the Declaration of London." Grey had indicated no such disposition. Bryan appreciated the "announcement by British Government that shipments to Netherlands of foodstuffs in neutral bottoms will not be interfered with."[44] Grey had made no such announcement, but rather had promised that Britain would not interfere with food shipments as long as the Dutch government embargoed food exports to Germany. If Bryan lacked the legal knowledge to catch these discrepancies, Lansing certainly must have recognized them. But the counselor, after his September 28 conversation with Wilson, saw only what he and the president wished to see.

Lansing recognized that the measures outlined in the British proposal involved substantial and systematic violations of American neutral rights, as well as an almost total end to American trade with Germany and restrictions on American trade with the European neutrals. This fact did not distress him. He was concerned, however, that such extensive interference with American commerce and such blatant disregard for American rights would provoke a public reaction not only against Britain, but against the administration that tolerated them. The British and American governments had a common interest in finding some plausible legal justification for actions that could not be justified under customary maritime law. Lansing believed, and had convinced Wilson, that such a justification was available in the Declaration of London.

In essence, the counselor had adopted the view of many of the declaration's British critics during the 1911 debate: vague language in certain key articles would permit broad extensions of belligerent rights not possible under existing law. On October 2 Lansing explained in detail to Spring Rice how Britain might issue an order adopting the declaration in toto, then interpret Articles 23 and 25 in such a manner as to justify the present policy of

44. Bryan to Page, tel, 1 Oct 14, SD(M)M-367/189.

intercepting practically all goods destined directly or indirectly for Germany. This interpretation would not be within the spirit of the declaration and clearly would be contrary to the intent of the 1909 conference. But it would allow both governments to make a plausible case that Britain was remaining within the letter of the agreement, which had been negotiated and approved by the Senate under a Republican administration. Such an arrangement, Lansing argued, would meet both British military and American political requirements.[45]

Spring Rice had reported on October 1 that Bryan seemed "satisfied" with the progress of the Page-Grey talks.[46] Lansing's counterproposal therefore came as a surprise to London. British pressure had finally induced the Netherlands to prohibit food exportation, and a general ban on export of any item on the British contraband lists seemed likely in the near future.[47] Grey had ordered an end to interference with food shipments to Dutch ports on October 1,[48] and two days later he had told Page that the new order in council, drafted in accordance with Lansing's suggestions on September 28, was almost ready for submission to the American government.[49] Suddenly, just when Britain seemed to have reached a general accommodation with all the important neutrals, Lansing appeared to raise new issues and new problems.

Grey immediately cabled Spring Rice that Britain could not accept the suggestion that it adopt the Declaration of London in toto. Article 23 might well be interpreted to allow the addition of raw materials to the absolute contraband list. Other sections might also be interpreted in a way favorable to British requirements. But Article 35 stated explicitly that the doctrine of continuous voyage could not be applied to conditional contraband. The British government regretted, but might not be able to avoid, the necessity of taking "more effective steps" to prevent conditional contraband

45. Lansing to Spring Rice, 2 Oct 14, and Lansing, memo of conversation, 2 Oct 14, ibid./241; Spring Rice to Grey, tel, 2 Oct 14, FO 372/601.

46. Spring Rice to Grey, tel, 1 Oct 14, FO 372/601.

47. F. Oppenheimer (British commercial agent, the Netherlands), memo, 3 Oct 14, FO 368/1027.

48. Hurst, memo, 1 Oct 14, ibid.

49. Page to Bryan, tel, 3 Oct 14, SD(M)M-367/188.

from reaching Germany through the European neutrals. These steps must involve the application of continuous voyage. National security demanded that Britain retain a freedom of action incompatible with Article 35 of the Declaration of London. The British government could harldly adopt the declaration in toto while repudiating one article, so it could not follow Lansing's suggestion.[50]

The unpleasant task of transmitting this rejection fell to Spring Rice. He tried to soften the blow by emphasizing his government's eagerness to meet American wishes in specific cases and even pointed to what he considered analogies with the American Civil War:

> It is possible that this war and especially the struggle for the liberty of Belgium may entail heavy losses on the American producer.... But if losses ensue in consequence of this struggle in which so great issues are at stake, Americans may remember that in 1861, when the whole labouring population of Lancashire was thrown out of work in consequence of the blockade of the southern ports, those very men on whom starvation fell were most steadfast in repudiating the demand that our fleet should break the blockade.[51]

This emotional plea did not deflect Lansing. He did not object to British goals, even when they damaged American rights and economic interests, but he did believe that the British government had failed to recognize its own self-interest when it refused to act, at least nominally, within the framework of the Declaration of London. On October 5 the counselor explained to Spring Rice that he understood Grey's objection and believed it could be met. If Britain would issue an order adopting the declaration in toto, it could then issue supplementary regulations, to which the United States would make no objection, allowing continuous voyage to be applied to conditional contraband in necessary instances. In essence, the second highest ranking official in the State Department was telling the British government that if it adopted the declaration in form it need pay no attention to it in fact.[52]

50. Grey to Spring Rice, tel, 4 Oct 14, ibid.
51. Spring Rice to House, 4 Oct 14, House Papers; cf. Spring Rice to Wilson, 5 Oct 14, W. Wilson Papers, (M)63.
52. Spring Rice to Grey, tel, 5 Oct 14, FO 372/601.

If Lansing's October 2 suggestion has surprised Grey, the October 5 proposal seems to have stunned him. The foreign secretary patiently explained that if his government issued an order adopting the declaration in toto, then issued a rule explicitly contrary to the declaration, the prize court might well ignore the rule and enforce the order. For this reason, reservation of the right to apply continuous voyage to conditional contraband must be in the order itself. Yet to issue an order adopting the declaration in toto and at the same time repudiating one article of it would make the government appear not only unjust, but ridiculous. Lansing's attempts to be helpful were appreciated, but Britain simply could not accept the Declaration of London without reservation as he proposed.[53]

While these exchanges continued, Grey was moving ahead on the basis of the accommodation already discussed. With cabinet approval, he provided Page with a copy of the draft order in council.[54] But Washington, under increasing pressure for its apparently weak attitude, did not regard the new proposal with favor. John Bassett Moore, who had returned to private practice and was representing American exporters, complained of "the London Declaration, which we at the same time have and have not, having all its disadvantages, with added aggravations, and none of its benefits!"[55] Other voices complained as well. Against this background of rising discontent, Lansing warned Spring Rice on October 12 that the administration would have "some difficulty" accepting the draft order.[56]

With the assistance of Scott's Joint Neutrality Board, the counselor drafted the formal American reply. It was a blunt rejection of the British proposal. Lansing explained to Wilson that "the sum total of the objections is that the Order in Council of August 20th is repealed in no particular, but on the contrary is reenacted with changes and additions which make its provisions even more objectionable."[57] Although Spring Rice made a last-minute appeal

53. Grey to Spring Rice, tel, 7 Oct 14, ibid.
54. Draft order, n.d., ibid.; Asquith to George V, cabinet letter, 9 Oct 14, CAB 41/35/51.
55. Moore to W. Libby, 11 Oct 14, Moore Papers, 197.
56. Spring Rice to Grey, tel, 12 Oct 14, FO 372/601.
57. Lansing to Wilson, 15 Oct 14, SD(M)M-367/188; Joint Neutrality Board to Lansing, 16 Oct 14, ibid./172.

for reconsideration, again citing supposed Civil War precedents,[58] Wilson authorized dispatch of this message without significant modification.

The American note of October 16 was exceptionally blunt for a diplomatic communication, and particularly for one from a supposedly neutral nation. It began by stating that "the desire of this Government is to obtain from the British Government the issuance of an Order in Council adopting the Declaration without any amendment whatsoever." The United States government "fully understands and appreciates the British position, and is not disposed to place obstacles in the way of the accomplishment of the purposes which the British representatives have so frankly stated." Britain must realize, however, that the Order in Council of August 20 and the proposed new order in council were unacceptable to the United States. Page was to propose, as "your personal suggestion and not one for which your Government is responsible," that Britain adopt the Declaration of London in toto in return for American acceptance of the expanded lists of contraband and of Britain's right to treat a neutral that permitted export or reexport of contraband to Germany as a base of supplies for the enemy.[59]

These instructions did not please Ambassador Page. He was tired of maritime rights disputes and eager to devote his full attention to the more important business of helping Britain win the war. On October 6 he had offered the president his own solution to the current difficulties: the American government should place an embargo on all exports to Germany while openly supplying Britain with arms and munitions. This action would bring Germany to its knees, allow the British government to force Russia and Japan to disarm, and create a worldwide *pax Anglo-Americana*.[60] On October 15, the day before Lansing sent his rejection of the draft order in council, Page warned Wilson that the United States must either accept the British proposal or go to war against Britain. He advised acceptance, perhaps accompanied by

58. Spring Rice to Wilson, 15 Oct 14, FO 800/84.
59. Lansing to Page, tels, 16 Oct 14, Savage, II, 215–219.
60. Page to Wilson, 6 Oct 14, W. Wilson Papers, (M)63; cf. Page to Wilson, 21 Oct 14, ibid., (M)64.

a pro forma reservation of rights to satisfy the writers of legal textbooks.[61]

Because Page was both a personal friend and an influential political supporter, Wilson accompanied Lansing's rejection of the draft order with a personal message. The president begged his ambassador not to consider the administration's position "merely academic." Lansing's suggestions would permit Britain to accomplish its military objective of starving out Germany "without the least friction with this government and without touching opinion on this side of the water on an exceedingly tender spot." The only American objective was to put accommodation with the blockade "in unimpeachable form." Anglo-American maritime differences, Wilson argued, were not an inherent conflict between belligerent necessity and neutral rights. They were simply a question of which of two possible legal justifications the British government would use for mutually accepted actions. The present British justification was unacceptable to America, but a justification based on the Declaration of London would be acceptable. Wilson indicated again that he was willing to concede acceptance of the substance of the blockade in return for a concession on form meaningless to Britain but vital to the political position of his administration.[62]

Despite this personal explanation, Page refused to follow the State Department's instructions. He explained to the president that a gentleman does not lie, even in the service of his country. The ambassador condescended to present the scheme to Grey as that of his government, but withdrew it immediately when, "with some approach to irritation," the foreign secretary asked, "Do you mean that we should accept it [Declaration of London], and then issue a proclamation to get around it?" Page concluded that Grey

61. Page to Wilson and Bryan, tel, 15 Oct 14, Savage, II, 213–215.
62. Wilson to Page, tel, 16 Oct 14, ibid., 219. May, *World War*, p. 61, argues that during these negotiations Wilson "was prepared to press the British unrelentingly until they accepted the law, as he understood it, and agreed to spare American trade," but relented because he deemed it "urgent to end the controversy before inflammatory speeches and editorials began to appear." This assessment ignores the president's systematic disregard of legal advice and overestimates his commitment to protection of American rights and trade, but correctly emphasizes his determination to avoid public controversy with Britain. "American maritime policy remained undefined and ambivalent" at the end of October 1914, but only in regard to details of the Anglo-American accommodation. Wilson's basic goals and priorities had been established weeks earlier.

was "courteous, appreciative, and willing to go to any length he can to meet us," but that his government was adamant in rejecting the Declaration of London.[63]

Lansing now had no alternative but to advise Wilson to fall back on international maritime law as traditionally defined. On October 22, with the president's permission, he instructed Page to inform the British government that the United States had abandoned its appeal for acceptance of the declaration. Henceforth the American government reserved all rights under customary Anglo-American prize law and intended to enter a "protest or demand in each case in which those rights . . . are violated."[64]

This policy reversal, with its references to customary law, "protest," and even "demand," might have seemed to herald an American challenge to the flagrantly illegal aspects of the British economic campaign. But Woodrow Wilson still controlled foreign policy, and Wilson still believed that neutral rights were not worth a quarrel with the nation fighting for the cause of civilization. The president had been willing to use the threat of an overt rejection of the draft order in council in an attempt to persuade the British government to accept the Declaration of London proposal. When the British resisted this persuasion, however, Wilson once again found himself caught between carrying out the threat and possibly creating a public confrontation with Britain, or allowing the British government to commit more extensive violations of American neutral rights. Given the president's basic outlook and assumptions, there was no real choice. On October 21 Spring Rice reported Lansing's assurances that there would be no general challenge to the new order, although the United States would protest individual cases.[65] Page made essentially the same statement to Grey two days later.[66] The foreign secretary immediately circulated this information within the cabinet as evidence that no serious American objection need be feared, thus clearing the way for issuance of the new order.[67]

63. Page to Bryan, tel, 19 Oct 14, Savage, II, 219–221; Page to Wilson, 21 Oct 14, W. Wilson Papers, (M)64.
64. Lansing to Wilson, 20 Oct 14, SD(M)M-367/241; Lansing to Page, tel, 22 Oct 14, Savage, II, 221.
65. Spring Rice to Grey, 21 Oct 14, FO 372/602.
66. Page to Bryan, tel, 23 Oct 14, SD(M)M-367/188.
67. Grey to Spring Rice, 23 Oct 14, CAB 37/121/140.

From August 4 to August 20, the American government had hoped that all belligerents would accept its proposal for general adoption of the Declaration of London for the duration of the present war. When the Order in Council of August 20 demonstrated that the British government intended, for reasons of military necessity, to take certain measures incompatible with either existing maritime law or the declaration, the Wilson administration had found itself facing a peculiar dilemma. The president and his senior advisers did not object to the British measures per se. They did fear that such flagrant violations of neutral rights would generate a popular outcry in the United States which the administration would be unable to control. From late August until late October, the American government wrestled with its British counterpart and with itself as it sought to resolve this dilemma.

The president's advisers offered three basic policy options. The first, represented by the Scott-Lansing note, was to lodge an official protest against the blockade on legal grounds. This policy would establish the administration's determination to maintain neutrality in the eyes of the American people, but would risk confrontation with Britain. The second option, advocated by Ambassador Page, was to accept the blockade in principle while making a pro forma reservation of rights and protesting abuses in individual cases. This policy would reduce the danger of confrontation with London, but increase the risk that the American people would consider administration efforts in defense of rights and commerce inadequate. The third option, advocated by Lansing after he recognized that the president would not sanction a formal protest, was to negotiate a secret modus vivendi based on British acceptance of the Declaration of London in return for American acceptance of an interpretation of that document favorable to Britain. This policy offered the administration a convincing excuse for not challenging the blockade, yet at least in the view of Washington presented no serious obstacle to the Allied goal of strangling Germany by economic pressure.

Although Lansing initially recommended a formal protest on September 27, Wilson rejected this option the next day. From September 28 until October 22, the administration pursued an accommodation based on an interpreted Declaration of London. This diplomatic effort failed because the British government was unwilling to agree to any legal system that might limit its future action. By the end of October, Wilson's rejection of the protest option and British rejection of the modus vivendi option left the administration little choice but to adopt Page's strategy of pro forma reservations and individual protests.

Any judgment on American maritime neutrality during the first three months of World War I rests directly on the standard the historian selects. By Wilson's privately stated standard, American policy had been successful. The British had been able to establish an effective economic weapon for use against Germany, while, despite some grumbling from shippers and their representatives, American public opinion generally remained calm in the face of Allied violations of neutral rights. By Wilson's publicly stated standard of neutrality "in thought as well as in action," on the other hand, the administration had failed utterly. The private statements of Page, Scott, Lansing, House, Wilson, and other high officials prove conclusively that the men who made American foreign policy between August and October 1914 shared an overwhelming pro-Allied, anti-German bias.

A third standard also existed in 1914 as a measurement of American neutrality: the standard of international law and American history. In this context the record of the Wilson administration can only be termed abysmal. Britain had committed violations of neutral rights on a monumental scale, and the American government had not even made a formal protest. In some cases, such as the conversation between Lansing and Spring Rice on September 28 and that between Page and Grey the next day, American representatives actually had encouraged and helped to plan more extensive British violations of neutral rights. As James Brown Scott had warned, de facto acceptance of an obviously illegal blockade constituted a failure to fulfill American obligations to Germany or to United States citizens who wished to continue their legitimate trade. By the end of October 1914 the United States was neutral in the eyes of its president and the vast majority of its people, but it was not neutral under the law of nations. The American government had become a partner, and not always a silent partner, in the Allied economic campaign to strangle Germany.

CHAPTER TEN

✻

Evolution of the Anglo-American Blockade, November 1914 to January 1915

The Order in Council issued by the British government on October 29, 1914, opened a new phase in both the blockade and the American relationship to it. There has, however, been widespread misunderstanding evident in historical accounts of the nature and effects of the new British regulations. Arthur Link has asserted that "the maritime system . . . was in all its main features based soundly upon international law and practices which, though not formally sanctioned, enjoyed a near legality through custom and usage by all maritime powers, including the United States."[1] Arthur Marsden's recent study concludes that the Order represented major concessions to American claims of neutral rights and substantially weakened the economic campaign.[2] Either of these interpretations would have astounded the men who devised, approved, and enforced the new rules.

The Order in Council of October 29 revoked its predecessor of August 20 in law, although, as Lansing had already noted of the draft, it did not in fact remove any of the objectionable aspects of the earlier Order.[3] The burden of proof remained on the neutral merchant. The foreign secretary was granted power to declare a neutral state to be a base of supplies for the enemy, thereby allowing interception of all goods on the contraband lists shipped to that country. Iron ores, lead, copper, aluminium, rub-

1. Link, *Wilson*, III, 127; cf. Smith, *Great Departure*, p. 32.
2. Arthur Marsden, "The Blockade," Hinsley, ed., *British Foreign Policy*, p. 494.
3. See Chapter 9, at n. 57.

ber, and oil were added to the absolute contraband list.[4] Overall, the Order was more restrictive of neutral rights than the draft to which Lansing had objected so strenuously two weeks before and certainly more restrictive of neutral rights than the Order of August 20.

The Order in Council of October 29 in fact bore little relationship to any previous British or American statement of international maritime law. Britain's procurator general, who had to justify seizure of neutral ships in prize court, pointed out to the Foreign Office that the new rules created an absurd situation in which it would be "more difficult to obtain a condemnation of Absolute Contraband than of Conditional Contraband."[5] British shippers complained that their own government was creating precedents that would make international commerce impossible in the future whenever two nations were at war.[6] Nevertheless, the cabinet continued to tighten the blockade and to disregard legal objections and warnings of future complications. The casualty lists from the western front were coming to dominate any discussion of maritime rights.

The Order of October 29 represented only the first step in a general intensification of the economic campaign. Pressure for stronger action had been building for some time. The navy and the French government had advocated more rigorous measures, particularly against food and cotton.[7] Members of the cabinet had received heartrending appeals from parents of soldiers at the front to win the war by economic pressure rather than by the "needless sacrifice of our children."[8] Churchill sneered that the European neutrals were "playing Germany's game" and should not be considered "at all." The first lord admitted that the United States could not be dismissed quite so cavalierly, but maintained that there should be no concessions on the blockade "until it is

---

4. Order in Council and Contraband Proclamation, 29 Oct 14, Savage, II, 228–231.

5. Procurator general to FO, 31 Oct 14, FO 372/602.

6. E.g., Liverpool Steam-Ship Owner's Association to Asquith, 9 Nov 14, FO 368/1192; Hurst, memo of conversation with shippers' representatives, 7 Dec 14, ibid.

7. E.g., Jellicoe to Adm, 2, 14 Oct 14, Adm 137/1915; Crowe, memo of conversation, n.d. [ca. 28 Oct 14], FO 800/94.

8. E.g., J. Pillman to Grey, 4 Oct 14, FO372/601.

certain that persistence will actually & imminently bring the United States into the field against us."[9] Members of the Opposition warned that they intended to raise the issue of Government weakness on economic welfare when Parliament met.[10]

As this pressure had mounted during October, it had been resisted mainly by one man. Herbert Henry Asquith, with support from Simon and other ministers, had conducted a masterful campaign of delay based on the argument that Britain could not afford to lose American goodwill at any cost. While Grey, Churchill, Lloyd George, Kitchener, and other colleagues demanded more restictions on neutral trade and more extensive contraband lists, the prime minister continued to warn of possible American opposition. But when Grey reported that although the American government did not like the new Order in Council, it would not lodge a formal protest, Asquith had to admit that the balance now lay with the military advantages of a tightened blockade rather than the diplomatic advantages of conciliating a neutral government that apparently did not wish to be conciliated.[11]

The prime minister's surrender opened the way for a flood of actions strengthening the economic campaign. The Order in Council was issued on October 29. A day later Fisher replaced Battenberg as first sea lord. Supporters of a more vigorous policy were pleased, although Balfour's political secretary worried that perhaps Asquith had conceded too much: "Fisher will exercise a very strong influence upon policy towards Neutral shipping— wisely or unwisely I don't say: but you know that when Jacky is out on business *nice* considerations do not trouble him much."[12] Exactly how little they troubled him became clear on November 3, when the Admiralty announced that "the whole of the North Sea" had become a military area sown with mines. The locations of the minefields would not be revealed, although neutral ships might be given sailing directions through safe areas by calling at a

9. Churchill to Grey, 27 Oct 14, FO 800/88.
10. E.g., Sandars to Balfour, 29 Oct 14, Balfour Papers, AM 49768.
11. Walter Runciman (president of the Board of Trade) to Grey, 27 Oct 14, FO 800/89; Grey, n.d., minutes on Crowe to Grey, 28 Oct 14, FO 372/602; Grey to Bertie, 19 Oct 14, FO 372/601; Grey to Crewe, 21 Nov 14, Crewe Papers, C/17; Grey to Spring Rice, 23 Oct 14, CAB 37/121/140.
12. Sandars to Balfour, 4 Nov 14, Balfour Papers, AM 49768; Marder, *From the Dreadnought*, II, 89–91.

British port or stopping a British warship before entering the North Sea.[13]

Together the Order in Council of October 29 and the mine announcement of November 3 established almost total British control over the North Sea trade of neutral Norway, Sweden, Denmark, and the Netherlands. Neutral ships entering the North Sea without British sailing directions risked being blown up on British mines sown in international waters. Neutral ships that did ask for sailing directions found themselves diverted into British ports and held until they provided proof that none of their cargo of a contraband nature might reach Germany directly or indirectly. Long detentions, often without a shadow of legal justification, became common.

As the new British restrictions took effect, a wave of protest grew in the United States. Congressmen inundated with complaints[14] joined their constituents in pressing the State Department for action.[15] Spring Rice warned that "agitation in the press" on maritime questions was increasing, although he continued to express confidence that Wilson would resist the demand for any meaningful anti-British action. The United States might try to maintain its commerce and commercial rights in some ways, the ambassador predicted, but it would not defend "the interest of the Standard Oil, the richest corporation in the world, and of the Copper Syndicate" at the risk of a quarrel with Britain.[16]

Private conversations with Lansing, House, and Wilson confirmed Spring Rice's own judgment. The counselor assured the ambassador that "the United States Government fully appreciated the necessities of the situation, but in view of the organized attack now being made on the Department by parties interested in copper, &c., they were compelled before Congress met to make some strong representations."[17] House warned that the administration might have to make "some serious protests" against the new measures, but expressed confidence that American public opinion was

13. Grey to Spring Rice, 3 Nov 14, Savage, II, 226–227.
14. E.g., Papers of Senator William Borah, 23.
15. See SD(M)M-367/189–191 for examples of these protests, which form the bulk of several reels of microfilm.
16. Spring Rice to Grey, 3 Nov 14, FO 800/84.
17. Spring Rice to Grey, tel, 9 Nov 14, FO 368/1192.

shifting in favor of the Allies despite the maritime rights agitation.[18] Wilson explained that the danger of "violent racial division" in the United States as a result of the war would force him to make some protest against the blockade in order to avoid any appearance of unneutrality. All led Spring Rice to believe that any protest would be an "ex parte statement" for "the benefit of Congress and in order to show that they have not been neglectful of American interests."[19] Not surprisingly, when the United States did present protests on November 7 and November 10 against illegal detention and illegal rules of evidence, the British government ignored them.[20]

As Grey had predicted, the American government responded to the new measures with individual protests, but no general challenge. With Page in charge of these case-by-case negotiations, the British had little reason for concern. The ambassador often proclaimed the vigor of his efforts in defense of American trade in letters to Wilson,[21] but British records provide little support for his claims. On the contrary, a memo in the Foreign Office archives indicates the real degree of support American shippers could expect from the embassy in their struggle with the British contraband control bureaucracy. After a private conversation with a senior member of Page's staff, a Foreign Office official reported that "the Embassy were surprised at the readiness with which their requests in regard to contraband were met. There was a feeling that even more was conceded than was asked, much less expected, and the Embassy did not really welcome all our concessions."[22] Although Wilson did express concern that Page might be losing touch with American opinion, he continued to entrust the ambassador with the main role in his effort to keep the maritime differences from boiling over into a major crisis.[23]

Encouraged by Washington's passivity, the British decided on

18. Spring Rice to Grey, tel, 9 Nov 14, FO 800/84.
19. Spring Rice to Grey, tel, 13 Nov 14, ibid.
20. Lansing to Spring Rice, 7 Nov 14, and Bryan to Page, tel, 10 Nov 14, Savage, II, 231–232, 233–234.
21. E.g., Page to Wilson, 21 Oct, 30 Nov 14, W. Wilson Papers, (M)64, 65.
22. C. Orde (FO official), memo, 19 Oct 14, FO 372/602; note Grey's initials.
23. E.g., Wilson to House, 29 Oct 14, W. Wilson Papers, (M)64.

even stronger measures against American trade. During October British agents in the United States had reported large purchases of canned meats by "German agents."[24] Britain had been seizing food destined for Germany, or for European neutrals who failed to provide guarantees against reexport to Germany, since August 20. The official justification for this action had been that the German government had assumed control of all food supplies and that food imports therfore were good prize under the provision of the Declaration of London making property of the enemy government conditional contraband.[25] The legal basis for this position had long since vanished because the British government had repudiated the declaration and had received conclusive evidence that the German government did not exercise control over food supplies.[26] Nevertheless, on November 5 a British warship seized the *Alfred Nobel,* a neutral ship carrying American meat to Copenhagen. In subsequent weeks similar captures were made as part of a deliberate attempt to deny food to the German civilian population.[27]

International law as defined by Britain and the United States permitted food to be seized as contraband only when the captor could demonstrate that a particular cargo was destined for the enemy armed forces. The Declaration of London had expanded that rule to permit seizure when the captor could prove destination to the enemy government. In the *Alfred Nobel* and other "Meat Packer" cases, Britain claimed the belligerent right to seize a neutral ship carrying food to a neutral nation, without any requirement for the captor to establish destination to the enemy, much less to his army or government.

When news of the food seizures reached the United States, pressure mounted on the administration to take some action. On November 24 Spring Rice warned that the State Department was becoming impatient with Page's failure to produce results by

24. Spring Rice to Grey, tel, 15 Oct 14, FO 368/1104.
25. See Chapter 8, following n. 39.
26. E.g., Johnstone to Grey, 19 Oct 14, with minute by Simon, 27 Oct 14, FO 372/601.
27. For details of these cases, see John B. Aspinall, ed., *Lloyd's Reports of Prize Cases,* 10 vols. (London: Lloyd's, 1915–1924), III, 167ff.

negotiating with Grey on individual cases.[28] When it became clear that the British were holding neutral ships for carrying food to a neutral, and not simply to search for concealed contraband, a deputation of meat industry representatives called on Lansing. The Republican leader in the House of Representatives accompanied them. The counselor sent the group on to the British Embassy to present their concerns to Spring Rice personally and added his own warning that the British would have only themselves to blame if the administration lost control of public opinion.[29]

Spring Rice quickly produced an attempt to justify the food seizures under supposed American precedents.[30] He warned Grey privately, however, that such expedients had reached the limits of their usefulness. The maritime agitation had become "very serious," the Wilson administration did seem to be losing control over public and congressional opinion, and "violent agitation" against the blockade must be expected when Congress met.[31]

These warnings had little effect on the British government. Successive predictions of American resistance by Slade, Sturdee, Hurst, Simon, and Asquith all had proved inaccurate. Too many false alarms had created a general disregard for the possibility that the United States might offer serious opposition to any British action. Hurst admitted privately that Britain had "no adequate 'legal' ground" for seizing the food shipments destined for Copenhagen. The Contraband Committee had ordered the captures "as a matter of expediency and as a wholesome check to shipowners." The committee now urged Grey to make no concession to the American position, despite the fact that Britain was admittedly acting illegally.[32] The foreign secretary softened the suggested language but made no substantive change in passing

28. Spring Rice to Grey, tel, 24 Nov 14, FO 368/1162.
29. Spring Rice to Grey, tel, 2 Dec 14, ibid.
30. Spring Rice to Lansing, 2 Dec 14, SD 763.72112/441.
31. Spring Rice to Grey, tel, 3 Dec 14, FO 368/1162; Spring Rice to Grey, 3 Dec 14, FO 800/84.
32. Contraband Committee, minutes, 4 Dec 14, FO 368/1195; on the absence of legal justification for these seizures in the opinion of the men who were charged with justifying them in prize court, see procurator general to FO, 8 Feb 15, FO 372/787.

this message to Washington.[33] The captured ships continued to sit in British ports, denied even the opportunity for defense in prize court.

The same day Grey notified Spring Rice that there would be no special concessions to American meat exporters, Page informed the State Department of his latest scheme to avoid controversy over maritime rights. He had persuaded the Foreign Office to accept an accommodation under which the American government would prevent its citizens from exporting to Germany or to a neutral that might reexport to Germany any item on the British contraband lists. In return, Britain would promise to provide favorable treatment for noncontraband American trade and to sell British-produced products vital to American industry.[34] This proposal, which Page considered a wise modus vivendi, would have made the United States government a branch office of the British contraband control authorities.

Grey's rejection of legally unimpeachable American complaints on the food issue, combined with the latest evidence of Page's strange view of neutrality, convinced the State Department that further negotiations along current lines were likely to do little or nothing to mitigate the treatment of neutral commerce or the political pressures building on the administration. Some action was necessary. On December 11 Bryan instructed American diplomatic and consular representatives to render "all proper assistance" to citizens who wished to trade in conditionally contraband articles.[35] This order had little practical effect because the British disreagarded consular protests as easily as Page's complaints, but it did demonstrate that attitudes within the State Department were hardening.

Further evidence of this stiffening emerged in a series of meetings between Lansing and Spring Rice during the second week of December. The counselor stated flatly that the United

33. Grey to Spring Rice, tel, 6 Dec 14, FO 368/1195. The characterization of British policy as "vigorous appeasement" in Marsden, "The Blockade," p. 494, is ludicrous in light of the Contraband Committee minutes and the reality of British seizures.

34. Page to Bryan, tel, 6 Dec 14, Savage, II, 235–238.

35. Bryan to diplomatic and consular officers, circular, 11 Dec 14, ibid., 238–239.

States would "never" admit that food shipped in a neutral bottom to the civilian population of a belligerent, much less to the civilian population of a neutral, could legally be seized as contraband. He suggested privately that the administration would not object to' a secret agreement between the British government and American exporters which would prevent suspicious shipments from being made, but demanded more "liberal" treatment for food shipments that were made. The president wished to maintain good relations with Britain because he believed it essential for his hopes to mediate an end to the war, but pressure from Congress and the public were forcing him to take a more vigorous position on maritime rights. Spring Rice concluded his series of reports on these conversations by predicting that "we may face serious crisis in our relations with this country."[36]

If a serious Anglo-American crisis was impending, few in London were inclined to make any effort to avoid it. The minutes of the Contraband Committee for December 14 epitomize this no-compromise attitude: "The Committee have decided to detain this [Norwegian] vessel pending enquiries though they realize that they have no legal justification for doing so. . . . The Committee omit to inform the Norwegian Minister in this instance as they are at a loss to know what to tell him."[37] Four days later the same committee ordered another neutral ship carrying food to Denmark detained, although it admitted that there existed "no power under the Order in Council to put the consignment in the Prize Court."[38] The Admiralty ordered that neutral ships refusing to cooperate voluntarily with the contraband control authorities be treated with extraordinary harshness even when innocent, in an effort to encourage voluntary cooperation on future voyages.[39] Grey, despite repeated and explicit promises to Page, ordered all items on the absolute contraband list held "for as long as we can" even when there was "no very strong evidence for use

36. Spring Rice to Grey, tels, 6, 8, 10 Dec 14, FO 368/1162; Spring Rice to Grey, 11 Dec 14, FO 800/84.
37. Contraband Committee, minutes, 14 Dec 14, FO 368/1195.
38. Contraband Committee, minutes, 18 Dec 14, ibid.
39. Adm to Jellicoe, 11 Dec 14, Adm 137/977; presumably this is another example of Marsden's "appeasement" by Britain.

in the Prize Court."[40] Military expediency had been a dominant factor in the development of the blockade since the outbreak of the war. By December it seemed to be the only factor.

Public pressure on the Wilson administration continued to mount. On December 16 the lawyers for a group of injured American exporters told Spring Rice that because the British government and the State Department appeared to be unwilling to respect the established legal rights of American citizens on the high seas, the shippers had decided to appeal to Congress for direct retaliation against Britain.[41] The State Department solicitor, Cone Johnson, agreed that the administration had failed in its legal obligation to protect its citizens. The policy of having Page seek case-by-case redress in private talks with Grey obviously had failed. Johnson proposed to "drop a flea into the ear" of Sir Edward Grey and to commend to the attention of Walter Hines Page the words of Thomas Jefferson in 1793: "Great Britain might indeed feel the desire of starving an enemy nation; but she can have no right of doing it at our loss, nor of making us the instrument of it."[42]

On December 16 Johnson submitted the draft of a protest note to Lansing. Its tone was friendly, and it contained no overt threat. But it described the situation in regard to the blockade as "critical." If Britain did not cease its flagrantly illegal acts and return to the established standards of international law, the United States, however reluctantly, would have no alternative but to consider "resistance."[43]

The counselor revised Johnson's draft slightly, then forwarded it to Bryan with a favorable recommendation. His covering letter emphasized that American exporters already had complained of the State Department's failure to act effectively on their behalf. If the administration did not act soon, congressional and

40. Grey, 19 Dec 14, quoted in Leverton Harris, "Copper for Switzerland," 26 Feb 15, CAB 37/124/53. More "appeasement"?

41. Spring Rice to Grey, 16 Dec 14, FO 368/1162.

42. Johnson to Lansing, 14 Dec 14, SD(M)M-367/190; Johnson to Lansing, 21 Dec 14, ibid./149.

43. Johnson, "Draft of a Proposed Instruction to the American Ambassador at London," 16 Dec 14, SD 763.72112/545A.

popular outrage might take the opportunity for rational and appropriate action away from the executive and plunge into a confrontation with the most dire consequences. To present Johnson's protest would not only emphasize the strength of American feelings on the issue to London, but might "avoid serious criticism" of the administration at home. Lansing warned that an anti-British tide of opinion was growing. In his opinion the administration now faced a choice between running with this tide, in an attempt to direct it, or resisting the tide at the risk of being swept away by it.[44]

Bryan, who had only the barest understanding of the maritime issues but a strong political sense, forwarded the draft note to the president on December 17.[45] That evening, for the first time since September 27, Wilson found a general protest against the British blockade on his desk. In the earlier instance House had persuaded him that informal talks offered a better solution than a formal diplomatic protest. That strategy had been tried, in various forms, for almost three months. The solicitor, counselor, and secretary of state now joined in advising that it had failed and that the situation was in fact worse than it had been in September. The State Department recommended a formal protest, which it considered essential for commercial, diplomatic, and political reasons.

Colonel House, however, was not yet ready to admit that his advice had been wrong. He persuaded the president to return the draft to the State Department for the purpose of having the technical legal language replaced by "good and understandable English." House then made a last attempt at informal accommodation. Might not something, he asked almost apologetically of Spring Rice, be done to appease American public opinion?[46] Grey offered no hope. The British government had no desire to quarrel with the United States, but military necessity precluded any substantive concession on the blockade.[47]

44. Lansing to Bryan, 16 Dec 14, SD(M)M-367/190.
45. Bryan to Wilson, 17 Dec 14, ibid.
46. House, diary entry, 18 Dec 14, House Papers; Spring Rice to Grey, tel, 19 Dec 14, FO 800/84.
47. Grey to Spring Rice, tel, 21 Dec 14, copy in House Papers, "Grey"; Spring Rice to Wilson, 21 Dec 14, W. Wilson Papers, (M)66.

This latest evidence of intransigence finally convinced the president that some formal protest was necessary. On December 26 he approved the State Department's revised draft, which was cabled to London that same day.[48] It asserted that the seizure of cargoes without proof of enemy destination, the inconsistency of British authorities and regulations, the treatment of both absolute and conditional contraband, and the detention of ships without prize court proceedings constituted violations of well-established American rights. Britain's treatment of food was especially distressing because it contradicted the principles stated by Lord Salisbury in 1900. The United States did not object to enforcement of legitimate belligerent rights against its commerce, but it could not admit that British actions fell within any recognized definition of belligerent rights. Nevertheless, the United States retained its confidence in "the deep sense of justice of the British nation." The note concluded with an expression of hope that the British government, despite the passions and demands of war, would henceforth "conform more closely to those rules governing the maritime relations between belligerents and neutrals, which have received the sanction of the civilized world, and which Great Britain has, in other wars, so strongly and successfully advocated."[49]

The American protest of December 26 was mild and in places amost apologetic in tone. It was pathetically weak when compared to the protests Hay had dispatched to London and St. Petersburg in response to far less serious assaults on neutral rights in 1900 and 1904. Not surprisingly, Wilson's note won no concessions from the British government. It was, in fact, not even taken seriously in London.

British statemen who commented on the American protest expressed little but disdain and contempt for its authors and their motives. Spring Rice reported that the "message is for consumption of Congress, German vote and commercial interests affected," and did not represent the real view of the administration.[50] Hopwood complained that "this American business is a

---

48. Wilson to Bryan, 26 Dec 14, SD(M)M-367/190.
49. Bryan to Page, tel, 26 Dec 14, Savage, II, 240-244.
50. Spring Rice to Grey, tel, 29 Dec 14, FO 368/1162.

bore—Wilson's Cabinet is not in a particularly strong position and is 'window dressing' for the delectation of 'Parliament.'" He suggested that the easiest way to end the controversy would be to "give a good retainer to Senator O'Gorman" of New York.[51] Asquith considered the note a "nuisance." He admitted that the United States had "some technical points" of law in its favor, but did not see that law was relevant to a life and death struggle to save Western civilization. Wilson had acted only because his political "position becomes daily more precarious," and he "dare not offend the powerful money interests."[52]

This evident disdain was the product, ironically, of Wilson's efforts to maintain a special Anglo-American relationship in private while maintaining an appearance of neutrality in public. The British were unable to understand why anyone who recognized the moral and strategic implications of the war, as the president claimed to do, could continue to raise obstacles that hindered employment of one of the Allies' most effective weapons. Spring Rice had reported that the president drew an analogy between present circumstances and the War of 1812,[53] but from Britain's perspective it only seemed to confirm the picture of a leader who would do anything to defend civilization except endanger his own reelection. A Wilson who shared the British view of the war and led the United States to accept the blockade would have been loved and respected in London. A Wilson who took a firm stand on the legal and historical roots of American neutrality would have been disliked but respected. But the Wilson who assured Spring Rice that everything he loved most in the world was riding on Allied victory, then asked for restrictions on a vital Allied weapon because he could not control his own legislature or public, did not appear to deserve either admiration or respect.

Despite these widespread feelings about Wilson and his administration, the British government acknowledged that it did have to return some answer to the protest of December 26. Grey, who had not asked for the Law Officers' opinion on the Orders in

---

51. Hopwood to Grey, 30, 31 Dec 14, FO 800/88.

52. Asquith to Stanley, 29 Dec 14, Stanley Papers; cf. Asquith to Stanley, 16 Jan 15, ibid.

53. E.g., Spring Rice to Grey, 1 Oct 14, FO 800/84.

Council or supplementary measures,[54] now sought Simon's advice on the best legal justification for a blockade the attorney general had opposed from its beginnings. Simon explained sardonically that there was no plausible legal case. The requirement that a neutral exporter prove the innocence of his goods "really is rather startling" and was not supported by "any authority." The rules on conditional contraband were "unnecessarily wide and harsh" and created the legal absurdity of making conditional contraband easier to condemn than absolute contraband. These principles might well be justifiable as a matter of expedient policy, as the cabinet had decided, but they certainly were not defensible under international law. The legal issues raised in the American note should be dodged as adroitly as possible because Britain's case would not stand even the most cursory examination.

Simon did offer one suggestion. The American note had stated that "commerce between countries which are not belligerents should not be interfered with by those at war unless such interference is manifestly an imperative necessity to protect their national safety." This passage, which was either grossly incompetent drafting or a loophole deliberately left open, offered Britain a way out of the legal embarrassment. The government could make this section of the American note "the basis of our defence," as it "in effect" admitted that "the traditions of international law may be properly modified to suit modern conditions, as long as belligerent necessity calls for such an adjustment." Simon advised Grey to state that all British actions were vital to national security, however violative of American rights and interests, and therefore must be accepted under the principle so wisely admitted by the United States.[55]

The foreign secretary made this recommendation the basis of his draft note, which he circulated to the cabinet and read to Page on January 2. Grey explained that Britain did not disagree with the American interpretation of international law stated in the note of December 26. But German aggression had forced the

54. Contrast the frequency of Law Officer reports on maritime rights questions in FO 834/19 (Boer War) and FO 834/21 (Russo-Japanese War) with the absence of such reports in FO 834/23 and 24 (1914–1915).
55. Simon, memo, n.d. [ca. 29 Dec 14], FO 800/89.

Allies to take extraordinary measures to defend themselves. The British government regretted this necessity, but could not avoid it. Fortunately, the United States recognized the right of a belligerent to take such action, so there could be no dispute in principle between the two nations. Britain remained willing to discuss any specific case in which Washington believed an American citizen had been treated unfairly and appreciated the friendly tone of the American note.[56]

Page described this response as "frank and friendly in tone and conciliatory in substance."[57] Lansing took a rather different view. He reported to the president that the tone of the British reply was indeed "conciliatory" and the argument "adroit," but the substance was unacceptable. Britain's case was "transparently illogical in many particulars to one familiar with the facts." The purpose of the note obviously was "allaying public irritation in this country without giving any assurance that trade conditions with neutral countries will be relieved." The counselor doubted that the note would achieve this purpose and recommended continued pressure until London made some substantive concessions.[58] Wilson took this advice under consideration, but made no immediate decision for or against further protests.

While the president pondered, the British government continued to expand its drive to block enemy imports. In doing so it continued to demonstrate its contempt for the American government and for the possibility of serious American opposition. On New Year's Day the commander of a British cruiser squadron recorded that one of his captains had made a "sad mistake," hoisting the Royal Navy's White Ensign over the American flag as he brought a diverted ship into port. The admiral noted that "the Yankees will fume" at having one of their ships treated like a defeated enemy, but he did not seem overly distressed at the prospect.[59] Board of Trade President Walter Runciman discovered that so many neutral ships were being detained in British ports that the Allies could not charter enough to meet their own

56. Draft note, 2 Jan 15, CAB 37/124/57; Page to Bryan, tel, 2 Jan 15, SD(M)M-367/190.

57. Page to Bryan, tels, 2, 7, 8 Jan 15, SD(M)M.367/190 and 191.

58. Lansing to Wilson, 11 Jan 15, ibid./191.

59. Admiral D. de Chair, diary entry, 1 Jan 15, de Chair Papers, P/38.

needs. His solution, illegal but effective, was to release those ships whose owners would agree to accept British charters but continue to hold those whose owners refused.[60] Eyre Crowe wrote on January 11 that the Wilson administration was so weak it could not carry out a meaningful program of opposition to the blockade even in the unlikely event it could make a decision to resist. He advised that London waste no more time considering Washington's complaints, but simply move ahead to tighten the blockade wherever possible.[61] Each of these incidents, and many others like them, demonstrates not only the failure of Wilson's efforts to maintain neutrality but also the contempt that failure inspired in Britain.

The full measure of the president's failure became apparent on January 21, when Spring Rice presented Bryan with the most insolent communication a British diplomat had addressed to the American government since the days when "Copenhagen" Jackson had plagued James Madison. The note accused the United States of being dominated by "a body of men linked together by joint sympathies of blood and lineage," determined "to compass by any and every means the success in Europe of the German cause." The pro-German attitude of these so-called Americans had convinced many Englishmen that the United States was "not neutral but hostile." Unless the United States acted to curb the unneutral activities of its citizens, British resentment of this aid to the enemy would poison Anglo-American relations "beyond our generation."[62] Spring Rice's lecture on the requirements of neutrality provides an ironic but appropriate counterpoint to Wilson's effort to win British trust by tilting American neutrality to favor the Allies.

Any evaluation of American neutrality during the first six months of World War I must begin with the recognition that the Wilson administration permitted, and in some cases encouraged, systematic British violation of American neutral rights on a scale unprecedented at the height of the Napoleonic Wars. Wilson,

---

60. Grey to Simon, 8 Jan 15, and Simon to Grey, n.d., FO 800/89.

61. Crowe, 11 Jan 15, minute on Spring Rice to Grey, tel, 7 Jan 15, FO 372/785; Crowe, 31 Jan 15, minute on Spring Rice to Grey, tel, 30 Jan 15, FO 382/184.

62. Spring Rice to Bryan, 21 Jan 15, CAB 37/124/15.

who possessed every advantage in his dealings with the British government, had given away the very neutral rights which Washington, Adams, Jefferson, and Madison had refused to yield, at gunpoint. The American response to the blockade was not neutrality, as Arthur Link argues, or "benevolent neutrality," as Ernest May argues.[63] It was simple unneutrality.

During the first month of war, the British government had repudiated the Declaration of London. It had every right to do so because it was under no legal obligation to abide by an unratified agreement. But London had subsequently enforced belligerent rights admittedly unrecognized under customary maritime law with the justification that those rights were recognized in the declaration. Wilson had first offered to accept the declaration's definition as a substitute for that of existing law and then, when the British government rejected this compromise, had stated that the United States would recognize only those belligerent rights sanctioned by existing law. When the British rejected this principle also and enforced belligerent rights from both legal systems while recognizing none of the safeguards each provided for neutrals, the only American response was the case-by-case importunings of Page and the equally impotent protest note of December 26.

This failure to hold the British maritime system within some recognized legal system paralleled a failure to maintain specific doctrines of maritime law traditionally upheld by the United States. In five broad areas, British measures constituted substantial departures from existing Anglo-Amercan prize law. In none of these areas had the Wilson administration taken effective action by the end of January 1915 to assert American rights or interests.

During the first six months of war, British authorities had systematically eroded the distinciton between absolute and conditional contraband. In most cases the contraband control officials made no effort to prove that a particular cargo was destined for enemy military use, and indeed they sometimes disregarded con-

---

63. Link, *Wilson*, III, 127 and *passim;* Arthur Link, "Wilson and the Ordeal of Neutrality," in Link, ed., *The Higher Realism of Woodrow Wilson* (Nashville: Vanderbilt University Press, 1971), p. 91; May, *World War*, pp. 34–53.

clusive evidence that a cargo was desined for use by neutral civilians. In 1904 John Hay had lectured the Russian government: "The established principle of discrimination between contraband and noncontraband goods admits of no relaxation or refinement. It must be either inflexibly adhered to or abandoned by all nations. There is and can be no middle ground. The criterion of warlike usefulness and destination has been adopted by the common consent of civilized nations." The secretary of state had concluded with the warning that the United States could never recognize as a principle or accept as a policy belligerent seizure of goods as contraband unless the captor could prove military destination.[64] Ten years later Wilson proved this statement wrong. For two months his administration ignored British violations of the military usage rule far more extensive than Russia's 1904 violations. It then tried for another three months to negotiate an informal compromise before finally delivering a protest so weak that it inspired contempt rather than respect.

The British government had added raw materials such as iron ore and copper to the absolute contraband list, contrary to both the Declaration of London and customary Anglo-American law. Ores and metals were on the free list of the declaration and thus could not be declared contraband of either sort under that agreement. They might be declared conditional contraband under existing law, but capture could be justified only when the captor could prove destination to the enemy armed forces. The British, by their own admission, were never able to provide this proof during World War I. They seized the metals anyway, with only pro forma objections from Washington.

The British government had declared food to be conditional contraband. It had then, on the basis of unfounded rumors that the German government had assumed control of food stocks, seized both direct and indirect food shipments to Germany on grounds that they would become the property of the German government and thus were good prize under the Declaration of London. The British continued to seize food shipments after they had formally repudiated the declaration and after they had re-

64. Hay to Mc Cormick, 30 Aug 04, FRUS, 1904, pp. 760–762. See above, Chapter 2 at n. 95.

ceived incontrovertible evidence that German food imports did not come under government control. Again, Washington did nothing.

The British government also had claimed the right to seize as contraband any cargo on either contraband list for which a neutral state of destination would not provide a guarantee against either reexport to Germany or export of an equivalent domestically produced product. This rule violated the sovereignty of the importing neutral, which was blackmailed into not selling its domestic products to Britain's enemy. It violated the right of the neutral exporter to maintain his trade with another neutral state. These actions could be justified under neither the Declaration of London nor customary maritime law. Yet Washington not only failed to protest against this naked coercion of friendly neutral governments and United States citizens, but actually encouraged the practice.[65]

The administration's record in the second broad area of conflict between British policies and neutral rights, the nature of the evidence that would justify seizure of a neutral ship by a belligerent, was as unneutral as its record in regard to contraband. The British government claimed and enforced the right to seize neutral ships on mere suspicion. It then required the owners of the ship and cargo to prove their innocence, at their own expense, to the satisfaction of British contraband control authorities. The penalty for failure to establish innocence ranged from continued detention at enormous expense to outright confiscation. This rule of "presumed guilty until you prove yourself innocent" was contrary to every principle of Anglo-Saxon jurisprudence, to the Declaration of London, to customary international law, and to the sovereign rights of neutral citizens and states. Britain had been ready to go to war rather than submit to enforcement of a more limited version of this rule by Russia in 1904.[66] When Britain applied the principle to American trade by *force majeure* on a far more extensive scale a decade later, Wilson made only the mildest protest.

65. E.g., Lansing's 28 Sep 14 comments to Spring Rice, Chapter 9, following n. 28.
66. See Chapter 2 at n. 86.

The administration was only slightly more active in a third area of concern, that of visit and search. The British government claimed and enforced a belligerent right to divert neutral ships found on the high seas into British ports, where they would be searched at the convenience of British officials and often held for prolonged periods without prize court proceedings. This practice violated both the Declaration of London and customary international law. It violated most grievously the rule of law defined by Britain's own Law Officers in 1899 and 1904. The British government had threatened war when Russia attempted to enforce a version of this rule less offensive to neutral rights in 1904.[67] Wilson's response in 1914 was to have Ambassador Page ask the Foreign Office for relief in individual cases. This action won the release of few American ships or cargoes and certainly did nothing to challenge a flagrantly illegal practice.

In a fourth area, the doctrine of continuous voyage, British practice also went far beyond either the Declaration of London or established international law. The system of controls Britain established over Dutch, Danish, Swedish, and Norwegian imports was deliberately designed to keep those neutrals so short of food, raw materials, and other products that they would have no surplus for export to Germany.[68] This application of continuous voyage was illegal under both the Declaration of London and customary law. It violated the sovereignty of the affected European neutrals, as well as that of the United States. Wilson accepted this illegal system with hardly a whimper.

The American government also accepted the British proclamation of November 3, 1914, which declared the North Sea a war zone. Neutral ships that failed to call at a British port for sailing instructions—and not incidentally a thorough and likely prolonged inspection by contraband control officials—risked destruc-

---

67. Ibid. The U.S. navy and the French government both considered the British detention policy unacceptable, and Runciman, normally among the strongest cabinet supporters of the blockade, admitted privately that the delays sometimes were capricious and unreasonable. See General Board to secretary of the navy, 3 Mar 15, General Board Papers, serial #338; Jessup, *Neutrality*, III, 39; Runciman to Grey, 16 Jan 15, FO 800/89.
68. CID, Historical Section, "Report on the Opening of the War," 1 Nov 14, CAB 17/102B.

tion by British mines. By sowing mines in international waters, Britain deliberately replaced the belligerent right of visit and search in the North Sea with a new rule: explode and sink. This action, which threatened to send American ships, seamen, and cargoes to the bottom simply for exercising their basic right to sail the high seas, was a direct contradiction of the principle of freedom of the seas. Wilson ignored it.

By the end of January 1915, the British government was systematically violating every rule of international law which it believed might hinder its campaign against German imports. Only the Declaration of Paris remained in theory, although British seizure of conditional contraband under the neutral flag without evidence of enemy military destination constituted de facto violation of that agreement. Yet the United States, traditionally a strong advocate of neutral rights, had offered no meaningful resistance and only the most apologetic, pro forma protest.

Why had the American government refused to act? George Washington had accepted the humiliation of Jay's Treaty because Britain possessed overwhelming naval and economic superiority in 1794. But Thomas Jefferson, who also had accepted maritime humiliation rather than challenge British power in war, wrote in 1801 that the day was coming "when we may say by what laws other nations shall treat us on the sea."[69] By 1914 that day clearly had arrived. Had Wilson chosen war to defend American rights, as Wambaugh advised he was legally entitled to do, Britain would have been almost helpless. With the Royal Navy already strained by the need to contain Germany's High Seas Fleet, British trade routes and overseas possessions would have been at the mercy of American naval forces. Page's predictions that Britain would go to war with the United States rather than make substantive concessions on the blockade[70] ignored one fact the British government could not afford to ignore: that a Britain strained to the limit by its conflict with Germany had essentially nothing left with which to fight the United States.

Less drastic remedies also were available to the American gov-

69. Quoted in Gardner et al., *Creation of the American Empire*, p. 65.
70. E.g., Page to Wilson and Bryan, tel, 15 Oct 14, Savage, II, 213–215; Page to Wilson, 21 Oct 14, W. Wilson Papers, (M)64.

ernment in 1914. Wilson could have ordered warships to escort American merchantmen, as John Adams had done in 1798. Grey admitted after the war that he had feared neutral convoy more than any other form of American resistance.[71] The president could have ordered a British merchant vessel or cargo detained in an American port for each American ship or cargo detained by Britain. He could have followed the example of Jefferson and Madison and relied on economic pressure to bring the British government to heel. A partial embargo would have hurt the Allies severely; a total denial of access to American resources almost certainly would have cost them the war. Grey wrote later that his guideline from 1914 to 1916 had been "to secure the maximum of blockade that could be enforced without a rupture with the United States."[72] Even Churchill, the most militant of the militant proponents of economic warfare, admitted that a choice between weakening the blockade and active American hostility was really no choice at all.[73] The British government was prepared to back down at the first concrete evidence of American resistance. Yet during six months of systematic violation of American neutral rights Wilson never used, or made a convincing threat that he would use, American power to force substantive British concessions.

Historians have offered varied explanations for this failure to resist the blockade. The most commonly held modern views emphasize that British actions never presented a direct challenge to American rights and interests. Arthur Link has argued that the British maritime system was "based soundly upon international law" and that American resistance therefore would have constituted an unneutral failure to recognize established belligerent rights.[74] Ernest May maintains that "the conciliatory policy of the

71. Grey, *Twenty-Five Years,* II, 115–116; cf. Hankey, "Blockade and the Laws of War," 31 Oct 27, and Richmond, "A Note on 'Freedom of the Seas à l'Americaine'," n.d., Richmond Papers, 13/6.

72. Grey, *Twenty-Five Years,* II, 107.

73. Churchill to Grey, 27 Oct 14, FO 800/94.

74. Link, *Wilson,* III, 127 and passim. Marsden, "The Blockade," p. 494, goes further and asserts that Wilson did force significant restriction of established belligerent rights: "The Americans were quite ready to deny Britain belligerent rights which they had claimed for themselves in the past, especially during the Civil War." He then cites the "rights" to detain and search neutral ships in port

British government," reflected in "the fact that Britain did so little damage to American interests," induced Wilson "to view legal differences as technicalities, to trust in British morality, and to evade public controversy."[75] Neither of these interpretations is sustainable in light of the evidence now available. The blockade was flagrantly illegal, as Asquith and several other British leaders acknowledged privately. The British government attempted to maintain an appearance of conciliation in its dealings with Washington, but was adamantly nonconciliatory on matters of substance. Protests from Americans injured by the blockade fill box after box in the State Department archives.

The president ultimately refused to challenge the British economic campaign because the shadow of 1812 haunted him. He believed that Germany represented a threat to Western civilization and that the Allies were defending the United States as well as themselves against that threat. The greatest danger, in Wilson's view, was that an unsophisticated American public, aroused by legalistic arguments over maritime rights but unaware of the far greater threat posed by German aggressiveness, would repeat its error of a century before and force an unjustifiable conflict with Britain. The primary factor shaping Wilson's response to the blockade was his determination that no Anglo-American differences be allowed to recreate the chain of events he believed had forced an unwilling Madison into a war in which the United States unwittingly fought on the side of tyranny against that of civilization.

A secondary factor, also vital to an understanding of American neutrality policy, was the president's hope of playing a major role in restructuring the world and the basic patterns of international relations at war's end. The complex history of Wilson's mediation efforts would require a volume of their own.[76] But the

---

without prize court proceedings, to demand coercive guarantees against reexport from neutral governments, and several other British World War I practices which the United States had never claimed or attempted to enforce during the Civil War or at any other time in its history.

75. May, *World War,* pp. 66, 305, and passim; cf. the similar view expressed in Cooper, *Page,* p. 281.

76. There is no satisfactory general study of Wilson's mediation efforts, but see May, *World War,* pp. 79–89; Devlin, *Too Proud,* pp. 217–282; Smith, *Great Departure,* pp. 67–74; and C. M. Mason, "Anglo-American Relations: Mediation and 'Permanent Peace'," Hinsley, ed., *British Foreign Policy,* pp. 466–487.

key for American neutrality was that Wilson regarded the active cooperation of the British government as the first prerequisite for any successful mediation. He expected his greatest ally in the pursuit of a liberal, healing peace to be Sir Edward Grey. A confrontation over maritime rights would have placed the foreign secretary in an embarrassing position and perhaps have led to his replacement by someone less sympathetic to liberal goals. In this context, abstract neutral rights and a few cargoes of canned ham or copper appeared less important than preservation of Grey's power to speak for Britain in foreign policy to a president whose moral and religious outlook made him long for peace with every fiber of his being.[77]

Did Wilson then deliberately mislead an isolationist public with promises of neutrality, all the while pursuing a "realistic" policy of nonbelligerent aid to the Allies under the justification of national security and in hope of creating a better world? The evidence indicates that such was his effect but not his intent. The president saw no contradiction between his public promises of neutrality and his unneutral actions on maritime rights because he never admitted, in public, in private, or to himself, that those actions were in any way unneutral. He continued to believe that the blockade was substantially within the rules of international law, although admitting that there might be occasional technical variations from traditional American principles. He continued to believe that the blockade did little real harm to legitimate American commerce with Europe and that any problems which did arise were best dealt with privately on a case-by-case basis. He continued to believe that the British government in general and Sir Edward Grey in particular were honest and conciliatory, and that Grey was doing his best to lead Britain and its Allies to adopt liberal war aims. These beliefs were ludicrously wrong, but Wilson held to them tenaciously, despite overwhelming contrary evidence, because they fit so comfortably his perceptions of the war and his vision of the peace.

Ironically, the president's misunderstanding of Grey's character and policies contributed significantly to undermining his hopes both for quiet resolution of maritime rights differences and for a

77. There has been little scholarly attention to the Wilson-House efforts to influence British politics. The best source remains House's diary.

liberal peace. Far from being an advocate of healing peace terms, the foreign secretary led the anti-German faction in the cabinet and had done so for a decade. Although not as militant in rhetoric as Lloyd George or Churchill, Grey was the last member of the Government who would have accepted a peace not dictated in Berlin after decisive Allied victory. He continued to speak of Belgium and national honor after August 4, 1914, as he had done earlier. But this rhetoric should not be allowed to disguise his firm commitment to an "absolutely secure" Triple Entente and a European balance of power unfavorable to Germany. Because Russia and France were essential to the war effort and their terms could not be imposed on Germany without decisive victory, Alsace-Lorraine and Constantinople became as much sine qua non for Grey as restoration of Belgium, destruction of German sea power, or prevention of German hegemony. The London agreements of September 1914 and April 1915 were not forced on the foreign secretary, but negotiated by him.[78] It was ironic, but characteristic, that Wilson should choose as his ally in the destruction of the old balance of power diplomacy Britain's strongest advocate and most skilled practitioner of the balance of power since Lord Palmerston.

The president's vision of Grey in relation to British maritime rights policy was equally unrealistic. There was a group in the cabinet that favored a conciliatory policy. Simon took such a position consistently and at various times found support from Asquith, Haldane, and other ministers. Grey, on the other hand, had been directly responsible for the objectionable aspects of the Order in Council of August 20. He had been the strongest proponent of the expanded campaign against raw materials in September and October. While Lloyd George and Churchill made angry speeches about the need to "blockade" Germany and most of neutral Europe, the foreign secretary devised the means to translate this rhetoric into reality. More than any other minister, the man Wilson trusted to be conciliatory and honest was responsible for the British failure to make substantive concessions to the United States during the first six months of war.

78. Michael G. Ekstein, "Russia, Constantinople and the Straits, 1914–1915," Hinsley, ed., *British Foreign Policy*, pp. 423–435, is particularly effective in illuminating how Grey's concept of a European balance of power shaped his wartime diplomacy.

There were people in the British government, and even in the cabinet, in 1914, who would have been willing to make concessions to the American position on the blockade and to work for a liberal peace. But by failing to resist violations of neutral rights, Wilson undercut the very people who would have helped him and encouraged those who would not. As long as the United States remained satisfied with Grey's conciliatory appearance, the British government had no reason to provide substance to support that appearance. Rarely if ever has an American president based so vital a policy on so complete a misunderstanding of a foreign nation and leader. Wilson saw in Grey what he wished to see, another in his long series of self-deceptions concerning the war and the blockade.

At the heart of this tenacious refusal to recognize reality was the president's system for receiving and acting upon information concerning the war. Reports reached the White House already filtered through pro-British advisers such as Page, Lansing, and House. Wilson then interpreted this slanted evidence in the light of his own pro-Allied prejudices. He would believe and act on the most absurd stories of Germany hostility, as when in November 1914 he instructed his his intelligence services to investigate his suspicion that German agents were building "concrete foundations for great guns" disguised as tennis courts in the United States in preparation for an invasion.[79] Yet a few days after reading the evidence of blatant British violations of American neutrality contained in the Scott-Lansing note, Wilson assured Spring Rice that "it is a real source of comfort and reassurance to me that this serious matter is in the hands of real friends on both sides." The American press would try to "make a solution difficult and as embarrassing as possible, . . . but that need not daunt us, for we mean to do the right and wise thing."[80] The "right and wise thing" in Wilson's view was to give Britain the benefit of every possible doubt, while viewing each German action with hostility and suspicion.

Against this background, it is not difficult to understand how Wilson could continue to believe what he desperately wanted to believe: that the British blockade and the administration response

79. House, diary entry, 4 Nov 14, House Papers.
80. Spring Rice to Grey, tel, 1 Oct 14, FO 372/601.

to it did not violate American neutrality. Those in the press and elsewhere who argued the contrary were only trying to "make a solution difficult" and to embarrass the administration for their own unworthy purposes. Those like Lansing who urged a direct challenge to the blockade on legal grounds were confusing true neutrality with legalistic technicalities. The entire maritime rights controversy was to the president a misunderstanding among gentlemen, which they could settle with little difficulty if only troublemaking newsmen, hyphenated Americans, and publicity-seeking politicians did not interfere. Convinced of the accuracy of this view and of his own moral superiority, Wilson simply believed that he could define true neutrality better than lawyers and textbooks.

Once this intellectual foundation is understood, the other elements of American policy fall into place. The concessions Wilson sought from Britain were matters of form, not of substance. His effort to secure general adoption of the Declaration of London was intended to pacify the American press and public, not to safeguard neutral commerce. Administration protest notes to London served a similar purpose and also alerted Grey to potentially irritating British actions. Page's case-by-case discussions with the foreign secretary gave an appearance of support to shippers and producers injured by the blockade and thereby discouraged the groups with specific, documentable grievances from resorting to public anti-British and antiadministration agitation. The talks also increased Grey's prestige and influence within his own government, allowing the foreign secretary to point to his success in securing American acceptance of the blockade. The situation at the end of January 1915 seemed to indicate that Wilson had reached an effective equilibrium. The blockade was being tightened steadily and Grey's prestige had never seemed higher, but press and public agitation against Britain remained a relatively minor factor in the United States.

✿

CHAPTER ELEVEN

The German Submarine Campaign, the British Blockade, and the United States, February to April 1915

On February 4, 1915, the Imperial German Government announced that "beginning on February 18th, 1915 it will endeavour to destroy every enemy merchant ship that is found" within a war zone including "all the waters surrounding Great Britain." This campaign was to be conducted primarily by submarines and admittedly would not be in accordance with the rules of cruiser warfare in existing international law. In addition, because Allied shipping often flew neutral flags as a *ruse de guerre*, the German proclamation acknowledged the possibility that a submarine might sink a neutral merchantman in the mistaken belief that it was an enemy hiding under the neutral flag. Germany regretted, but could not promise to avoid, such flagrant violations of neutral rights. Nevertheless, Britain had pleaded its "vital interests" to justify violation of established maritime law, and "the neutral powers seem to satisfy themselves with theoretical protest." The German government expected all true neutrals to accept the submarine with the same attitude.[1]

Six days later, on February 10, William Jennings Bryan instructed the American ambassador in Berlin to lodge an immediate protest. The note was signed by the secretary of state, but the words were those of President Wilson:

If the commanders of German vessels of war should act upon the presumption that the flag of the United States was not being used

1. Germany, Foreign Ministry, memo, 4 Feb 15, Savage, II, 265-267.

in good faith and should destroy on the high seas an American vessel or the lives of American citizens, it would be difficult for the Government of the United States to view the act in any other light than as an indefensible violation of neutral rights which it would be very hard indeed to reconcile with the friendly relations now so happily subsisting between the two governments.

If such a deplorable situation should arise, the Imperial German Government can readily appreciate that the Government of the United States would be constrained to hold the Imperial German Government to a strict accountability for such acts of their naval authorities and to take any steps it might be necessary to take to safeguard American lives and property and to secure to American citizens the full enjoyment of their acknowledged rights on the high seas.

In marked contrast to the apologetic tone of American notes to London during previous months, the "Strict Accountability" note had the unmistakable ring of an ultimatum.[2]

Unlike John Hay in 1904, Wilson had not waited for an overt act to protest. He had warned Berlin a week before the campaign was to begin that the United States would not tolerate illegal submarine attacks on American ships or on Allied ships carrying American citizens or their property. There would be no informal negotiations and no case-by-case discussions. "Any steps it might be necessary to take" would be taken to guarantee American citizens "the full enjoyment of their acknowledged rights on the high seas" against deliberate or accidental German violations.

Wilson's anger was in ironic contrast with the glee the submarine announcement provoked in London. Churchill saw it as evidence that Allied economic warfare was hurting Germany and as an excuse for further restrictions. He openly hoped that American ships would be sunk, thus bringing the United States into the war on the Allied side.[3] The Royal Navy had no fear of the tiny number of submarines the enemy could deploy against the enormous British merchant marine.[4] Haldane's view was typical: "The submarine business is annoying but that is all."[5] The general perception was that the first lord was correct in seeing the

2. Bryan to Gerard, tel, 10 Feb 15, ibid., 267–269.

3. Asquith to Stanley, 28 Jan 15, Stanley Papers; Asquith to George V, cabinet letter, 3 Feb 15, CAB 41/36/3; Churchill to Runciman, 12 Feb 15, Runciman Papers, 301.

4. Marder, *From the Dreadnought,* II, 345.

5. Haldane to M. Haldane, 2 Feb 15, Haldane Papers, MS 5993.

German announcement as an opportunity rather than a threat to the Allies.

The question for the British government in February 1915 was not whether to retaliate, but how. Churchill proposed explicit repudiation of the Declaration of Paris, including the "free ship, free goods" principle. Asquith considered this suggestion too risky, especially if applied to American cotton exports, but could not convince his colleagues. On February 10 the cabinet approved in principle a retaliatory declaration authorizing seizure of any ship or cargo "of presumed enemy destination, ownership, or origin." In essence it made all neutral trade with Germany, contraband or noncontraband, import or export, direct or through European neutrals, subject to confiscation by the Allies.[6]

This action shocked the French government. Although Paris had pressed for tighter restrictions on enemy trade since the outbreak of war, the French considered the plan to seize "American ships carrying non-contraband cargo to Germany and to neighbouring neutral ports, without proclaiming any blockade" so blatantly illegal that it was sure to provoke "the most extreme protest" from the United States.[7] Asquith agreed and continued to press for less restrictive measures. For the first time Grey sided with the prime minister, warning that "the proposed reprisals being obviously more injurious to neutral commerce & interests than the more or less illusory German threat," the United States "very likely" would begin convoying its merchantmen with warships. Despite the foreign secretary's defection, however, Churchill, Lloyd George, and McKenna retained the support of the cabinet majority. On February 16 a "unanimous" cabinet decided to go ahead with the reprisals despite the admitted risk, but to pass without interference merchant ships escorted by American warships.[8] Two days later the Government made the final decision to proceed with an all-out campaign of economic strangulation.[9] The British

6. Asquith to George V, cabinet letters, 3, 10 Feb 15, CAB 41/36/3 and 4; Asquith to Stanley, 6, 10 Feb 15, Stanley Papers; Churchill, memo, 6 Feb 15, revised 10 Feb 15, CAB 37/124/21.

7. Crowe, memo, 13 Feb 15, FO 382/185.

8. Asquith to George V, cabinet letter, 17 Feb 15, CAB 41/36/6; Hobhouse, diary entry, 16 Feb 15, David, ed., *Inside Asquith's Cabinet*, p. 222.

9. Asquith to George V, cabinet letter, 19 Feb 15, CAB 41/36/6; Asquith to Stanley, 18 Feb 15, Stanley Papers; "Reprisals against Germany, Draft Declaration," n.d., CAB 37/124/49.

recognized that they were bluffing and that the new policy would have to be modified or abandoned altogether if the United States resisted. But the potential for victory through economic warfare seemed sufficient to justify taking that risk.

Grey conveyed the outlines of this decision to Page on February 19. He expressed regret that measures so restrictive of neutral commerce were necessary, but argued that the barbarous submarine campaign of the enemy left Britain no choice. Under the circumstances, the British government "confidently expect that such action will not be challenged on the part of neutral States by appeals to laws and usages of war whose validity rests on their forming an integral part of that system of international doctrine which as a whole their enemy frankly boasts the liberty and intention to disregard."[10] Asquith used essentially the same justification in announcing the reprisals to the House of Commons on March 1: "The words 'blockade' and 'contraband,' and other technical terms of international law, do not occur, and advisedly so. In dealing with an opponent who has openly repudiated all the principles, both of law and of humanity, we are not going to allow our efforts to be strangled in a network of juridical niceties."[11] Germany had cited British violations of international law to justify the submarine campaign, which Britain then cited to justify more extensive violations of its own.

To the limited degree that the belligerents attempted to provide serious legal justification for their new measures against neutral commerce, they cited the doctrine of retaliation. This doctrine, which had existed for centuries on the fringes of international law without winning general acceptance, permitted a belligerent to respond to extraordinary enemy provocation with extraordinary measures of its own directed against the enemy. The most common use had been in response to violations of the laws of war, as when Britain in 1814 had justified the burning of public buildings in Washington as retaliation for American burning of Canadian public buildings earlier in the War of 1812. Only in rare cases had a belligerent attempted to strike at his enemy by extend-

10. Grey to Page, 19 Feb 15, FO 382/184.
11. Asquith, House of Commons speech, 1 Mar 15, Great Britain, 5 *Parliamentary Debates* (Commons), LXX (1915), 600.

ing the doctrine to cover actions against a neutral trading with the enemy. In the most notable instance, the British and French seizures of neutral ships trading with their respective enemies at the height of the Napoleonic Wars, the United States had refused to accept the principle, had resisted the actions of both nations by economic reprisals, and finally had gone to war with Britain. The Treaty of Ghent had been silent on the the subject, but subsequent belligerents had shown no eagerness to adopt the Anglo-French position. Even Russia in 1904, despite the provocation of Japan's flagrantly illegal sneak attack on Port Arthur, had not dared to cite retaliation as justifying interference with noncontraband neutral trade with its enemy. But in February 1915 both Britain and Germany were clinging to the doctrine as the only possible fig leaf of legal respectability for the submarine and surface blockades. Wilson already had warned Germany that the United States would not accept this argument.[12]

The British government, after announcing its reprisals policy, waited with a sort of bored resignation for the expected protest from Washington. Spring Rice had pictured the Wilson administration as drifting aimlessly, without strength or leadership. He warned that this combination of a weak executive with a volatile Congress and public was explosive and could thrust the United States into a crisis at any time. He urged his superiors to "strain a point against ourselves when necessary" rather than risk an Anglo-American confrontation that might easily escape the control of either London or Washington.[13] The cabinet had disregarded this advice by adopting the retaliatory measures announced on March 1. When Spring Rice proposed informal

12. Devlin, *Too Proud*, pp. 161–164 and passim argues that retaliation was a legitimate, if controversial, legal doctrine which did provide a reasonable justification for the Order in Council of 11 Mar 15. He admits, however, that the British government in 1915 did not consider that position sufficiently strong to justify making the doctrine the basis for British explanations to the United States. Devlin's statement that "at the start in 1914 Britain and Germany both adopted the belligerent doctrine" (p. 163) is not correct in regard to maritime rights. The British did not cite retaliation to justify interference with neutral commerce until March 1915, seven months after the outbreak of war. Until that point the campaign against German imports had been conducted, at least nominally, entirely under the doctrine of contraband.

13. E.g., Spring Rice to Grey, 12 Feb 15, FO 800/241.

negotiations to ease American acceptance of the new regulations, Crowe spoke for many when he minuted that the ambassador "has invariably shown himself more alarmed than subsequent events justified." Britain had no need to seek "any agreement with the State Department at all." The proper policy was to inform the American government "very fully exactly what we propose to do, and to use every argument to show the reasonableness of our action." There was no room for discussion, but only for explanation of decisions already made in London.[14]

During February and March British leaders seemed to demonstrate an almost willful disregard for the realities of American power. Esher and Bertie agreed that "there is no fear of the Americans breaking with us if we are firm and conciliatory; we should yield nothing." Esher noted confidently that "100 years ago the United States went to war with us, and yet the war went on not unsuccessfully to its ending at Waterloo."[15] Lloyd George, as chancellor of the exchequer, knew precisely how dependent the Allies were on American money, munitions, food, and other vital supplies,[16] yet adamantly opposed any concessions on the blockade to win American confidence. Only Asquith, Simon, Grey, and Crewe seemed to appreciate the reality of American power or the risk Britain ran by challenging it. The rest of the cabinet was willing to yield only if the alternative was an exchange of gunfire between British and American warships.

London's adamant attitude left Washington as essentially the sole determinant of how dangerous the Anglo-American dispute over maritime rights became. Grey could continue to play a conciliatory role by his presentation of the new measures and his manipulation of American leaders. But his colleagues had left him no room for substantive concessions. For six months Wilson had sought to avoid a confrontation between the blockade and American neutrality, which he feared would turn public opinion against the Allies and recreate the pressures that had forced Madison to fight in 1812. The administration had bent and even

14. Spring Rice to Grey, tel, 2 Mar 15, with minutes by Crowe and Grey, 3 Mar 15, FO 382/185.
15. Esher, diary entry, 5 Mar 15, Esher Papers, 2/14.
16. E.g., Lloyd George to Balfour, 6 Mar 15, Balfour Papers, AM 49692; C. P. Scott, diary entry, 15 Mar 15, Scott Papers, AM 50901.

broken international law to assure itself and the American people that British actions somehow did not really violate neutral rights. Now the British prime minister had stated publicly that his government regarded neutral rights as "juridical niceties" deserving no further attention from the Allies. Even such dedicated Anglophiles as Robert Lansing and James Brown Scott believed that Wilson, in the wake of his "Strict Accountability" stand against Germany, could no longer postpone a confrontation with the British blockade.

The president's advisers offered several policy options. Page, who already had assured Grey that the "obvious necessity" of the British reprisals "would not give rise to any trouble with the United States,"[17] counseled continuation of the informal, case-by-case negotiations which he and Grey had been conducting since the end of September.

> In view of the decisive effect of the British reprisals which brings the war into its final stage, in view of the unparalleled power with which the British will be left when peace comes, and in view of this government's courteous regard for us and our rights, and in view of British public opinion which is more thoroughly aroused and more firmly united than ever before in English history, I most earnestly recommend the following:
>
> That we content ourselves for the present with a friendly inquiry how the proposed reprisal will be carried out and with giving renewed notice that we hold ourselves free to take up all cases of damage to our commerce and all unlawful acts on their merit as they occur. This will enable us to accomplish all that we can accomplish by any sort of note or protest.[18]

Colonel House, who was in London at the time hoping to prepare the way for peace discussions, took essentially the same position. Although he warned Grey that the administration would not be able to control American public opinion "if the Allies went too far," he continued to believe that public confrontation could be avoided by informal accommodation.[19] Neither House nor Page considered the British reprisals objectionable per se. The

17. Grey to Spring Rice, 1 Mar 15, FO 382/185.
18. Page to Bryan, tel, 3 Mar 15, SD(M)M-367/192. House claimed (diary entry, 4 Mar 15, House Papers) to have persuaded Page to cut out most of the "pro-British argument" before finally sending the text as quoted.
19. House, diary entry, 3 Mar 15, House Papers.

essence of their advice was that Wilson accept the new measures in fact, while giving his acceptance the best possible appearance for the sake of American public opinion.

James Brown Scott's Joint Neutrality Board took the diametrically opposed position. It argued that the actions Asquith had announced simply could not be tolerated by the United States. The economic interests of American citizens engaged in perfectly legitimate business demanded protection from their government, although such material considerations paled before the real issues at stake. The British reprisals constituted a direct assault on the very fabric of international law. The world's most powerful neutral had both a moral and a legal obligation to preserve "the public law of the world" against Britain's "lapse into barbarism." Scott warned that a normal diplomatic protest would be insufficient, given the magnitude of the offense. He advised that the United States tell Britain, as it already had told Germany, that violation of "certain broad principles" of law was simply unacceptable.[20]

A third American option emerged from a conversation between the secretary of state and German Ambassador Johann von Bernstorff on February 15. Bryan had raised the submarine issue, and his visitor had explained that Berlin regretted the necessity for such measures but could not allow its people to be starved by the Allied food blockade without striking back. The secretary expressed sympathy for those denied adquate nourishment by illegal Allied actions, but argued that the submarine campaign would create more problems for Germany than it solved. Might the German government withdraw the submarine decree, he asked, if the United States could persuade the Allies to stop interfering with food for German civilians? When Bernstorff replied that he believed his government would welcome such a compromise, Bryan requested and received the president's permission to submit this proposal to London.[21]

Wilson welcomed the suggestion of a maritime modus vivendi because it seemed to offer a convenient escape from the dilemma that the submarine, the food blockade, and the new British re-

20. Joint Neutrality Board to Lansing, memos, 3, 6 Mar 15, SD(M)M-367/173.
21. Bryan to Wilson, 15 Feb 15, ibid./191; Bryan to Wilson, 18 Feb 15, Bryan Papers, 66; Bryan to Page, tel, 19 Feb 15, SD(M)M-367/192.

prisals posed for American neutrality. When Page presented the proposal to the British government, however, he found London in no mood for compromise. Hurst wrote that he saw no reason to "purchase the safety of a few tramp steamers at the price of . . . prolongation of the war."[22] Slade and Hopwood, with Churchill's endorsement, denounced the proposal as "an unblushing attempt to assist our enemy." Why, they asked, should Britain abandon a weapon that might win the war while Germany gave up only a submarine campaign that in any case could do little harm to the Allies? If the American government wished a reason for Britain's rejection, it should be invited to ponder Gereral William T. Sherman's campaign in Georgia.[23] With the Admiralty expressing contempt for the submarine and with confidence in the food blockade rising in light of the new reprisals policy, the cabinet's decision was not difficult. Grey explained that he personally could see much merit in Bryan's suggestion, but the British people would never accept it.[24] Although negotiations dragged on for weeks, neither belligerent would accept terms its enemy would approve.[25]

The failure of compromise left Wilson the hard choice between Page's policy of accommodation and Scott's policy of confrontation. The president bought some time by sending what Asquith characterized as a "Pecksniffian American note" asking for details of the reprisals announced on March 1.[26] Britain's answer was formal publication of an Order in Council on March 11 giving legal form to the prime minister's speech. Grey's covering note acknowledged that the new regulations were not in accordance with customary international law, but justified them as appropriate retaliation for illegal German submarine attacks. On Spring

22. Page to Grey, 22 Feb 15, with minute by Hurst, 22 Feb 15, CAB 37/124/41; cf. Nicolson to Grey, 24 Feb 15, FO 800/95.

23. Slade, Hopwood, et al., "Observations," 28 Feb 15, with covering letter by Churchill, CAB 37/124/56. Churchill and Gilbert, *Churchill*, III, companion volumes, pt. 1, pp. 588–590, incorrectly attributes the memo rather than the covering letter only to Churchill.

24. House, diary entries, 23, 27 Feb 15, House Papers.

25. On continuation of the modus vivendi negotiations after 27 Feb 15, see Devlin, *Too Proud*, pp. 209–211.

26. Asquith to Stanley, 12 Mar 15, Stanley Papers; Bryan to Page, tel, 5 Mar 15, Savage, II, 273–274.

Rice's advice, the foreign secretary's gloss made a single, substantively meaningless concession to American sensibilities: it used the word "blockade" in relation to the new measures, despite Asquith's explicit repudiation of such "juridical niceties" and despite the fact that the Order itself did not proclaim a blockade.[27]

The vital importance of this entirely semantic concession became evident on March 19, during a meeting of the president's cabinet to consider the American response. Wilson began to expound the view that the United States was obligated to submit to the measures contained in the new Order in Council because of precedents established when the United States had been belligerent and Britain neutral during the American Civil War. The British were only claiming the right of blockade the Union had asserted fifty years before, so the American government had no legal basis to protest. The proper policy for the United States was to accept the recently proclaimed British blockade as legitimate and to continue protesting cases in which the British authorities exceeded their established belligerent rights.

This argument did not convince the secretary of war. Lindley Garrison agreed with the president's statement that the United States must accept a British blockade conducted under the existing rules of international law, but maintained that the present Order in Council bore no relationship to blockade as defined by the Union in 1861. Whatever language Grey's note used, the Order itself did not proclaim a blockade. The new measures were utterly lacking in justification under existing law, and the United States would forfeit the legal status of "neutral" if it failed to resist them. Unless the administration took a firm stand against Britain, Garrison warned, Germany would have every legal right to treat the United States as an enemy.[28]

Wilson, never at his best in debate, adjourned the cabinet without announcing a formal decision. He had, nevertheless, made that decision. Immediately after the cabinet members left he reduced his thoughts to "an outline sketch of the substance of a

27. Grey to Page, 15 Mar 15, and Order in Council, 11 Mar 15, transmitted in Page to Bryan, tel, 15 Mar 15, Savage II, 274–277; Spring Rice to Grey, tel, 6 Mar 15, FO 382/185; Devlin, *Too Proud,* pp. 203–206.
28. Wilson to Bryan, 19 Mar 15, SD(M)M-367–193; Garrison to Wilson, 20 Mar 15, W. Wilson Papers, (M)69.

reply to the British note which accompanied the recent Order in Council." He entitled his draft "Note in reply to ours received, notifying us of the establishment of a blockade of the coasts of Germany which it is intended to make in all respects effective." The title itself is an indication of its author's confusion, the British having given no such notification. Wilson went on to express confidence that the British government did not intend to violate the established rules of international law, ignoring the explicit statements to the contrary in Grey's note, in Asquith's speech, and in the Order itself. Whatever the difficulties, the president was determined to continue his policy of assuming that the blockade did not violate neutral rights, then having Page raise individual cases in which British actions seemed to conflict with British intentions as Washington defined them.[29]

Wilson's draft note stunned Robert Lansing. The counselor already had stated his own opinion: the reprisals Order was "manifestly without warrant under the rules of International law." It did not proclaim a blockade, and the doctrine of contraband, by definition, could not be applied to justify the seizure of noncontraband.[30] Yet the president was now proposing to recognize the existence of a blockade the British government had not proclaimed! Lansing and Chandler Anderson, a leading expert on maritime law and as strong an Anglophile as the counselor himself, agreed that if the United States took no stronger stand than that outlined in Wilson's draft "the Administration would be very severely criticized, and . . . our Government would have failed in its obligation to protect our national interests."[31]

Garrison had reached the same conclusion independently. In a memo submitted to the president the day after their disagreement over the cabinet table, the secretary of war restated his argument that the United States could not maintain the legal status of neutral unless it protested British violations of American rights as vigorously as it had protested German violations. The "whole order in council contravenes international law," and Britain

29. Wilson, draft note, 19 Mar 15, SD(M)M-367/193; for further evidence of the president's extraordinary confusion and ignorance on the subject of blockade, see Wilson to House, 23 Mar 15, House Papers.
30. Lansing, memo, 19 Mar 15, SD(M)M-367/193.
31. Anderson, diary entry, 20 Mar 15, Anderson Papers.

"should be so notified and be told that we will hold her to 'strict accountability', that being the same phrase which we used to Germany."[32]

Lansing took essentially the same view two days later when he sumitted a delicately worded alternative to the president's draft note. He began by asserting that the measures announced in the Order in Council and in Grey's covering note were illegal under any existing standard of international law. He reviewed these illegalities in detail, then expressed confidence that the British government would remove them as soon as they were brought to its attention. His draft warned, however, that if Britain persisted in violating American rights Washington would have no choice but to hold London "responsible for any loss or damage which citizens of the United States may incur." Lansing did not recommend that the phrase "strict accountability" be used in the note to Britain, but his draft did constitute a firm defense of neutral rights.[33]

The Lansing-Garrison position received somewhat unexpected support on March 24, when the navy's General Board responded to the secretary of the navy's request for a formal opinion on the reprisals Order. Under the signature of Admiral George Dewey, probably the most fervent Germanophobe in the entire American government, the board sounded a ringing indictment of the "sweeping claims put forth in the British Order in Council, claims which might be readily interpreted into a claim of universal sovereignty of the sea,—to the exclusion of all other nations,—on the part of the power issuing the order." The United States must reject this usurpation of sovereignty and maintain "its traditional policy of freedom of the sea for innocent commerce between neutral ports and belligerent unblockaded ports, and freedom of commerce of all kinds between neutral and neutral except contraband in transit to a belligerent." Dewey had been willing to share the seas with Britain in 1906, but he was not willing to surrender them to the Royal Navy in 1915.[34]

Wilson now had two draft replies to the Order in Council. The

32. Garrison, memo, 20 Mar 15, enclosed in Garrison to Wilson, 20 Mar 15, W. Wilson Papers, (M)69.

33. Lansing, "Suggestions for Answer," 22 Mar 15, SD(M)M-367/193.

34. General Board (Dewey) to secretary of the navy, 24 Mar 15, General Board Papers, serial #344.

first, his own, embodied the position of Page and House. The second, Lansing's, embodied the advice of Garrison, Lansing, Anderson, Dewey, and the Joint Neutrality Board. Had the American response been determined by majority vote, the proponents of a firm and formal rejection on legal grounds would have won. Under the Constitution, however, a president, his friend, and an ambassador to London outweigh a secretary of war, a State Department counselor, the admiral of the navy, and any number of lower-ranking diplomatic, legal, and naval advisers. Woodrow Wilson retained the power of decision, and he had decided that no "Strict Accountability" note would be sent to London.

On March 24 Lansing made a last attempt to persuade the president to take a stronger stand against the blockade. This time the counselor returned to his earlier argument concerning the political danger to the administration from public reaction to apparent weakness in the face of British provocation:

> Unless the reply contains a declaration of the legal rights of the United States based on the principles of international law, with which the press has made the public more or less familiar, the American people will consider the Government either indifferent to or ignorant of its rights. Furthermore the declaration must be urged with sufficient vigor to remove any impression that the Government is submitting without objection to violations of such rights.

Lansing warned that a general statement "based on expediency rather than legality," such as the president's draft note, would "invite strong criticism and furnish the opponents of the Administration with a plausible argument as to the weakness of our foreign policy." The United States need not defend its neutral rights against Britain with "drastic measures," because public opinion would be satisfied to "file a *caveat,* to permit their violation under protest deferring settlement until peace has been restored." But the American people would demand some show of strength, and their president's note provided none.[35]

Wilson admitted that "these notes by Mr. Lansing are admirable and convincing." But if presented to London they would lead

---

35. Lansing, memo, 24 Mar 15, SD(M)M-367/193.

"only to debate, and debate with the British Government (which for the time being consists of the War Office and the Admiralty) is at present of no avail." In words that were a direct echo of Page's, the president stated that "we are face to face with something they are going to do, and they are going to do it no matter what representations we make." The United States would hold Britain to "a strict accountability for every instance of rights violated and injury done," but the phrase "strict accountability" would not be used in the communication to the British government.[36] Wilson had responded to the choice between Page's policy of accommodation and Scott's policy of confrontation by accepting the advice of the ambassador.

The American note sent to London on March 30, like that sent to Berlin on February 10, conveyed the ideas of Woodrow Wilson under the signature of William Jennings Bryan.[37] That was the only similarity between the two notes. The protest to the British governement closely followed the text of Wilson's draft reply that had so distressed Lansing and Anderson. Its operative paragraph was a far cry from the "Strict Accountability" note's overt threat of war with Germany:

> The possibilities of serious interruption of American trade under the Order in Council are so many, and the methods proposed are so unusual and seem liable to constitute so great an impediment and embarrassment to neutral commerce that the Government of the United States, if the Order in Council is strictly enforced, apprehends many interferences with its legitimate trade which will impose upon His Majesty's Government heavy responsibilities for acts of the British authorities clearly subversive of the rights of neutral nations on the high seas. It is, therefore, expected that His Majesty's Government having considered these possibilities will take the steps necessary to avoid them, and, in the event that they should unhappily occur, will be prepared to make full reparation for every act, which under the rules of international law constitutes a violation of neutral rights.[38]

Anderson characterized the note as "stern on the face of it but has a twinkle in the eye."[39] It had absolutely no effect in persuading

---

36. Wilson to Bryan, 24 Mar 15, Savage, II, 280–281; cf. Page to Bryan, tel, 3 Mar 15, SD(M)M-367/192.
37. For various drafts of this note, see W. Wilson Papers, (M)69.
38. Bryan to Page, tel, 30 Mar 15, Savage, II, 281–286.
39. Anderson to Root, 29 Mar 15, Anderson Papers, 5.

the British government to show more respect for American rights.

The ultimate measure of American neutrality during World War I is a comparison between the February 10 protest to Berlin and the March 30 protest to London. When Germany had warned that it would regret but might not be able to avoid violation of certain American martime rights in the course of military operations directed against the Allies, Wilson took six days to send an ultimatum. When Britain committed what Grey privately admitted were more serious and more extensive violations, Wilson took a month to send a note that even Eyre Crowe, who was coming to dislike Americans almost as much as Germans, had to admit was "altogether friendly" in tone.[40] The differences in substance and in tone between the two notes demonstrate the gulf between the president's public calls for neutrality and his actions.[41] As Scott, Lansing, and Garrison had warned, the American failure to enforce neutral rights equally against the two belligerents constituted under international law a hostile act against the German Empire. By the end of March 1915, the United States was no longer entitled to the legal status of "neutral."

Wilson and Lansing later claimed that they protested more vigorously against the submarine than against the blockade because the latter took property, which was replaceable, whereas the former took lives, which were not.[42] This position must be regarded as an ex post facto rationalization for unneutral behavior and an inconsistent one at that. No such distinction appears in the "Strict Accountability" note, which stated explicitly that the United States would hold Germany accountable for destruction of "American lives *and* property," and would secure "to American

40. Crowe, 7 Apr 15, minute on Page to Grey, 2 Apr 15, FO 382/186.

41. The contemporary judgments of Lansing, Anderson, Crowe, and most other informed observers to this effect seem more convincing than the argument of Link (*Wilson*, III, 348 and passim) that Wilson treated the submarine and the reprisal blockade in essentially the same way. Although there were ambiguities in the "Strict Accountability" note that could have been interpreted to imply a limited acceptance of submarine warfare against commerce, and although the note to London also contained ambiguities that could have been interpreted to imply a serious challenge to the blockade, the president already had made it clear that such interpretations were not likely to be adopted. Only the most strained reading can make the note to Germany less than an ultimatum or the note to Britain more than a slap on the wrist.

42. E.g., Lansing to Wilson, 21 Dec 15, *FRUS, Lansing Papers*, I, 221-222.

citizens the full enjoyment of their acknowledged rights on the high seas."[43] Nor had Wilson made any effort in November 1914 to defend the right of American ships to free passage through Britain's North Sea war zone. The German war zone was to be enforced by submarines, whose captains were ordered to make every effort to spare neutral ships. The British war zone was enforced by automatic contact mines, which could not distinguish a German battleship from an American tanker carrying oil between two neutral ports. Yet the administration was willing and even eager to assert the right of Americans to sail unmolested through the German zone, while citizens who entered the British zone did so at their own risk. The real difference between blockade and submarine in Wilson's view was not that the former took property and the latter took lives, but that the former was British and the latter was German.

Two years to the day after Page presented the American note of April 2, 1915, to Grey, Woodrow Wilson asked the Congress of the United States to declare war on Germany. He emphasized in his request that, although other concerns had influenced his decision, the primary motivation had been defense of American maritime rights against the German submarine: "We enter this war only where we are clearly forced into it because there are no other means of defending our rights."[44] At best this statement indicates Wilson's capacity for self-delusion; at worst it demonstrates his capacity for hypocrisy. The system of international law Wilson claimed to be defending in 1917 had been undermined two years earlier by his own failure to maintain American neutrality. The United States went to war not in defense of neutral rights, but to enforce the principle that a nation purporting to be neutral could violate the rules of neutrality while avoiding the consequences of belligerency.

43. Bryan to Gerard, tel, 10 Feb 15, Savage, II, 268.
44. Wilson, speech to a Joint Session of Congress, 2 Apr 17, Baker and Dodd, eds., *Public Papers*, V, 15.

Epilogue

The history of maritime rights in Anglo-American relations from 1899 to April 1915 falls conveniently into two parts. The first fifteen years were a story of apparent success, during which the Great Powers, warned by the Boer and Russo-Japanese Wars, sought to reduce the potential for international conflict inherent in opposing claims of belligerent and neutral rights. This effort culminated in the International Prize Court Convention, the Declaration of London, and the Anglo-German agreement of June 1914 which seemed to clear the way for their ratification. During the first eight months of World War I, however, the story became one of failure and even tragedy. The new legal order constructed over the past decade was stillborn because of Britain's refusal to accept the Declaration of London. The old customary legal order, evolved over the centuries, broke down because the United States refused to defend its neutral rights against Britain. The result, despite Woodrow Wilson's attempts after April 1915 to create a new legal order to replace the one he helped to destroy, has been an enduring anarchy on the seas. Historical evaluation of these events is difficult but necessary.

In 1899 both Britain and the United States were wedded to fossilized policies on maritime rights. William McKinley advocated immunity for private property at sea to please the peace movement and because support for immunity was a traditional American position. Lord Salisbury rejected the proposal because he had little faith in international law and much faith in the Royal

Navy's ability to hurt potential enemies by enforcing belligerent
rights. Each nation's position was shaped by historical reflex.
Neither was based on a systematic analysis of how the national
interest might have changed since 1815. Balfour's lament at having to "expound the policy of a Government which had none" was
echoed by Mahan, but by few others.

This era of general satisfaction with traditional positions on
maritime rights came to an abrupt end with the Boer War. Salisbury's disdain for international law and faith in the fleet led him
to authorize enforcement of belligerent rights without serious
consideration of the issues involved and without ensuring that the
South African authorities knew what they were doing. The result
was the spectacle of neutral ships seized for "trading with the
enemy," open cabinet revolt against the prime minister, a
humiliating retreat under German and American pressure, and
payment of substantial compensation to injured neutrals. This
experience convinced the generation of British statemen and
strategists who came to power after 1899 that a broad reconsideration of the national position on maritime rights was long overdue.

Such a review took place between 1900 and 1907. The result
was the policy first suggested under the Balfour Government in
1904 and formally adopted by its Liberal successor in 1907, the
policy that remained Britain's basic position on maritime rights
until after the outbreak of World War I. Throughout the decade
before 1914, the British government opposed immunity for private property or any significant limitation on the right of blockade. It consistently favored limitation or even abolition of the
doctrines of contraband and continuous voyage.

Because continuous voyage and contraband became the foundation for Britain's wartime economic campaign against Germany, while blockade and capture of enemy ships played little
role in that campaign, historians have had enormous difficulty
trying to understand the government's prewar position. Recent
scholars have characterized it as "inconsistent," "bizarre," and
"wellnigh incredible."[1] From a post-1914 perspective, such criti-

---

1. Marsden, "The Blockade," p. 488, and Clive Perry, "Foreign Policy and
International Law," Hinsley, ed., *British Foreign Policy*, pp. 102–103.

cisms seem amply justified. Yet Balfour, Grey, and the others responsible for prewar policy were neither stupid nor careless. Their decisions were thoroughly considered, based on the best professional advice available, and justified by what seemed at the time excellent reasons.

Four basic assumptions underlay the conclusion that British interests would benefit from limitations on contraband and continuous voyage: that Britain would be neutral in most world conflicts, that any war in which Britain was involved would be a limited war for limited aims, that powerful nations such as the United States would not tolerate a return to the neutrals-be-damned practices of the Napoleonic Wars, and that commercial blockade of the German coast remained possible. Each of these assumptions proved invalid during World War I. Yet this failure of foresight was neither as obvious nor as great as historians with the advantage of hindsight have made it seem.

The inaccuracy of one premise certainly should have been recognized before the outbreak of war. As Arthur Marder has shown, British naval officers had expressed increasing doubts concerning the continued feasibility of close blockade from 1904 on. In 1912 it had been deleted from the war plan entirely.[2] In spite of these doubts, however, Fisher had endorsed the strengthening of blockade rights at the expense of contraband and continuous voyage in 1907. Successive Boards of Admiralty had taken the same position through 1914. Although Bonar Law and others had pointed out the contradiction between this increased emphasis on blockade rights and the decreasing ability of the Royal Navy to enforce those rights, it is hard to fault the Asquith Government for preferring the opinion of its responsible professional advisers to that of a few Tory orators. The failure to recognize that blockade was obsolete and that any effective economic campaign under modern conditions would have to be based on the doctrine of contraband rests squarely on the Admiralty. Fisher, Arthur Wilson, Slade, Ottley, and other senior officers simply did not understand that the technological changes which made close blockade suicidal had rendered an effective commercial blockade of Germany impossible.

2. Marder, *From the Dreadnought,* I, 369–371.

From a post-1914 perspective, two of the other prewar assumptions seem as unrealistic as continued faith in blockade. Britain did not remain neutral in World War I, and neither did it fight a limited war for limited maritime aims. Even Henry Wilson's prewar vision of Continental intervention paled before the bloody reality of Ypres and the Somme. Yet British intervention in a Franco-German war and dispatch of the BEF to France seem far more inevitable in retrospect than they did when the Declaration of London was signed in 1909 or even in July 1914. The peacetime cabinet never committed itself either to war or to Continental military operations. The most ardent interventionists feared that Britain would stand neutral until the invasion of Belgium united the cabinet for war. The Government's August 2 decision not to send the BEF to France and Grey's August 3 depicition of a cheap naval war to the House of Commons demonstrate that a limited conflict to destroy German sea power remained a serious option up to and even after the declaration of war. In this light, British maritime rights policy appears less "bizarre." What does seem "wellnigh incredible" is that successive prewar Governments had never resolved the basic contradiction between two mutually exclusive grand strategic concepts. For this failure, Asquith, Grey, and their colleagues bear a heavy responsibility.

The assumptions that close blockade remained feasible and that Britain would either remain neutral or fight a limited maritime war help to explain the intellectual gap between prewar maritime rights policy and the economic campaign that began in August 1914. The inaccuracy of the fourth assumption, that neutrals could and would defend their rights, ultimately made that campaign possible. Britain could not have established the wartime blockade without unprecedented expansion of the doctrines of contraband and continuous voyage. Such extensive violations of existing international law would have been impossible had the United States acted to defend its neutrality. Only Hankey and a few Unionist politicians had predicted before 1914 that Britain could safely dismiss neutrals in applying economic pressure against future enemies. Their arguments had been based on a simplistic assertion of national will and sea power, not on any rational consideration of possible neutral resistance. Grey, Slade, and the others responsible for prewar policy failed to predict that one man, Woodrow

Wilson, would have both a higher regard for the Anglo-American relationship than for traditional American neutrality and the ability to impose his view on the nation he led. Had the president of the United States in 1914 been prepared to defend neutrality, the British government would have been forced to choose between a limited economic campaign as called for in prewar planning and a more aggressive campaign resulting in Anglo-American confrontation. Given the reality of American naval and economic power, it is hard to believe London would have chosen confrontation.

British prewar policy on maritime rights failed to survive the test of war, but not because it was unrealistic or carelessly formulated. It failed because the assumptions on which it had been based were rendered invalid by changed circumstances in 1914. Some of these changes should have been foreseen, others might have been foreseen, and at least one, the failure of the United States to defend its neutrality, was totally unforeseeable. However unrealistic Britain's prewar maritime rights policy may seem in hindsight, it appears understandable and almost inevitable in light of the assumptions that shaped its formulation.

British policy appears in a particularly favorable light when contrasted with the disorganized, even amateurish way the United States formulated its maritime rights policies between 1899 and 1914. The Naval War Code of 1900 and the next year's prize law course at the Naval War College demonstrate the navy's recognition of the need for reconsideration and reform. But the American government never succeeded in translating this concern into a coherent national position. The closest it came was in 1906, when Mahan's initiative led the Navy and State Departments to reexamine traditional support for broad neutral rights and immunity for private property. This study concluded that the old policies no longer were in the national interest and should be reversed, but President Roosevelt dismissed the recommendation without bothering to explain why. The United States went to the Second Hague Conference in 1907, as it had gone to the first in 1899, with a delegation formally instructed to support immunity and a naval delegate personally determined to defeat it. This confusion continued during the Declaration of London negotiations, when the American government devoted most of its efforts to blocking

British efforts to safeguard and strengthen neutral rights. When the Taft administration proposed and the Senate approved ratification of the declaration and the International Prize Court Convention, they acted from historical reflex and bureaucratic inertia rather than from a systematic analysis of national interests under twentieth-century conditions. The United States had no Walton Committee to prepare for The Hague, no Desart Committee to prepare for London, and certainly no CID to coordinate policy on a grand strategic level. Any understanding or evaluation of the American position on maritime rights between 1899 and 1914 must begin with recognition of this administrative disarray and intellectual confusion.

The only serious challenge to the traditional American position came from a small group of senior naval officers. Mahan, Dewey, Sperry, and others argued that stronger, not weaker, belligerent rights were in the national interest under modern conditions. In their view a common concern with German aggressiveness already was pushing Britain and America into de facto alliance. The United States should recognize this trend and understand that sea power was the only effective weapon the Anglo-Americans would have to deter or resist a German attack. To limit belligerent rights had been in the national interest a century earlier, but now would reduce the effectiveness of sea power and thereby threaten national survival when the inevitable clash with Germany came.

Should the United States have adopted this advice and deliberately sought to strengthen the belligerent rights essential for victory in an Anglo-American economic campaign against Germany? Although this question was never systematically considered by the American government, it is a fair one for the historian to raise. The Mahan-Dewey prediction of Anglo-American cooperation against Germany was fulfilled, although not under the circumstances its authors had expected. In 1914 the United States did permit Britain to expand belligerent rights because its president considered sea power a vital weapon defending American as well as Allied interests. Had he not done so, the result might well have been a crippled blockade and a German victory in Europe, followed by an assault on the Monroe Doctrine. Yet it is hard to criticize McKinley, Roosevelt, Taft, or Wilson for not easing the way to wartime acceptance of broader belligerent rights by publicly breaking with the traditional policy before 1914. Given the support for commercial rights in the peace movement and the business community, as well as the more vague support of public opinion in general, the political consequences of a prewar break would have been incalculable. Even after the outbreak of war in Europe, Wilson was careful to disguise his accommodation with the blockade in a cloak of neutral rhetoric. American prewar policy was amateurish in many ways, but it was firmly grounded in political reality.

The British declaration of war against Germany on August 4, 1914, transformed the context in which both Britain and the United States formulated their maritime rights policies. During the next four years the British government would evolve and impose a blockade on a scale unimagined during the harshest days of the Napoleonic Wars. It would do so with the passive, and eventually with the active, cooperation of the United States government. The blockade would become a decisive factor in the ultimate breakup of the German, Austro-Hungarian, and Ottoman empires and in the other consequences that flowed from World War I.[3]

British maritime rights policy during the war thus clearly was a success. Historians have proved too willing, however, to credit this success to deliberate planning by British strategists and wise judgments by British statesmen. Hankey's boast that "from the King to the printer everyone knew what he had to do"[4] was true for the limited economic campaign planned by the prewar Admiralty, but not for the broad effort initiated in the Order in Council of August 20. One scholar's recent assertion that confiscation of "all contraband on its way to the enemy" was a major objective defined in the war plan[5] simply is not accurate. Battenberg, Sturdee, and Slade, the men profesionally responsible for the economic aspects of the naval war plan, continued to argue as late as

---

3. There is no adequate modern study of the blockade's effects, but see ibid., V, 297–299, and Bell, *Blockade,* pp. 671–703 and passim. Kennedy, *Rise and Fall of British Naval Mastery,* p. 254, sees the economic campaign as less decisive.

4. Hankey, *Supreme Command,* I, 139; cf. the more accurate picture in Bell, *Blockade,* pp. 31–32.

5. Marsden, "The Blockade," p. 488.

August 16, 1914, that conditional contraband destined for Germany could not be intercepted effectively under the doctrine of continuous voyage. The wartime blockade in fact had no prewar roots. Instead it was improvised in the ten days after August 10 to exploit inaccurate rumors of enemy food shortages and to satisfy a vague desire to strike some sort of blow. The real historical precursor of the Order in Council of August 20 was the panic of Black Week in 1899, when an unsubstantiated belief in the vulnerability of enemy food supplies had also led a British government to an unconsidered and unprecedented assertion of belligerent rights.

The policy adopted in the Boer War had led to humiliating retreat. Essentially the same policy adopted fifteen years later laid the foundation for decisive success. The key difference was neutral reaction. In both cases a British government had decided on a broad assertion of belligerent rights without serious consideration of possible opposition. In 1899 Germany and the United States had insisted that their neutrality be respected. In 1914 the Wilson administration permitted, and in a few cases even encouraged, violation of neutral rights. The success of the blockade was determined in Washington. Wilson's refusal to defend American neutrality against Britain created a vacuum that a surprised London rushed in to fill. The British role in the blockade's success was to recognize the existence of this vacuum, to devise and enforce measures to take advantage of it, and to manipulate the American government so Washington would continue its unexpected accommodation.

Personal credit for the development of the economic campaign is relatively easy for the historian to assign. Churchill and Grey devised the Order in Council of August 20, and Hurst drafted it. McKenna provided the fig leaf of legal respectability which made the break with prewar concepts of limited economic warfare acceptable to the cabinet. These three ministers, with the support of Lloyd George and usually Kitchener, constituted a group committed to more rigorous economic warfare and generally able to carry the Government in that direction. Fisher was a strong proponent of a more militant policy both before and after his return to the Admiralty. The Hopwood and Contraband Committees bore primary responsibility for recommending the specific measures that curtailed trade with the enemy; the Royal Navy intercepted the neutral ships and directed them into British ports; and the prize courts, "as much distinguished for their patriotism as for their impartiality,"[6] refused to enforce rules of either international or municipal law which might have embarrassed the war effort.

Credit for recognizing that the United States would not defend its neutral rights, and for successfully manipulating the American government, is more difficult to assign. Historians commonly have seen Grey as the great conciliator, deliberately using his dominant influence on foreign policy to limit the rigor of the blockade in order to maintain Wilson's trust.[7] This view is not supported, however, by a detailed examination of the British archives. There is no indication that the foreign secretary advocated substantive restriction of the economic campaign for the purpose of conciliating the United States at any time prior to February 1915, when he joined Asquith and Simon in opposition to Churchill's reprisals proposal. On the contrary, Grey appears repeatedly as a leader of the cabinet faction favoring greater restrictions on neutral trade. Far from being a passive spectator who, in Ernest May's words, "apparently made no objection" to adoption of the Order in Council of August 20,[8] the foreign secretary had personally directed Hurst to draft the Order and, with Churchill, had been its most vigorous proponent in the cabinet discussions. During September and October he had been the most consistent advocate of adding a broad list of raw materials to the contraband lists. In November he had objected to permitting American food relief shipments to the Belgian civilian

6. Devlin, *Too Proud,* p. 160.
7. May, *World War,* pp. 3-33 and passim, esp. p. 12; Cooper, *Page,* p. 289; Robbins, *Grey,* pp. 314-315. Even scholars with access to the relevant cabinet and Foreign Office archives have accepted the picture of Grey limiting the blockade in order to conciliate the United States. Gregory, *Origins,* p. 35, asserts that "documents show that he felt exactly the same way," but fails to cite any such documents. Marsden, "The Blockade," p. 493, maintains that "there was not much doubt what Grey himself would advocate. It was a policy involving no risk." He documents this statement, made in relation to the Order in Council of 29 Oct 14, with reference to Grey's own memoirs, to George Macaulay Trevelyan's hagiographic biography *Grey of Fallodon* (London: Longmans, Green, 1937), and a recorded comment by the foreign secretary on 22 Jul 15 made under entirely changed circumstances.
8. May, *World War,* p. 17.

population because he feared they might be diverted to German use. More than any other minister, Grey bore responsibility for devising and carrying into effect the economic campaign. More than any other minister, he blocked substantive concessions to the United States on maritime rights during the first six months of war.

Although the picture of Grey advocating conciliatory policies is largely a myth, he did make one substantial contribution to American acceptance of the blockade. His management of Page, House, and Wilson was masterful. His reputation for probity and candor, however undeserved it appears in retrospect, was a great asset in persuading the American president to regard violations of neutral rights as honest differences among gentlemen rather than deliberate denials of American sovereignty and neutrality. His reputation as a liberal idealist in foreign affairs, although often contradicted by his private actions, was a major asset in persuading Wilson that the man who negotiated the London agreements of September 1914 and April 1915 was a kindred spirit and would be an invaluable ally in the quest for a healing peace. Although the foreign secretary's policies led to potential confrontation, his public image and diplomatic skill were vital in preventing the realization of that potential.

Far more important than anything Grey did or said in winning American acceptance of the blockade, however, was a factor historians too often overlook in their search for rational patterns of motivation and causation: simple, blind, unpredictable luck. British leaders, including the foreign secretary, made policy decisions based on a frequently ludicrous ignorance of American realities.[9] British press and intelligence reports from the United States reflected little more than glowing accounts of pro-Allied and anti-German sympathies.[10] The British government reached the correct conclusion—that the United States would not offer serious resistance to practically unlimited expansion of belligerent rights by the Allies—by a process of wishful thinking and trial and

9. E.g., Spring Rice to Grey, 5 Oct, 3 Nov 14, FO 800/84; Spring Rice to Grey, 6 Dec 14, FO 368/1195; Board of Trade to FO, 9 Dec 14, FO 368/1162; Spring Rice to Grey, 15 Jan 15, FO 800/241; Grey to Spring Rice, 26 Feb 15, FO 382/185; FO, memo, 26 Jan 15, CAB 37/123/52; Hobhouse, diary entries, 9 Oct 14, 2 Mar 15, David, ed., *Inside Asquith's Cabinet*, pp. 197, 225.

10. E.g., *The Times*, 14 Sep 14, p. 6; WO, Intelligence Summaries, 9, 12, 17, 26 Aug 14, WO 106/299.

error rather than by sound reasoning based on an accurate assessment of American conditions.

Ultimately, success or failure of the blockade rested on Woodrow Wilson's twin capacities to delude himself and to delude the American people. Grey's manipulation of American leaders was possible only because they so desperately wanted to be manipulated. Only the president's ability to believe that Britain was not violating American neutrality despite all the evidence to the contrary, only his ability to continue to believe that his beloved England would not actually do the very things its prime minister had boasted it already was doing in a public session of the House of Commons, prevented an Anglo-American confrontation over maritime rights that Britain could not have won. William Wordsworth, Walter Bagehot, and the other paragons of liberal idealism who shaped Wilson's romantic view of English civilization in the final analysis deserve more credit for the success of the economic campaign than Grey, Churchill, or anyone else in the British government in 1914.

One final question must be asked concerning the British side of the maritime rights issue. Given the commitment to a Continental war and American acquiescence, the Government's decision to scrap the plans for a limited economic campaign in favor of an improvised but far more rigorous blockade obviously was correct. But was the decision for a Continental war rather than neutrality or a limited maritime war itself a correct one? The neutrality option remained available until August 4 and the limited war option until August 6. It is possible to imagine Britain standing aside while France, Russia, Germany, and Austria-Hungary fought for Continental domination. But every indication of modern scholarship is that such a policy would have proved disastrous. Wilhelmine Germany was determined, for reasons essentially irrational, to challenge the British Empire.[11]

11. On the German determination to challenge Britain at some point, see Holger H. Herwig, "Admirals *versus* Generals: The War Aims of the Imperial German Navy, 1914-1918," *Central European History*, 5 (1972), 208-233; Jonathan Steinberg, "A German Plan for the Invasion of Holland and Belgium, 1897," *Historical Journal*, 6 (1963), 107-119; Imanuel Geiss, *German Foreign Policy, 1871-1914* (London: Routledge & Kegan Paul, 1976), pp. 82-83, 85-86, 92-95, 106-110, 130-132, and passim; L. L. Farrar, *The Short War Illusion* (Oxford: A. B. C.-Clio Press, 1973), pp. 102-116; and Fritz Fischer, *Germany's Aims in the First World War* (New York: Norton, 1967), pp. 25-41 and passim.

Had Britain not joined France and Russia in 1914, it almost inevitably would have faced a future conflict with a Germany free of Continental distractions and able to command the resources of Europe. In August 1914 Asquith and his colleagues did not have the option of canceling decades of misperceptions and mistakes on both sides and starting over with a clean slate. There is much to criticize in British policy toward Germany during the years before the outbreak of war, particularly Grey's pursuit of an "absolutely secure" Entente which implied insecurity for Germany. The Cabinet's decision for war in August 1914, however, must be considered prudent and in the national interest.

That decision cost the British Empire almost a million lives over the next four years, most of them on the Western Front.[12] The British government could have refused to pay this price. It could have maintained the August 2 decision against committing the BEF to the Continent and adopted Fisher's strategy of limited maritime war. This option seems particularly attractive in retrospect because it offered an alternative to the offensive carnage that made the Somme and Passchendaele synonyms for wanton butchery. Yet Fisher's strategy was a pipe dream under the conditions actually existing when Britain went to war. The French and British General Staffs, committed to offensive doctrines, would not have accepted a plan that called for the French army to stand on the defensive while British troops raided the enemy coasts and seized offshore islands from which a tight legal blockade could be maintained. The British and French governments would not have been willing to limit their war aims to those essential for a lasting, healing peace. The British and French peoples would not have been willing to wait patiently for a wide spectrum of pressures to become effective against Germany. From an abstract point of view there is much to be said for Fisher's strategy of limited war, just as there is much to be said for British isolation from Continental conflicts. But the political, military, and diplomatic realities facing the Asquith Government in August 1914 denied it the luxury of taking such abstract views.

The hard fact is that on the outbreak of war the British gov-

12. R. Ernest Dupuy and Trevor N. Dupuy, *The Encyclopedia of Military History*, rev. ed. (New York: Harper & Row, 1977), p. 990, gives British losses as approximately 940,000.

ernment found itself painted into a corner. The demands of foreign policy, whether defined as preservation of the European balance of power or as fulfillment of honorable obligations to Belgium, exceeded the capabilities of the armed forces. Fisher had recognized this discrepancy before the war and advocated that national aims be redefined in more limited terms appropriate to Britain's limited military capabilities. The government had refused to accept this advice. But neither had it taken the steps necessary to increase its military capabilities. When war came, Kitchener improvised a mass, ultimately conscripted, army while Grey, Churchill, and others improvised an effective economic campaign. In both instances prewar policies actually hindered and embarrassed wartime efforts. The ministers who served in successive Governments prior to 1914 must bear a heavy responsibility for this failure to recognize or to deal with the imbalance between the ends of British foreign policy and the means provided to achieve those ends.

Questions also remain concerning American policies. The Wilson administration's actions on maritime rights between August 1914 and April 1915 were incomprehensible to British leaders. They have seemed almost equally so to historians, despite the opportunity to examine the documents that detail the formulation of those actions. The overall pattern is one of confusion and contradiction, unified only by the president's commitment to three fundamental assumptions. Wilson believed that German victory in Europe would endanger American national security, that neutral rights were not sufficiently important to justify a clash with Britain, and that American public opinion must not be allowed to become so outraged by the blockade that it compromised his leadership as it had compromised that of James Madison in 1812. Because Wilson revealed these guidelines only to House and Lansing, while defining his views in entirely different terms to other members of his administration and to the public, the confusion of American neutrality policies and the historians who study them is not surprising.

Woodrow Wilson publicly pledged in August 1914 to maintain American neutrality. He did not keep this pledge, as Arthur Link maintains he did. Nor was his policy "benevolent neutrality," as Ernest May argues. American policy toward Britain during the

Boer War had been benevolent neutrality. American policy during World War I was precisely what James Brown Scott had warned it would be if the United States failed to defend its rights against flagrant British violation: "non-neutrality toward Germany" and "a manifest failure to safeguard the interests of United States citizens engaged in perfectly legitimate business." American maritime neutrality during the first eight months of World War I was incompatible with the traditional American principles contained in John Bassett Moore's magisterial 1907 *Digest of International Law,* incompatible with John Hay's statements during the Boer and Russo-Japanese Wars, incompatible with the Naval War Code of 1900 and the teachings of the Naval War College, incompatible with the positions taken by the United States at the Hague and London Conferences, and incompatible with the recommendations of the president's own Anglophilic advisers such as Lansing, Scott, Dewey, and Anderson. Only by Wilson's personal definition, which had no reference to either international law or American history, was the United States entitled to the status of "neutral" by March 1915.

Several historians have concluded from this evidence that Wilson deliberately compromised American neutrality in order to aid the Allies and eventually bring the United States into the war at their side.[13] For the first eight months of war, at least, this interpretation overestimates Wilson's deviousness and underestimates his capacity for self-delusion. The president did shape American neutrality so it aided the Allies, but there is no evidence that he recognized his actions were in any way unneutral. On the contrary, surrounded by advisers eager to present Allied actions in the best possible light and convinced of his own moral superiority, Wilson continued to believe that he could define true neutrality better than could lawyers and textbooks. Lansing and Garrison saw the flaw in this reasoning—than other nations were more likely to accept the rule of law than to accept the rule of Wilson—but they were never able to make the president see it. The best

13. E.g., John Kenneth Turner, *Shall It Be Again?* (New York: B. W. Heubsch, 1922), pp. 20-23 and passim. Tansill, *America Goes to War,* seems to waver between Wilson as a conspirator and as the semiknowing dupe of Lansing, Page, and House. Millis, *Road to War,* p. 79 and passim, charitably concludes that the president was a dupe of "the shrewd spokesmen of the Entente."

summation of Wilson's attitude on maritime rights was written by Shakespeare in regard to Cardinal Wolsey: "His own opinion was his law."[14]

If Wilson's personality explains how he could continue to believe in all sincerity that his administration was neutral despite overwhelming evidence to the contrary, another explanation is needed for the failure of the American people to insist on strict adherence to traditional policies. The president's greatest fear was a public outcry against the blockade which would compromise his leadership and thus recreate the "tragical" circumstances of 1812. Lansing and others warned consistently that British actions were on the verge of provoking such a reaction. Yet the outcry never developed, despite obvious British violations of neutral rights and the evident failure of the administration to prevent them. The fact that public opinion ultimately turned against Germany, and not against Britain, the initial offender, is one of the most puzzling aspects of American maritime rights policy.

The first, and most important, factor working against a popular demand that Wilson follow traditional neutrality policies was that a majority of the American people sympathized with the Allies.[15] Two decades of Anglo-American rapprochement, historical friendship with France, both real and imagined German brutality in Belgium, and other influences had predisposed most Americans to accept administration claims that Anglo-American differences over the blockade were technical and relatively minor. The complexity of maritime law prevented all but a handful from understanding the real issues involved, and both London and Washington deliberately sought to maintain this confusion. The most vocal Republicans, led by Theodore Roosevelt, openly supported the Allies and thus allowed Wilson to picture himself as the

14. *King Henry VIII*, act IV, scene 2; cf. Mahan to Henderson, 7 Nov 13, above, Chapter 9 at note 12.
15. Public opinion is extremely difficult to evaluate for any historical period before the advent of scientific polling techniques, but see Smith, *Great Departure*, pp. 1–5; Gregory, *Origins*, pp. 7–12; John Milton Cooper, *The Vanity of Power* (Westport, Conn.: Greenwood, 1969), pp. 19–22 and passim; May, *World War*, pp. 35–37, 140; and Frederick C. Luebke, *Bonds of Loyalty* (DeKalb: Northern Illinois University Press, 1974), pp. 83–151. Link, *Wilson*, III, 6–43, correctly emphasizes the commitment to neutrality felt by the great majority of Americans, but would seem to underestimate the degree of general sympathy for the Western Allies.

man of peace dedicated to true neutrality.[16] Grey and Spring Rice were careful to justify British actions in terms least likely to offend American sensibilities, as when the ambassador cited supposed Civil War precedents and the foreign secretary used the word "blockade" inaccurately but effectively to describe the reprisals Order in Council of March 1915. The Allies eased the pain their economic campaign inflicted on such key American industries as copper, cotton, and meat with huge purchases of their own.[17] All these factors joined to create the extraordinary passivity of American public opinion in response to the blockade and the administration's failure to challenge it effectively.

To say that Wilson was unneutral and that he led the United States into an unneutral policy on maritime rights is not to say that he was necessarily wrong in what he did. Link, though wrong in asserting that the president did maintain neutrality, makes a convincing case for the position that the failure to challenge the blockade was a wise strategic decision:

> The results of destroying the British blockade would have been the wrecking of American friendship with the two great European democracies and the probable victory of the Central Powers, without a single compensatory gain for the interests and security of the United States. Only the sure achievement of some great political objective like a secure peace settlement, certainly not the winning of a commercial advantage or the defense of doubtful neutral rights, would have justified Wilson in undertaking a determined challenge to British sea power.[18]

This argument is particularly impressive in light of what is now known of German war aims. There no longer is room for doubt that the Kaiser's government, from shortly after the war began to shortly before it ended, was committed to a massive program of territorial aggrandizement. The details of this program remained vague, but two essential elements were Continen-

16. May, *World War*, p. 140; Blum, *Republican Roosevelt*, pp. 151–156; John Allen Gable, *The Bull Moose Years* (Port Washington, N. Y.: Kennikat Press, 1978), pp. 233–239; *TR Letters*, VIII, 822–825 and passim.

17. Leverton Harris to Churchill, 3 Mar 15, Churchill and Gilbert, *Churchill*, III, companion volumes, pt. 1, p. 618; Hobhouse, diary entry, 12 Jan 15, David, ed., *Inside Asquith's Cabinet*, p. 216; Siney, *Allied Blockade*, pp. 56–59.

18. Link, *Wilson the Diplomatist*, p. 43; cf. Link, *Wilson*, III, 129.

tal domination and destruction of British maritime supremacy.[19] Had Germany achieved this position, a challenge to the Monroe Doctrine almost certainly would have followed.[20]

The failure to challenge the illegal aspects of the Allied blockade thus gained one clear advantage for the United States. The economic campaign proved a decisive factor in preventing a German victory that would have threatened American security. Britain and France remained Great Powers for two more decades, during which American power grew enormously. When the United States did have to face a victorious Germany in 1941, it was far more ready for the challenge than it would have been in 1914. Wilson's fears of German agents building heavy artillery emplacements in the United States and disguising them as tennis courts were paranoid fantasies, but his belief that German victory in Europe would pose an unacceptable threat to American national security seems entirely realistic.

Evaluation of American maritime rights policy thus rests on weighing this advantage against the costs of unneutrality. For there were costs, despite the president's failure to acknowledge or even to recognize them. By aiding the Allies in order to block German aggrandizement, Wilson's policies ultimately identified the United States with the postwar aggrandizement of Britain, France, Japan, and Italy. He compromised not only the American tradition of neutrality in colonial and European conflicts, but the entire system of international relations based on the concepts of neutrality and limited war. He sacrificed on the altar of Anglo-American friendship any possibility that the United States could use its immense power to preserve the existing international system, to mitigate the horrors of war for neutrals and perhaps for belligerent civilians, and to mediate a compromise peace. Wilson ignored these costs, but the historian must weigh them in his balance.

19. The literature on German aims during World War I is enormous. See especially, Fischer, *Germany's Aims;* Gerhard Ritter, *The Sword and the Scepter,* translated by Heinz Norden, vols. III and IV (Coral Gables: University of Miami Press, 1972 and 1973); and John A. Moses, *The Politics of Illusion: The Fischer Controversy in German Historiography* (London: G. Prior, 1975).

20. Herwig, *Politics of Frustration,* pp. 133–138, 150–151.

A sincerely neutral United States could have reduced wartime suffering among the weaker neutrals and among the civilian populations of the belligerents. The best indication of what might have been done in this regard is Wilson's success in using American power to delay the German decision for unrestricted submarine warfare by two full years. A similar stand against British interference with food shipments to the European neutrals, to Germany, and to Austria-Hungary would have saved innocent lives and prevented enormous suffering.[21] Such a stand also would have done much to establish American good faith in German eyes and perhaps would have opened the way to other limitations on war's barbarism.

Another cost of Wilson's failure to challenge the blockade, destruction of the existing legal order on the seas, is more difficult to evaluate. The general historical view, that the system of maritime rights existing in 1914 was "ambiguous," "obsolete," or "very nearly unworkable,"[22] would have found few supporters in either the British or the American government. Britain violated what its leaders privately acknowledged to be established international law for reasons of military expediency; the United States permitted these violations for reasons of presidential policy. Wilson had the power to command respect for neutral rights from all belligerents. He chose to use that power only against Germany. By doing so he forfeited America's claim to neutrality. The established system of international maritime law broke down in 1914 not because of its own flaws, but because one man refused to uphold it. Wilson tried to replace the system he destroyed with a new order, "freedom of the seas," but failed. The result has been an enduring anarchy.

The American failure to challenge the blockade destroyed more than traditional maritime law. Wilson perverted the very concept of neutrality and thereby undermined the entire system of international relations which had dominated Western civiliza-

21. Bell, *Blockade,* pp. 671–673 and passim; Siney, *Allied Blockade,* pp. 137–139, 248–249, 256–257; Olav Riste, *The Neutral Ally* (Oslo: Aas & Wahls Boktrykkeri, 1965); Amry Vandenbosch, *The Neutrality of the Netherlands during the World War* (Grand Rapids, Mich.: Wm. B. Eerdmans, 1927).

22. Link, *Wilson,* III, p. 105; Kennan, *American Diplomacy,* p. 64; Devlin, *Too Proud,* p. 159.

tion since the rise of the nation-state. The old system had drawn a clear distinction between belligerents and neutrals, and had defined certain rights and duties for each. The American failure to fulfill the obligations of neutrality was a primary factor in the disintegration of this distinction. Wilson instead drew a moral distinction between the Allies and the Central Powers and shaped American "neutrality" to favor the "good" belligerent. For the rest of his presidency he sought to build a new world order in which his own moral universalism would replace nationalism as the foundation of international relations. The heart of this order was to be the League of Nations, which was to replace national self-interest with international justice. The League's failure was also the failure of Wilson's vision.

The national system of international relations had its flaws, as World War I demonstrates. But it did deal with the twentieth century's dominant historical force, nationalism, more effectively than Wilson's system of moral universalism. The old system sought to limit and localize conflicts by providing guidelines for belligerent and neutral conduct which discouraged outside intervention. The new system invited nations not directly involved in a conflict to intervene in accordance with their moral judgments. The history of neither the League of Nations nor the United Nations supports Wilson's assurance that a world organization would evaluate such local conflicts fairly and ensure that any outside intervention would be on the side of justice. Like many before him, Woodrow Wilson learned that to destroy an existing system is easier than to replace it with a better system. His role in undermining the traditional national system of international relations might ultimately prove to have been the greatest cost of American unneutrality in 1914.

Evaluation of American maritime rights policy during World War I rests essentially on the answer to one question: could the United States have blocked a German victory while preserving its own neutrality within the existing system of international relations, avoiding identification with Allied aggrandizement, and preventing the innocent deaths and suffering caused by the blockade? This question can never be answered with certainty because the Wilson administration refused to explore any alternatives to its own policy. Nevertheless, it is possible to sketch a scenario in which both belligerent camps, denied by firm American resistance the sustaining hope of victory through illegal surface or submarine blockade, sicken of the carnage in the trenches. In such circumstances, with each side recognizing that supplies from America could sustain its foe indefinitely and with neither able to afford antagonizing the United States, the promise of American mediation and a compromise peace does not seem totally unrealistic. Ironically, it was the genius of Woodrow Wilson which recognized that a lasting peace must be "a peace without victory."[23] It was the tragedy of Woodrow Wilson that his own unneutrality would be a major factor in bringing about the decisive Allied victory that made a healing peace impossible.

23. Wilson, speech to the Senate, 22 Jan 17, Baker and Dodd, eds., *Public Papers*, IV, 410.

Bibliography

I. MANUSCRIPT SOURCES EXAMINED

UNITED STATES

Public Documents (National Archives unless otherwise specified)

Commerce Department, Bureau of Navigation
Congress, Senate Foreign Relations Committee
Justice Department, (Federal) Bureau of Investigation. The author was permitted to examine eight Justice-originated documents in the State Department records. His application for general access to Justice Department records on 1914–1915 neutrality was rejected by the F.B.I. director (C. M. Kelley to author, 1 Jul 74)
Navy Department
Navy Department, Naval War College (Newport, R.I.)
Navy Department, Operational Archives Branch, Papers of the General Board (Washington Navy Yard)
State Department
Treasury Department, Customs Service. Records of the Secret Service relating to 1914–1915 neutrality were not open to scholars
War Department

Private Papers (Library of Congress unless otherwise specified)

Aldrich, Nelson
Anderson, Chandler P.
Beveridge, Albert
Bonaparte, Charles
Borah, William
Bryan, William Jennings
Bryan, William Jennings (National Archives, Microfilm)
Burleson, Albert Sydney

Carnegie, Andrew
Choate, Joseph
Daniels, Josephus
Dewey, George
Dewey, George (Navy Department, Operational Archives Branch, Washington Navy Yard)
Fiske, Bradley
Foster, John W.
Hay, John
Hobson, Richard
House, Edward M. (Yale University Library)
Hull, Cordell
Knox, Philander C.
Lansing, Robert
McAdoo, William
McKinley, William
Mahan, Alfred Thayer
Moore, John Bassett
Norris, George
Olney, Richard
Page, Walter Hines (Houghton Library, Harvard University)
Porter, Horace
Reid, Whitelaw
Roosevelt, Franklin D. (F.D.R. Library, Hyde Park, N.Y.)
Roosevelt, Theodore
Root, Elihu
Scott, James Brown (Georgetown University Library)
Sherman, John
Sims, William S.
Sperry, Charles
Squire, George
Stimson, Henry (Yale University Library)
Stowell, Ellery
Straus, Oscar
Taft, William Howard
Walsh, Thomas J.
White, Henry
Whitlock, Brand
Wilson, Woodrow

GREAT BRITAIN

Public Documents (Public Record Office unless otherwise specified)

Admiralty
Admiralty, Naval Intelligence Department (Naval Historical Library, Ministry of Defence)

Board of Trade
Cabinet
Colonial Office
Foreign Office
Treasury Solicitor
War Office

Private Papers

Ardagh, John (PRO)
Arnold Forster, Hugh (British Museum)
Asquith, Herbert Henry (Bodleian Library, Oxford)
Balfour, Arthur James (British Museum)
Balfour, Gerald (PRO)
Battenberg, Prince Louis of (Imperial War Museum)
Beaverbrook, Lord (Beaverbrook Library—now in House of Lords Record Office)
Bertie, Sir Francis (PRO)
Blumenfeld, R. D. (Beaverbrook Library—now in House of Lords Record Office)
Bonar Law, Andrew (Beaverbrook Library—now in House of Lords Record Office)
Bridge, Sir Cyprian (National Maritime Museum)
Bryce, James, Lord (Bodleian Library, Oxford)
Bryce, James, Lord (PRO)
Buller, Sir Redvers (PRO)
Burns, John (British Museum)
Campbell-Bannerman, Sir Henry (British Museum)
Cawdor, Lord (Naval Historical Library, Ministry of Defence)
Cecil, Lord Robert (British Museum)
Chamberlain, Austen (Birmingham University Library)
Chamberlain, Joseph (Birmingham University Library)
Crease, T. E. (Naval Historical Library, Ministry of Defence)
Crewe, Lord (Cambridge University Library)
Cromer, Lord (PRO)
Crowe, Sir Eyre (PRO)
de Chair, Sir D. (Imperial War Museum)
Dilke, Sir Charles (British Museum)
Donald, Sir Robert (Beaverbrook Library—now in House of Lords Record Office)
Elibank, Alexander Murray, Master of (National Library of Scotland)
Elibank, Arthur Murray, Master of (National Library of Scotland)
Esher, Lord (Churchill College Library, Cambridge)
Fisher, Sir John, Lord (St. Andrews University, on deposit by the Duke of Hamilton)
Gladstone, Herbert (British Museum)
Grant Duff, Major A. (Imperial War Museum)

Greene, Sir William Graham (National Maritime Museum)
Grey, Sir Edward (PRO)
Haig, Sir Douglas (National Library of Scotland)
Haldane, R. B. (National Library of Scotland)
Halsbury, Lord (British Museum)
Hamilton, Sir Frederick (National Maritime Museum)
Hankey, Maurice (Churchill College Library, Cambridge)
Hankey, Maurice (PRO)
Hardinge, Sir Charles (Cambridge University Library)
Hardinge, Sir Charles (PRO)
Henderson, Sir William (National Maritime Museum)
Hood, Sir Horace (Churchill College Library, Cambridge)
Jellicoe, Sir John (British Museum)
Jerram, Sir Thomas (National Maritime Museum)
Kimberly, Lord (National Library of Scotland)
Kitchener, Lord (PRO 30/57 and PRO WO/159)
Langley, Sir Walter (PRO)
Lansdowne, Lord (PRO)
Lascelles, Sir Frank (PRO)
Lee, Arthur H. (Beaverbrook Library—now House of Lords Record Office)
Lloyd George, David (Beaverbrook Library—now House of Lords Record Office)
McKenna, Reginald (Churchill College Library, Cambridge)
Madden, Sir Charles (National Maritime Museum)
May, Sir William (National Maritime Museum)
Midleton, St. John Broderick, Lord (British Museum)
Midleton, St. John Broderick, Lord (PRO)
Milne, Sir Berkeley (National Maritime Museum)
Milner, Sir Alfred, Lord (Bodleian Library, Oxford)
Monson, Sir Edmund (Bodleian Library, Oxford)
Morley, John, Lord (India Office Library)
Nicolson, Sir Arthur (PRO)
Noel, Sir Gerald (National Maritime Museum)
Oliver, Sir Henry (National Maritime Museum)
Pease, Joseph (Nuffield College Library, Oxford)
Richmond, Sir Herbert (National Maritime Museum)
Ripon, Lord (British Museum)
Roberts, Lord (PRO)
Robinson [Dawson], Geoffrey (Naval Historical Library, Ministry of Defence)
Rosebery, Lord (National Library of Scotland)
Runciman, Walter (Newcastle-upon-Tyne University Library)
Salisbury, Lord (Hatfield House mss., 3d Marquess)
Sandars, Jack J. (Bodleian Library, Oxford)
Sanderson, Sir Percy (PRO)
Sanderson, Sir Thomas (PRO)
Satow, Sir Ernest (PRO)

Scott, C. P. (British Museum)
Seely, Sir John (Nuffield College Library, Oxford)
Selborne, Lord (Bodleian Library, Oxford)
Slade, Sir Edmond (National Maritime Museum)
Smith-Dorrien, Sir Horace (British Museum)
Spender, J. A. (British Museum)
Spring Rice, Sir Cecil (PRO)
Stanley, Miss Venetia (Private. Consulted in typescript by courtesy of
    Milton Gendel, Michael Brock, and Martin Gilbert)
Strachey, J. St. Loe (Beaverbrook Library—now in House of Lords Re-
    cord Office)
Sydenham, Sir George Clarke, Lord (British Museum)
Trevelyan, Sir Charles (Newcastle-upon-Tyne University Library)
Tweedmouth, Lord (Naval Historical Library, Ministry of Defence)
Villiers, Sir Francis (PRO)
Wilson, Sir Henry (Imperial War Museum)

II. PUBLISHED PRIMARY COLLECTIONS

Documents

Aspinall, John B., ed. *Lloyd's Reports of Prize Cases Heard before and Decided
    by the Right Honourable Sir Samuel Evans, P.C., L.L.D., President of the
    Probate, Divorce, and Admiralty Division during the European War which
    Began in August, 1914.* Reprinted from "Lloyd's List" by Direction of
    the Committee of Lloyd's. 10 vols. London: Lloyd's, 1915-1924.
*Debates in the British Parliament, 1911-1912, on the Declaration of London and
    the Naval Prize Bill.* Washington: U.S. Government Printing Office,
    1919.
Gooch, G. P., and Temperley, Harold, eds. *British Documents on the Origin
    of the War, 1898-1914.* 11 vols. London: His Majesty's Stationery Of-
    fice, 1927-1938.
Great Britain. Parliament. *Parliamentary Papers.* House of Commons and
    Command. 1905, vol. CIII, Cmnd. 2348.
_____. Privy Council. *The Prize Court Rules, 1914.* London: Darling and Son,
    under authority of His Majesty's Stationery Office, 1914.
Gregory, Charles Noble, ed. *Abstracts of Cases Contained in Lloyd's Reports of
    Prize Cases, Volumes 1, 2, 3, and 4.* Washington: U.S. Government
    Printing Office, 1919.
Hurst, C. J. B., and Bray, F. E., eds. *Russian and Japanese Prize Cases.* 2
    vols. London: His Majesty's Stationery Office, 1912.
Martin, Harold, and Baker, Joseph. *Laws of Maritime Warfare affecting
    Rights and Duties of Belligerents as Existing on August 1, 1914.* Washington:
    U.S. Government Printing Office, 1918.
Moore, John Bassett. *A Digest of International Law.* 8 vols. Washington:
    U.S. Government Printing Office, 1906.
Savage, Carlton. *Policy of the United States toward Maritime Commerce in*

War. 2 vols. Washington: U.S. Government Printing Office, 1934 and 1936.

Scott, James Brown, ed. *The Declaration of London, February 26, 1909.* New York: Oxford University Press, 1919.

———. *Instructions to the American Delegates to the Hague Peace Conferences and Their Official Reports.* New York: Oxford University Press, 1916.

———. *The Proceedings of the Hague Peace Conferences.* 5 vols. New York: Oxford University Press, 1920.

United States. Department of State. *Papers Relating to the Foreign Relations of the United States.* Washington: U.S. Government Printing Office, 1861 *et seq.*

———. ———. *Papers Relating to the Foreign Relations of the United States. The Lansing Papers.* 2 vols. Washington: U.S. Government Printing Office, 1939.

———. ———. *Papers Relating to the Foreign Relations of the United States. Supplement: The World War.* Washington: U.S. Government Printing Office, 1928–1933.

———. Naval War College. *International Law Topics and Discussions, 1896–1915.* Washington: U.S. Government Printing Office, 1896–1915.

———. Senate. *Journal of Executive Proceedings.* Vol XLII, 61st Congress, 3d session. Washington: U.S. Government Printing Office, 1942.

———. ———. *Journal of Executive Proceedings.* Vol. XLIV, 62d Congress, 2d session. Washington: U.S. Government Printing Office, 1946.

Private Papers

Baker, Ray Stannard. *Woodrow Wilson: Life and Letters.* Vol. V: *Neutrality, 1914–1915.* Garden City: Doubleday, Doran, 1935.

———, and Dodd, William E., eds. *The Public Papers of Woodrow Wilson.* 6 vols. New York: Harper & Brothers, 1925–1927.

Blake, Robert, ed. *The Private Papers of Douglas Haig, 1914–1919.* London: Eyre & Spottiswoode, 1952.

Borchard, Edwin, et al., eds. *The Collected Papers of John Bassett Moore.* 7 vols. New Haven: Yale University Press, 1944.

Brett, M. V., and Esher, Oliver, Viscount, eds. *Journals and Letters of Reginald, Viscount Esher.* 4 vols. London: Ivor Nicholson & Watson, 1934–1938.

Callwell, C. E., ed. *Field-Marshal Sir Henry Wilson: His Life and Diaries.* 2 vols. London: Cassell, 1927.

Chalmers, W. S. *The Life and Letters of David, Earl Beatty.* London: Hodder and Stoughton, 1951.

David, Edward, ed. *Inside Asquith's Cabinet.* London: John Murray, 1977.

Gwynn, Stephen, ed. *The Anvil of War: Letters between F. S. Oliver and His Brother, 1914–1918.* London: Macmillan, 1936.

———. *The Life and Friendships of Sir Cecil Spring Rice.* Vol II. London: Constable, 1929.

Hendrick, Burton J. *The Life and Letters of Walter H. Page.* 3 vols. Garden City: Doubleday, Page, 1924-1926.

Horsley, E. M., ed. *Lady Cynthia Asquith: Diaries, 1915-1918.* New York: Knopf, 1969.

James, Robert Rhodes, ed. *Winston S. Churchill: His Complete Speeches, 1897-1963.* 8 vols. New York: Chelsea House, 1974.

Kemp, P. K., ed. *The Papers of Admiral Sir John Fisher.* Vol. II. *Publications of the Navy Records Society,* Vol. CVI. London and Colchester: Spottiswoode, Ballantyne, 1964.

Lennox, Lady Algernon Gordon, ed. *The Diary of Lord Bertie of Thame, 1914-1918.* 2 vols. London: Hodder and Stoughton, 1924.

Link, Arthur S., et al., eds. *The Papers of Woodrow Wilson.* Princeton: Princeton University Press, 1966 *et seq.*

Marder, Arthur J. *Portrait of an Admiral: The Life and Papers of Sir Herbert Richmond.* London: Jonathan Cape, 1952.

_____, ed. *Fear God and Dread Nought.* 3 vols. London: Jonathan Cape, 1952-1959.

Morison, Elting, et al., eds. *The Letters of Theodore Roosevelt.* 8 vols. Cambridge: Harvard University Press, 1951-1954.

Patterson, A. Temple, ed. *The Jellicoe Papers.* Vol. I: *1893-1916. Publications of the Navy Records Society,* Vol. CVIII. London and Colchester: Spottiswoode, Ballantyne, 1966.

Riddell, Lord. *Lord Riddell's War Diary, 1914-1918.* London: Ivor Nicholson & Watson, 1933.

_____. *More Pages from My Diary, 1908-1914.* London: Country Life, 1934.

Seager, Robert II, and Maguire, Doris D., eds. *Letters and Papers of Alfred Thayer Mahan.* 3 vols. Annapolis: Naval Institute Press, 1975.

Seymour, Charles, ed. *The Intimate Papers of Colonel House.* 4 vols. Boston: Houghton Mifflin, 1926-1928.

Taylor, A. J. P., ed. *Lloyd George: A Diary by Frances Stevenson.* New York: Harper & Row, 1971.

Wilson, Trevor, ed. *The Political Diaries of C. P. Scott, 1911-1928.* London: Collins, 1970.

III. CONTEMPORARY SOURCES

Books

Anonymous. *Dod's Parliamentary Companion for 1911.* London: Whittaker, 1911.

Atherley-Jones, L. A. *Commerce in War.* London: Methuen, 1907.

Baty, T. *Britain and Sea Law.* London: G. Bell and Sons, 1911.

_____, ed. *Prize Law and Continuous Voyage.* London: Stevens & Haynes, 1915.

Bowles, Thomas Gibson. *Sea Law and Sea Power*. London: John Murray, 1910.

Brassey, Thomas, ed. *Brassey's Naval Annual, 1915*. London: William Clowes and Sons, 1915.

Bray, F. E. *British Rights at Sea under the Declaration of London*. London: P. S. King, 1911.

"Civis." *Cargoes & Cruisers: Britain's Rights at Sea*. London: Hodder and Stoughton, n.d. [ca. 1912].

Cohen, Arthur. *The Declaration of London*. London: Hodder & Stoughton, 1911.

Corbett, Julian. *Some Principles of Maritime Strategy*. London: Longmans, Green, 1911.

Hall, J. A. *The Law of Naval Warfare*. London: Chapman & Hall, 1914.

Loreburn, Robert Threshie Reid, Lord. *Capture at Sea*. London: Methuen, 1913.

Pyke, H. Reason. *The Law of Contraband of War*. Oxford: Clarendon, 1915.

Roosevelt, Theodore. *The Naval War of 1812*. New York: G. P. Putnam's Sons, 1882, reprinted 1910.

Smith, F. E., and Sibley, N. W. *International Law as Interpreted during the Russo-Japanese War*. Boston: Boston Book Co., 1905.

Wilson, Woodrow. *History of the American People*. 5 vols. New York: Harper & Brothers, 1902.

Articles

Bentwich, Norman. "International Law as Applied by England in the War." *American Journal of International Law*, 9 (1915):17-44.

Dewar, K. G. B. "Oversea Commerce and War." *Journal of the Royal United Service Institution*, 57 (1913):449-500.

Dugmore, E. V. F. R. "Commerce and War." *Journal of the Royal United Service Institution*, 57 (1913):721-772.

Garner, James. "Some Questions of International Law in the European War." *American Journal of International Law*, 9 (1915):372-401.

Tarle, A. de. "The British Army and a Continental War." Translated from the French by H. Wylly. *Journal of the Royal United Service Institution*, 57 (1913):384-401.

Wyatt, H. F. "England's Threatened Rights at Sea." *Journal of the Royal United Service Institution*, 54 (1910):5-33.

Pamphlets

Balfour, Arthur James. *The British Blockade*. London: Darling & Son, 1915.

———. *The Navy and the War*. London: Darling & Son, 1915.

Bryce, James, Viscount. *Neutral Nations and the War.* London: Macmillan, 1914.

Corbett, Julian. *League of Peace and a Free Sea.* New York: Hodder and Stoughton, 1915.

_____. *The Spectre of Navalism.* London: Darling & Son, 1915.

Davison, Charles Stewart. *The Case of the "Kronprinz Wilhelm" and "Bernstorffian Diplomacy,"* 1915 [no place or name of publisher].

_____. *A Letter to the State Department* [no facts of publication, but the letter is dated March 19, 1915].

De la Hautiere, R. *Conference Navale de Londres.* Bordeaux: Y. Cadoret, 1910.

Hurd, Archibald. *If the British Fleet Had Not Moved!* London: Darling & Son, 1915.

Wise, Bernard R. *The Freedom of the Seas.* London: Darling & Son, 1915.

IV. ESSAY ON SECONDARY SOURCES

Preparation of a suitable bibliography for a study of maritime rights in Anglo-American relations from 1899 to April 1915 poses a peculiar dilemma. Little has been written that is focused specifically on this topic. Instead previous historians have written of maritime rights piecemeal, as a secondary theme at most useful to illuminate larger issues in works centered on British prewar grand strategy or American neutrality during World War I. To review these works simply in terms of statements on blockade or contraband while ignoring each author's own emphasis would be both unfair and unhelpful to future researchers. As I have tried to show in this book, Britain and the United States did not formulate their maritime rights policies separately from their foreign and defense policies or from domestic politics. Only in this broad context, for which a sound knowledge of British and American history during the period is essential, can the decisions of Washington and London on maritime rights be understood. Unfortunately, a bibliography covering every significant book or article bearing in some way on the context of maritime rights policy would require a separate volume. The essay that follows provides a brief evaluation of those secondary sources that are most valuable in establishing the essential conceptual framework for understanding maritime rights and offers suggestions for future research and reassessment in that general area.

One work specifically focuses on, as its title states, "Great Britain and Belligerent Maritime Rights from the Declaration of Paris, 1856, to the Declaration of London, 1909." M. R. Pitt's 1964 University of London thesis is best on pre-1899 background, although it also provides useful insights on the Boer War period. Analysis of the Second Hague and London conferences is less satisfactory, largely because the narrow concentration on law tends to leave broader questions of policy unexamined. The work is now dated in some respects, but still repays the careful reader with material unavailable elsewhere in print.

The best source for background on the Royal Navy, the dominant influence on prewar maritime rights policy, unquestionably remains the first volume of Arthur Marder's *From the Dreadnought to Scapa Flow* (1961). This model of thorough research and clear writing is superb naval history, particularly in regard to personalities and materiel. It is disappointingly brief on grand strategy and plans for economic warfare, however, and much of the analysis of Admiralty relations with the CID and cabinet is now obsolete. These sections should be read in light of Nicholas d'Ombrain's *War Machinery and High Policy* (1973), which provides an essential corrective.

Marder's military equivalent is Samuel Williamson's *The Politics of Grand Strategy* (1969), by far the best source on the Anglo-French staff talks and preparation of the British army for Continental war. Unfortunately, the empathy with military thinking, which is the book's strongest point when focused within the army, becomes its greatest flaw when directed on relations with other institutions of government. The statements that the Anglo-German naval race "deprived the British army of money" (p. 135) and that the CID secretary was "prudent and sensible" to prepare detailed plans for landing British troops in France without informing anyone in the cabinet (p. 80) are only two examples of this tendency to accept the General Staff perspective somewhat uncritically. Although Williamson is invaluable on the War Office contribution to the decade of navalist-Continentalist chaos so vital for an understanding of British positions at Second Hague or London, the military emphasis must be recognized and set off with more balanced views such as those of d'Ombrain.

The student who seeks to understand maritime rights policy in the broad context of British diplomacy should begin with the institutional framework provided in Zara Steiner's *The Foreign Office and Foreign Policy, 1898–1914* (1969). The same author's *Britain and the Origins of the First World War* (1977) is the most thoughtful and provocative study of its topic, but unlike the earlier work is inexplicably flawed by several elementary errors in fact. It is difficult to comprehend how a scholar of this stature and proven competence could misdate the most important speech of Grey's career (p. 210), confuse a junior commander serving as assistant director of naval ordnance with the first sea lord (pp. 31 and 191), misdate by a full year the Second Hague Conference and the resignation of Grey's most persistent critic in the cabinet (pp. 132 and 147), and describe the first lord of the Admiralty as being "under" the foreign secretary (p. 48). *Britain* is a powerful tool for historical understanding because it asks many of the basic questions, missed by more specialized studies, about the drift into Continental war with what remained essentially a Victorian army. But it is a flawed tool, and the reader must recognize its dangers as well as its benefits.

A more detailed study of the shift from isolation to Continental commitment is George Monger's *The End of Isolation* (1963), which unfortunately concludes in 1907. There is no comparable work on the last seven years before the outbreak of war, although C. J. Lowe and M. L. Dockrill cover that period in *The Mirage of Power* (1972) from a strongly pro-British, pro-Grey perspective. Peter Rowland's *The Last Liberal Governments* (1968 and 1971) provides useful political background, but is often simplistic and sometimes inaccurate on foreign and defense policies. A. J. A. Morris, *Radicalism against War, 1906–1914* (1972), is a generally critical study of Grey's left-wing critics which perhaps is more eager to indict Morley, Loreburn, and their colleagues than to understand them.

Although British scholars are justly famed for their biographic skills, the record for the period 1899–1914 is spotty at best. John Wilson's *CB* (1973) provides a useful counter to the Asquith-Grey perspective on Liberal politics and policies, while Michael Fry's first volume in *Lloyd George and Foreign Policy* (1977) includes a superb analysis of the often contradictory thoughts and feelings of both its subject and the cabinet during the last days of peace.

Randolph Churchill and Martin Gilbert have published invaluable source materials in the companion volumes to *Winston S. Churchill* (1966 et seq.), although the biography itself tends to hagiography. Keith Robbins's *Sir Edward Grey* (1971), best of the many unsatisfactory biographies of the foreign secretary, is based on research in the Grey Papers but makes no use of Foreign Office and cabinet records available in the same PRO search room. *British Foreign Policy under Sir Edward Grey* (1977), a collection of essays edited by F. H. Hinsley, is most disappointing. The essays vary enormously in scope, quality, and interpretation of their subject, but the book never attempts to integrate this diverse material. Despite the wealth of documentation now available, a reliable, comprehensive analysis of Grey's career remains to be written, as do similar studies of Asquith, Haldane, McKenna, Henry Wilson, and so many others.

Although the debate sparked by the general opening of public and private archives during the 1960s has yet to produce a scholarly consensus on British grand strategy, the student of maritime rights policy before 1914 can learn much from the available archive-based works on institutions and individuals. The student of the evolution of Allied economic warfare after the outbreak of war is not so fortunate. Any number of books have been written during the past sixty years on the blockade of Germany, but their value tends to be as slight as the documentation available to their authors. There is likewise an enormous historical literature on Britain during World War I, but most is too narrow in scope or too dated by lack of archival access to be useful in establishing context. No area is more in need of further research than wartime Britain.

Only two books specifically on the blockade remain worth reading. A. C. Bell's official history volume, *The Blockade of the Central Empires, 1914–1918,* was published in 1937 but considered so sensitive it remained classified until 1961. The author had the limited access to official documents characteristic of the British official histories in general. His work, although poorly written and organized, contains a wealth of data on the mechanics and effects of the economic campaign. Marion Siney's *The Allied Blockade of Germany, 1914–1916* (1957), on the other hand, is a thoughtful, readable account written exclusively from published sources. Although badly dated and often inaccurate from lack of access to the archives, it is helpful in framing questions. Bell and Siney supplement one another, with the former providing data that can be fit into the latter's conceptual framework. The two books together, however, still fall far short of an adequate history of their subject.

Even less satisfactory are three modern studies: Marjorie Milbank Farrar's *Conflict and Compromise* (1974), Patrick Devlin's *Too Proud to Fight* (1975), and Arthur Marsden's essay "The Blockade" in Hinsley. Farrar's study of the French role in the economic campaign is so narrowly focused that it fails to consider the broader aims and concerns of Allied economic warfare planners. Devlin goes to the other extreme, offering provocative general insights but failing to document them adequately or integrate them into a coherent whole. Marsden essentially repeats Ernest May's interpretation of Grey deliberately weakening the blockade in order to appease the United States, adding documentation unavailable when May wrote. The use of evidence is highly selective, however, and what is cited is sometimes not convincing. All three works have something to offer the modern reader, but ultimately prove disappointing.

The analysis of British policy in Ernest May's *The World War and American Isolation, 1914-1917* (1959), the only significant attempt to write a comprehensive account of the Washington-Berlin-London relationship, requires special attention. This well-written, persuasive interpretation has tended to dominate subsequent accounts. It is, nevertheless, a perfect example of the dangers inherent in multinational diplomatic history written without multinational access to archives. The German and American sections reflect broad research in public and private archives, but the British section reflects mainly memoirs and official biographies. These sources contain much that statesmen with the advantage of hindsight wished they had done and said years earlier, but often fail to present an accurate picture of what they actually did say and do. May's transformation of Grey from the architect of the blockade revealed in the documents to the conciliator of American neutral rights pictured in *World War* is only the most striking example of the distortion that resulted from closed archives and incautious use of other sources. A general reassessment in light of the material now available seems not only appropriate but overdue.

Unfortunately, the historian who attempts such a reassessment will find little agreement on the general strategic context essential to understand British policy on maritime rights and the United States. The best survey of the topic remains Paul Guinn's *British Strategy and Politics, 1914–1918* (1965), although the reader must recognize and compensate for the strong "Western Front" perspective. The second volume of Marder's *From the Dreadnought* (1965) provides some insight into the Admiralty perspective Guinn tends to ignore or dismiss, but is primarily concerned with fleet operations rather than grand strategy or economic warfare. Cameron Hazlehurst offers a provocative analysis of strategic decision making on the highest level in *Politicians at War, July 1914 to May 1915* (1971). The account of the cabinet's internal dynamics is the best available, but the defense of Lloyd George against the charge of political opportunism in wartime is overstated and distorts the overall impression. Taken together Guinn, Marder, and Hazlehurst serve to establish a framework for further research, but a satisfactory synthesis on British wartime policy requires much additional work.

Many of the generalizations that can be made concerning secondary sources on British maritime rights policies apply equally to the United States. There is no comprehensive account of the evolution of American positions on blockade, contraband, immunity, and continuous voyage between 1899 and 1914, although Calvin Davis provides a conceptual framework and considerable administrative background in *The United States and the First Hague Peace Conference* (1962) and *The United States and the Second Hague Peace Conference* (1975). Richard Challener attempted to write a synthetic study of *Admirals, Generals, and American Foreign Policy, 1898–1914* (1973), but never quite overcame the problem of writing an organized, coherent history of disorganized, often incoherent policy making. The background material is invaluable, although there is little directly on maritime rights, but much remains undigested. *The Great Rapprochement* (1968) by Bradford Perkins, though not always accurate on details, captures the spirit of the developing "special relationship" between Britain and the United States. Much remains to be done, but Davis, Challener,

and Perkins provide a solid foundation of secondary studies unavailable for Britain or for American policy after the outbreak of
World War I.

One area in which further research is essential is German-
American relations. There is no general study comparable to Perkins on Anglo-American relations. Howard Beale's *Theodore
Roosevelt and the Rise of America to World Power* (1956), Raymond
Esthus's *Theodore Roosevelt and the International Rivalries* (1970),
and Frederick Marks's *Velvet on Iron* (1979) all devote considerable attention to Roosevelt's diplomacy with Germany, but none of
the three offers much insight on the German side. Holger Herwig's *The Politics of Frustration* (1976) provides a thoughtful introduction centered on German plans for war with the United States,
and his work must form a new beginning for further research and
writing in this complex but vital area of American diplomatic
history.

If the student of maritime rights in Anglo-American relations
finds little on his topic in existing literature for the period before
August 1914, he is overwhelmed by the mass of secondary material on the Wilson administration's response to the British blockade of Germany after the outbreak of war. American neutrality
policies were controversial in their own time and have remained
so ever since. Three books published in successive years stand at
the center of this controversy today, having made previous accounts obsolete and having dominated subsequent discussion:
Daniel Smith's *Robert Lansing and American Neutrality, 1914–1917*
(1958), Ernest May's *The World War and American Isolation, 1914–
1917* (1959), and volume III of Arthur Link's *Wilson, The Struggle
for Neutrality, 1914–1915* (1960). The student who would understand current interpretations of American neutrality must begin
with these three works.

Smith's *Lansing,* the earliest and least influential of the three
studies, focuses on the role of the counselor and later secretary of
state. It concludes that Lansing was personally pro-British, but
that his legal training led him to advise the president at least
during the first eight months of war to base the American response to the blockade firmly on international law. This view
probably overstates the counselor's concern for abstract legal
principles and underestimates his fear of political reaction against

an administration that appeared too soft on British violations of neutral rights in the eyes of the American public. *Lansing* is now somewhat dated by lack of access to British and some important American archival collections, but still provides a useful analysis of the Wilson-Lansing relationship and the formulation of neutrality policies.

Smith's emphasis on Lansing's role is particularly valuable as a contrast to *Wilson*. The strongest point of Link's biography is its author's unequaled knowledge of and empathy with Woodrow Wilson. Its weakest point is the inability to escape from the president's hypnotic spell and see events from other perspectives as well. The overall thesis, stated briefly, is that Wilson dominated the formulation of American policies toward the belligerents, that he sincerely wished to remain neutral, and that his actions did in fact meet the standard of neutrality established in international law. Link discusses the specific issues of maritime rights—especially blockade, contraband, continuous voyage, and visit and search—in far more detail than Smith or May. This discussion is grounded firmly in Wilson's official and private papers, but not in contemporary legal sources such as Moore's *Digest*. The lack of archival access, especially in Britain, tends both to date the research and to accentuate the tendency to see questions through the president's eyes. *Wilson* remains a valuable study, but the empathy with Wilson that accounts for its continuing value also should make the reader seek other perspectives on the men and events discussed.

While Link credits Wilson for maintaining strict neutrality, Ernest May argues that the American government tilted toward the Allies in "benevolent neutrality." Part of this tilt resulted from the pro-British attitude of the president and most of his senior advisers. The single most important factor, however, was the masterful, conciliatory diplomacy of Sir Edward Grey. In May's view Wilson was willing and even eager to give Britain the benefit of any possible doubt, but was not willing to tolerate clear-cut violation of American neutral rights. *World War* traces events in Washington, London, and Berlin to demonstrate how the pressure built within both belligerent governments for an all-out effort to break the military stalemate by a rigorous naval blockade in open defiance of traditional rules of maritime law. Grey resisted this pressure successfully, using his vast prestige to restrain those in Britain who demanded a rash challenge to the United States and to persuade Wilson that Anglo-American maritime rights disputes could be settled by honest negotiation. German Chancellor Theobald von Bethmann Hollweg, on the other hand, lost control and was forced to watch as submarine warfare against commerce plunged Germany into flagrant violation of neutral rights and inevitable confrontation with the United States.

This interpretation is well written, persuasive, and seemingly well documented. It has dominated historical understanding of American neutrality since its publication. It is also unsupported, and indeed contradicted, by an overwhelming volume of evidence in the Foreign Office and other British archives unavailable to its author. Grey did not restrict the blockade in order to conciliate the American government. He was instead the primary architect of its most restrictive and illegal features. By asserting that the foreign secretary's influence prevented British measures from seriously damaging American interests or violating American rights, May was able to bring the Wilson administration's failure to challenge those measures effectively within the limits of "benevolent neutrality." If the blockade did inflict serious harm on American economic interests, as both State Department and Foreign Office records seem to indicate, and if the Orders in Council did constitute a flagrant violation of American legal rights, as the papers of the Joint Neutrality Board, the Foreign Office, the procurator general, and the attorney general would seem to indicate, then another explanation must be found for Washington's failure to act against Britain as it acted against Germany. *World War* is superb diplomatic history written with shrewd use of limited sources. But like all history it must be reexamined as further evidence becomes available.

Less need be said of accounts of American neutrality written after 1960 because they tend to be dominated by the major synthetic works of Smith, Link, and May. Daniel Smith has developed his views further in *The Great Departure* (1965), the best modern survey of Wilson era foreign relations, while Ross Gregory follows the broad outlines of May's interpretation in *The Origins of American Intervention in the First World War* (1971). Both are intended primarily for undergraduate use. Gregory and John Milton Cooper have published biographies entitled *Walter Hines Page* (1970 and 1977), both of which underestimate their subject's influence in shaping Wilson's perception of the war. Patrick Devlin's *Too Proud to Fight* (1975) is essentially a psychohistory of Wilson focused on his neutrality policies. Its approach is innovative and many of its conclusions are stimulating, but the lack of chronological structure is often confusing and sometimes misleading. Rachel West's *The State Department on the Eve of the First World War* (1978) provides valuable background on organization and personnel, but is far narrower than Steiner's study of the Foreign Office. In general during the past twenty years some holes in the neutrality period have been filled in, but aside from Devlin little ground has been broken that is both fresh and fertile.

The student of maritime rights, like the student of related aspects of British and American history during the period 1899–1915, must approach his topic with a sound knowledge of the available secondary sources, a willingness to reexamine those sources in light of all available primary materials, a recognition that particular events can be understood only in a broad context, and an open mind. The need for books that integrate fresh archival research with the disparate approaches and contradictory conclusions so common in the present historical literature is enormous. The student who writes an intellectual history of the influence exerted on events by Woodrow Wilson's ideas of history or Henry Wilson's ideas of civil-military relations will make a substantial contribution not only to understanding the particular topics but to understanding the man, his intellectual environment, and the events he helped shape. The student who will dig through the mass of Foreign Office, Treasury Solicitor, Prize Court, and Admiralty records to provide data on ships and cargoes detained will finally provide a solid basis for generalization about the blockade and its specific effects on American trade. On a broader level, the need for modern histories of international law and of German-American relations seems obvious. The period offers not only the opportunity to contribute, but the excitement of discovery and debate.

Index

Library of Congress Cataloging in Publication Data

Coogan, John W.
  The end of neutrality.

  Bibliography: p.
  Includes index.
  1. United States—Foreign relations—Great Britain. 2. Great Britain—Foreign
relations—United States. 3. United States—Neutrality. 4. War, Maritime (International law) I. Title.
JX1428.G7C66   327.73041   81-66645
ISBN 0-8014-1407-5   AACR2